# Good Housekeeping
# STEP-BY-STEP
# VEGETABLE COOKBOOK

# Good Housekeeping

## STEP-BY-STEP
## VEGETABLE COOKBOOK

Edited by Susan Westmoreland

*Food Director*

Good Housekeeping

with the assistance of

Susan Deborah Goldsmith

*Associate Food Director*

and Elizabeth Brainerd Burge

HEARST BOOKS
NEW YORK

# GOOD HOUSEKEEPING

*Editor-in-Chief* Ellen Levine
*Food Director* Susan Westmoreland
*Associate Food Director* Susan Deborah Goldsmith

## A CARROLL & BROWN BOOK

Designed and produced by
Carroll & Brown Limited
20 Lonsdale Road
London NW6 6RD
England

*Publishing Director* Denis Kennedy
*Art Director* Chrissie Lloyd

*Project Editor* Theresa Reynolds

*Editors* Janet Charatan, Paula Disbrowe, Kate Fryer, Valerie Cipollone, Madeline Weston
*Assistant Editors* Joanne Stanford, Simon Warmer

*US Cooking Consultant* Elizabeth Brainerd Burge

*Senior Art Editor* Sally Powell
*Designers* Paul Stradling, Simon Daley, Hallam Bannister

*Photography* David Murray, Jules Selmes

*Production* Christine Corton, Wendy Rogers, Clair Reynolds

*Nutrition Consultant* Michele C. Fisher, Ph.D., R.D.

The contents of this book first appeared in *The Good Housekeeping Step-by-Step Cookbook* published by William Morrow and Company, Inc., in 1997.

This edition first published in the United States by
Hearst Books
959 Eighth Avenue
New York, N.Y. 10019

1 2 3 4 5 6 7 8 9 10

*Library of Congress Cataloging-in-Publication Data*
Good Housekeeping Step-by-Step Vegetable Cookbook.
p. cm.
Includes index.
ISBN 0-688-17851-0
1. Cookery (Vegetables)
TX801.G633    2000
641.6'5–dc21    99-049800

Reproduced in Singapore by Colourscan
Printed and bound in the United States of America by
Quebecor Printing Hawkins

# FOREWORD

As children, we were all told to eat our vegetables (and some of us even became experts at hiding the peas under the potatoes!). Happily, as adults, we can treat ourselves to a much broader and tempting array of vegetable recipes. With that in mind, I am pleased to present the *Good Housekeeping Step-by-Step Vegetable Cookbook*, third in the series of spiral-bound books based on material from the original *Good Housekeeping Step-by-Step Cookbook*. It follows *Good Housekeeping Step-by-Step Main Dishes* and *Good Housekeeping Step-by-Step Great Desserts*.

Whether you are looking for an appetizer, the perfect accompaniment to a main dish, a healthy main meal, or a delicious pasta recipe, you'll find dishes that have lots of appeal. With photos to instruct and entice, the recipes range from tasty starters like Fresh Tomato and Basil Soup or Eggplant-Stuffed Cherry Tomatoes to scrumptious dishes like Spinach and Ricotta Dumplings, Vegetable Paella, and Southwestern Style Pasta to delightful salads such as Spinach and Tangerine Salad and Roasted Potato Salad.

Main dishes are divided according to vegetable family, each section beginning with Know-How tips and general instructions. If you're not sure how to cut and prepare an artichoke, the step-by-step photographs will show you the way. You'll also find preparation and cooking times and a full nutrition profile with each recipe. And as always, every recipe has been triple-tested in Good Housekeeping's Test Kitchens.

Dig in and enjoy the recipes, the photos, the wealth of Know-How information and cooking tips. Our aim at Good Housekeeping is to give the information and recipes that make cooking a pleasure.

Susan Westmoreland

Susan Westmoreland
*Food Director*
Good Housekeeping

# CONTENTS

# EQUIPMENT KNOW-HOW

There's a piece of equipment out there for every cooking method imaginable. No one needs every new gadget on the market, but there are certain items that make kitchen life easier and more enjoyable. Here are all of our favorites, from time-honored basic cookware to specialized utensils for adventuresome home cooks.

## SHOPPING TIPS

Quality cookware can be expensive. But if you get the best, you'll have a lifetime investment that's reliable, durable, and a pleasure to use. The first step in judging quality? Check the price: Finer metals and manufacturing typically mean you'll pay more. (But not always; cast-iron pans, for instance, are cheap, heavy, and durable.) Invest in a few quality pieces, especially knives and sturdy pots and pans. Don't skimp on nonstick pans for low-fat cooking. You can cut corners on items like pasta pots, which simply boil water. Get extra mileage from your cookware by choosing products that work equally well in the oven and on the stove-top.

## STOVE-TOP STAPLES

Pots and pans come in many materials. Stainless steel is easy to care for but does not conduct heat well, so manufacturers often add an aluminum or copper core to improve its heat-conducting qualities. By contrast, copper is a superb heat conductor and a pleasure to cook in – but it's heavy, expensive, and a nuisance to polish. Aluminum and cast iron are much less costly and easier to care for; both are efficient heat conductors but can react with acidic foods, causing them to taste metallic or discolor.

In general, look for pots and pans with thick bottoms, which guard against scorching, and heatproof handles (or ones designed to stay cool). You're better off investing in pieces you know you'll use and avoiding prepackaged sets, which may contain some pans you won't need. For a well-equipped kitchen, you'll need the following:

**Saucepan** You'll need at least 3 or 4 (ranging from 1-quart to 4-quart), each between 3½ and 4 inches deep. They should have tight-fitting lids and ovenproof handles.

**Dutch oven** Great for the stove-top or oven; heavy ones are best, and enameled pans are pretty enough to serve in. A 5-quart size is most useful.

**Skillets** Have at least 3 sizes: small (8-inch), medium (10-inch), and large (12-inch). A good nonstick skillet is a must if you're trying to cook with less fat.

**Saucepot** This deep, wide, fairly light pot is used for soups, stews, and cooking pasta. A 5-quart saucepot with a tight-fitting lid will serve most needs.

**Stockpot** A tall, narrow pot used for cooking soups and stocks as well as bulky foods like corn on the cob and lobster. A 6- or 8-quart stockpot is recommended.

Stockpot

---

### SEASONING A CAST-IRON PAN

Regular (not enamel-coated) cast-iron skillets require seasoning before the first use to create a nonstick finish. Wash in hot, soapy water; dry. Using a cloth soaked in vegetable oil, rub the entire surface – even exterior and lid. Heat upside down in a 350°F oven 1 hour. Turn off oven; cool completely in oven.

---

## FOR THE OVEN

Roasting and baking results depend on how long the food bakes and at how high a temperature, and the dimensions of the vessel. Many materials will do the job: enameled cast-iron, which is easy to clean and transmits heat well; enameled steel, which is a reasonably priced, lightweight choice for roasting pans; stainless steel, which is durable and inexpensive; and heat-resistant glass and glass-ceramic, which can go directly from the freezer or refrigerator to the oven. Earthenware and stoneware are especially good for long, slow baking. For most cakes, shiny metal pans will yield the most delicate crusts. The following is a round-up of essentials.

**Baking dish** A large, fairly shallow, coverless oval or rectangular dish with sides about 2 inches high; usually made of glass or ceramic. Choose a variety in different sizes.

**Baking pan** Like a baking dish, but made of metal; the sides of this pan are 1½ to 2 inches high. Essential: an 8" by 8" square; a 9" by 9" square; a rectangular 13" by 9" pan.

**Casserole** Round, oval, square, or rectangular, this dish may be made of glass, ceramic, or enameled metal, and may have a lid. Have several sizes.

**Roasting pan** A large, deep pan typically made of stainless or enameled steel or aluminum. A low, open roasting pan with a rack is the most versatile.

---

## CARE AND CLEANING

**Aluminum** Scrub with a mild abrasive cleanser. If pan has darkened, fill with water and vinegar or lemon juice; boil 15 minutes.

Casserole    Roasting pan with rack    Metal baking pan

**Cast iron** Wash cast iron briefly so you don't wash away the seasoning (see box, page 10). Clean with boiling water and a paper towel or soft cloth, or use a nylon pad to scrub off food. Dry at once.

**Copper** Wash in hot, soapy water; dry immediately. Copper tarnishes quickly; use a polish to brighten. Most traditional copper pans are lined with tin and will need relining from time to time (reline if you can see copper through the tin).

**Earthenware or stoneware** Cool completely before washing to prevent cracking. Scrub with nylon pad, rinse, and air dry. Glazed stoneware is dishwasher-safe.

**Enameled metals** Soak in hot, soapy water; avoid abrasives.

**Glass, glass-ceramic, porcelain** Soak in hot, soapy water. All are dishwasher-safe.

**Nonstick surfaces** Clean with a sponge and warm, soapy water. Avoid abrasives.

**Stainless steel** Wash in hot, soapy water with a nylon pad. A stainless steel cleaner will help remove stubborn stains.

## UTENSIL ESSENTIALS

**Bristle brushes** Have at least two: one for cleaning pots, and one for scrubbing vegetables. Nylon bristles last the longest.

**Colander** This sink staple is indispensable for draining pasta and vegetables. Large colanders are best; look for one with solid feet at the base.

**Cutting boards** To avoid cross-contamination, have one board for raw poultry, fish, and meat, and another for bread, vegetables, and cheese. Scrub with hot soapy water after use, and sterilize weekly in a solution of 1 tablepoon bleach mixed with 1 gallon water. Sanitize plastic boards in the dishwasher. You may want to reserve a board just for fruit, to avoid tragedies like garlic-flavored apple pie.

**Grater** This flat or box-shaped tool can grate (fine holes), shred (medium holes), or slice (large slots) many foods. Stainless steel won't rust.

**Measuring spoons** Stainless steel are the most durable. For liquids fill to the rim. For dry ingredients, fill and level off.

**Mixing bowls** A set of these all-purpose bowls is invaluable. They are typically made of stainless steel, glass, or plastic, and range in size from tiny to 8 quarts. Avoid using plastic bowls to beat egg whites.

**Sieve/Strainer** Sifts dry ingredients or strains liquids. Have a few in various sizes and with different gauges of mesh.

**Spatulas** Use wooden or heatproof rubber ones for turning foods during cooking, plastic or rubber for mixing and folding. Long metal spatulas make frosting cakes a cinch.

**Tongs** Use to pick up foods that are hot, slippery or messy.

**Vegetable peeler** Easier than a paring knife for peeling potatoes, apples, and other fruit and vegetables, and great for shaving cheese and making chocolate curls. A swivel blade removes less peel than a fixed blade since it conforms to the vegetable's shape.

Grater    Sieve

## ALL THE RIGHT KNIVES

Quality knives are made of high-carbon stainless steel. If the knife has a tang (the narrower metal part at the base of the blade) that goes right through the handle, it's solidly made. A good knife should feel comfortable to hold.

Essential knives include a chef's knife (for chopping, slicing, and dicing; a 6- to 8-inch blade is the most popular), a small paring knife (for fruits and vegetables), and a large serrated knife.

Sharp knives are easier to use and safer too because they'll be less likely to slip. Take a cue from chefs, who sharpen their knives every day. For directions on how to use a sharpening steel, see page 180.

Paring knife    Chef's knife    Serrated knife

## THE LITTLE EXTRAS

**Apple corer** This cylindrical tool neatly cores apples as well as pears. Buy the larger size so you don't miss any core.

**Juicer** A device to extract fruit or vegetable juices – from a simple ridged cone onto which a halved citrus fruit is pressed to elaborate electric models used for carrot juice.

**Kitchen scissors** For cutting kitchen string, snipping fresh herbs, and trimming artichoke leaves. Shears, which are larger and spring-loaded, make sectioning poultry simple.

**Mortar and pestle** For grinding spices, herbs, and nuts. You crush with the pestle (a bat-like tool) in a mortar (the bowl).

**Potato masher** Perfect for mashing potatoes, other root vegetables, and cooked beans into a slightly chunky puree.

**Steamer** The collapsible metal style can fit into pots and pans of various sizes. A two-tier steamer pan looks like a double boiler (see page 10) but the top half has a perforated base to allow steam through. Bamboo steamers fit in a wok or over a pot of simmering liquid.

**Zester** Pulled across citrus fruit, it removes only the outer peel, avoiding the bitter pith underneath.

# FOOD SAFETY AND STORAGE

The following guidelines are ones that no cook should be without. Keeping food in good condition isn't difficult and shouldn't be daunting. But a safe kitchen does call for a few precautions. Here, we outline safety essentials, including how long you can safely store a range of foods.

## GOLDEN RULES OF FOOD SAFETY

• Keep a clean kitchen. Any area can harbor harmful bacteria, so always wash and dry your hands before handling food. Frequently wash kitchen towels, cloths, and sponges. Rinse fresh fruits and vegetables before eating. Wash cutting boards, knives, and other utensils with hot soapy water after every use – especially after handling raw meat and poultry. Wash cutting boards occasionally with a solution of 1 tablespoon bleach per 1 gallon water to sterilize them.
• Don't put raw meat, poultry, or fish on a plate with raw or cooked vegetables.
• To kill harmful bacteria that may be present in raw eggs, fish, poultry, and meat, it's essential to cook these foods thoroughly.
• It's unwise to cook foods in stages. Don't start to cook food, stop, and then return to it later. Even when food is stored in the refrigerator between cooking periods, safe temperatures might not be maintained and bacteria may develop.
• Refrigerate leftovers as soon as possible. Do not leave at room temperature longer than 2 hours. Divide large amounts among small, shallow containers for quicker cooling.
• In hot weather, don't leave protein foods such as chicken, egg salad, etc., out of the refrigerator for more than 1 hour.

---

### WRAP IT UP

**Aluminum foil** This provides optimal protection, molds easily, and can withstand extreme temperatures. The heavy-duty version is ideal for long-term storage.
**Freezer paper** This old-fashioned favorite protects food from freezer burn and is very easy to label.
**Plastic bags** Food storage bags are intended for room-temperature or refrigerated foods. Freezer bags are the thickest and sturdiest, and can even endure a quick zap in the microwave for defrosting and warming.
**Plastic wrap** The best offer a tight seal and protect food against moisture loss and odor transfer. Thinner wraps often cling better and are ideal for leftovers and brief microwave reheats (but should not be in direct contact with food when microwaved). For freezer storage, choose a heavy plastic wrap intended for that purpose.

## PACKING A SAFER PICNIC

• Use 2 small coolers rather than one large one – one that will be opened frequently (for fruit and beverages), and one for perishable items like meat, poultry, salads, and cheese.
• Chill foods thoroughly before placing them in a cooler (the cooler cannot chill foods that aren't already cold). To preserve the chill, don't open the lid longer than necessary.
• Pack perishable items next to ice packs. Keep delicate fruits and lettuce away from ice to prevent freezing.

## PANTRY STORAGE

Unless otherwise noted, these pantry staples fare best in a cool, dry place. For more information on basic ingredients (e.g., flour, pasta, grains), see appropriate Know-How pages.
**Baking powder** Once opened, keep it well sealed and it should be effective for up to 6 months. To test it, add 1 teaspoon to 1 cup hot water; it should bubble vigorously.
**Bread crumbs** Store dried bread crumbs in the pantry up to 6 months, or – for better flavor – refrigerate up to 2 years.
**Honey** It will last indefinitely; if it has crystallized, place opened jar in bowl of hot water. Stir until crystals dissolve.
**Hot-pepper sauce** After opening, store at room temperature up to 3 months, or refrigerate for longer storage.
**Olive oil** Keep in a cool, dark place up to 6 months. Don't buy more than you can use; it may become rancid, especially if stored in a warm place.
**Pancake syrup** This will keep up to 9 months (after that, syrup thins and flavor weakens). It can also be refrigerated. Pure maple syrup should be refrigerated after opening, or can be frozen. Store in glass jars, not plastic or metal containers.
**Soy sauce** Unopened, it will keep in the pantry for a year. Once opened, refrigerate to keep for an additional year.
**Spices and dried herbs** Keep in lightproof containers in a cool place up to 1 year. Store red spices (paprika, ground red pepper), poppy seeds, and sesame seeds in the freezer.
**Vegetable oil** Store in a cool, dark place (for 6 months).
**Vinegar** Unopened, it will keep indefinitely. Sediment that may appear is harmless and can be strained off. Once opened, store in the pantry for 6 months. Vinegar with added flavorings (e.g., fruits, herbs) should be strained into a clean bottle when vinegar level drops below top of ingredients.

## THE RIGHT WAY TO REFRIGERATE

• Make sure your refrigerator temperature remains between 33° and 40°F.
• To prevent spoilage, keep foods on a rotating system. Place new items at the back of the shelves and move older purchases to the front.
• Date all leftovers so you know how long you've had them.

- If you're unsure whether a food is safe to eat, discard it.
- Keep eggs in their carton so they don't absorb other food odors. For the same reason, store cheese, cream, milk, yogurt, margarine, and butter tightly closed or covered.

## FREEZER FACTS

- Frozen foods retain their color, texture, and nutrients better than foods preserved by other methods.
- Check the temperature of the freezer with a freezer thermometer to be sure that it is at 0°F. (Higher temperatures will draw moisture from the food, resulting in a loss of texture and taste.)
- It's time to defrost whenever there is ½ inch of frost on the sides of the freezer. If the frost has not solidified into hard ice, a plastic scraper makes light work of this job.
- Don't overload your freezer or add more than 2 pounds of food for each cubic foot of space in a 24-hour period. Either will cause temperature changes that may damage food.
- To avoid ice crystals, color or texture changes, or freezer burn, seal foods in airtight containers, or wrap them tightly in a wrap intended for freezer storage.
- Small "piece" foods such as individual appetizers (e.g., tartlets, phyllo triangles), drop cookies, or strawberries keep best when "tray," or "dry," frozen. This method freezes foods so they remain separate and you can remove only as many as you need. Simply spread the unwrapped food on a baking sheet; freeze just until firm, then package in zip-tight plastic bags. Tray-freezing is also ideal for firming foods such as cakes and pies so packaging material will not adhere to them.
- Liquid and semiliquid foods must be stored in leakproof containers; leave headspace for expansion of liquid during the freezing process (for wide-mouth containers, leave ½ inch for pints and 1 inch for quart cartons; for narrow-mouth containers, leave ¾ inch for pints and 1½ inches for quarts).
- Don't freeze raw vegetables (they'll lose crispness unless you blanch them first) or fried foods (they'll turn soggy). Also avoid freezing soft cheeses, mayonnaise, sour cream, custard, and pumpkin pies – they'll become watery or may separate.
- Label and date food packages, and note the weight of meats and poultry and number of portions.
- Prepare frozen foods right after thawing; growth of bacteria can occur rapidly in thawed foods left at room temperature (especially casseroles, pot pies, and gravy).

## STORING FRESH HERBS

- Most fresh herbs are highly perishable, so buy them in small quantities as needed. To store them for a few days, immerse roots or freshly cut stems in about 2 inches of water. Cover the leaves with paper towels or a plastic bag and refrigerate.
- To dry fresh herbs (this works best with sturdy herbs like rosemary and thyme), first rinse lightly and pat dry with paper towels. Hang them upside down by the stems in bunches, in a dry, warm spot out of bright light. When leaves become brittle (typically a few days to a week), pick them off and discard the stems; store dried leaves in tightly covered containers in a cool, dry place.
- To freeze herbs, rinse lightly, pat dry, remove the stems, and place in plastic containers or bags. The frozen herbs will darken in color, but the flavor will be fine. There's no need to thaw frozen herbs; just add them directly to the food you are cooking. Or, place a few herbs (leaves only) in ice cube trays; add just enough water to cover leaves and freeze. Simply add the cube to simmering soups or sauces.

## MICROWAVE TIPS

- Remember that the size of the food affects cooking time. Small or thin pieces cook faster than large or thick ones.
- Avoid microwaving large cuts of on-the-bone meat. The bones attract microwaves and the meat will cook unevenly.
- Pierce eggs and foods with tight skin (eggplant, potatoes). If not, they may explode from a buildup of steam.
- Use a dish that's large enough for stirring and boiling. Think of how full you'd want a saucepan, not a casserole.
- Don't reheat baked goods in the microwave – they'll be tough. However, you can thaw them in a paper towel.
- Use medium power (the microwave will cycle on and off) for delicate tasks, such as melting chocolate.
- Clean the oven with soapy water or multi-purpose cleaner.

### MICROWAVE SAFETY

- Use paper products only for cooking less than 10 minutes, or they could ignite. Don't use recycled paper, which can contain metal bits that will spark, or dyed paper products – the dye could leach into food.
- Don't use the twist ties that come with plastic storage bags – the metal could spark and possibly ignite. Also beware of glass or porcelain with a metal trim, or the metal content of some ceramic glazes.
- For safety, use plastic wrap designed for microwave use, and don't let the plastic touch the food.
- Always remove a tight cover carefully, opening it away from your face – steam can build up under the cover.
- Sugar attracts microwaves, so sweet foods can become extremely hot – be careful when you take a bite.

**OVEN TEMPERATURES**

| Celsius | Fahrenheit | Gas | Description |
|---|---|---|---|
| 110°C | 225°F | ¼ | Cool |
| 120°C | 250°F | ½ | Cool |
| 140°C | 275°F | 1 | Very low |
| 150°C | 300°F | 2 | Very low |
| 160°C | 325°F | 3 | Low |
| 170°C | 325°F | 3 | Moderate |
| 180°C | 350°F | 4 | Moderate |
| 190°C | 375°F | 5 | Moderately hot |
| 200°C | 400°F | 6 | Hot |
| 220°C | 425°F | 7 | Hot |
| 230°C | 450°F | 8 | Very hot |

**VOLUME**

| Metric | Imperial | Metric | Imperial |
|---|---|---|---|
| 25 ml | 1 fl oz | 500 ml | 18 fl oz |
| 50 ml | 2 fl oz | 568 ml | 20 fl oz/1 pint |
| 75 ml | 2½ fl oz | 600 ml | 1 pint milk |
| 100 ml | 3½ fl oz | 700 ml | 1¼ pints |
| 125 ml | 4 fl oz | 850 ml | 1½ pints |
| 150 ml | 5 fl oz/¼ pint | 1 litre | 1¾ pints |
| 175 ml | 6 fl oz | 1.2 litres | 2 pints |
| 200 ml | 7 fl oz/⅓ pint | 1.3 litres | 2¼ pints |
| 225 ml | 8 fl oz | 1.4 litres | 2½ pints |
| 250 ml | 9 fl oz | 1.5 litres | 2¾ pints |
| 300 ml | 10 fl oz/½ pint | 1.7 litres | 3 pints |
| 350 ml | 12 fl oz | 2 litres | 3½ pints |
| 400 ml | 14 fl oz | 2.5 litres | 4½ pints |
| 425 ml | 15 fl oz/¾ pint | 2.8 litres | 5 pints |
| 450 ml | 16 fl oz | 3 litres | 5¼ pints |

**SPOONS**

| Metric | Imperial |
|---|---|
| 1.25 ml | ¼ tsp |
| 2.5 ml | ½ tsp |
| 5 ml | 1 tsp |
| 10 ml | 2 tsp |
| 15 ml | 3 tsp/1 tbsp |
| 30 ml | 2 tbsp |
| 45 ml | 3 tbsp |
| 60 ml | 4 tbsp |
| 75 ml | 5 tbsp |
| 90 ml | 6 tbsp |

**US CUPS**

| Cups | Metric |
|---|---|
| ¼ cup | 60 ml |
| ⅓ cup | 70 ml |
| ½ cup | 125 ml |
| ⅔ cup | 150 ml |
| ¾ cup | 175 ml |
| 1 cup | 250 ml |
| 1½ cups | 375 ml |
| 2 cups | 500 ml |
| 3 cups | 750 ml |
| 4 cups | 1 litre |
| 6 cups | 1.5 litres |

**WEIGHT**

| Metric | Imperial |
|---|---|
| 5 g | ⅛ oz |
| 10 g | ¼ oz |
| 15 g | ½ oz |
| 20 g | ¾ oz |
| 25 g | 1 oz |
| 35 g | 1¼ oz |
| 40 g | 1½ oz |
| 50 g | 1¾ oz |
| 55 g | 2 oz |
| 60 g | 2¼ oz |
| 70 g | 2½ oz |
| 75 g | 2¾ oz |
| 85 g | 3 oz |
| 90 g | 3¼ oz |
| 100 g | 3½ oz |
| 115 g | 4 oz |
| 125 g | 4½ oz |
| 140 g | 5 oz |
| 150 g | 5½ oz |
| 175 g | 6 oz |
| 200 g | 7 oz |
| 225 g | 8 oz |
| 250 g | 9 oz |
| 275 g | 9¾ oz |
| 280 g | 10 oz |
| 300 g | 10½ oz |
| 315 g | 11 oz |
| 325 g | 11½ oz |
| 350 g | 12 oz |
| 375 g | 13 oz |
| 400 g | 14 oz |
| 425 g | 15 oz |
| 450 g | 1 lb |
| 500 g | 1 lb 2 oz |
| 550 g | 1 lb 4 oz |
| 600 g | 1 lb 5 oz |
| 650 g | 1 lb 7 oz |
| 700 g | 1 lb 9 oz |
| 750 g | 1 lb 10 oz |
| 800 g | 1 lb 12 oz |
| 850 g | 1 lb 14 oz |
| 900 g | 2 lb |
| 950 g | 2 lb 2 oz |
| 1 kg | 2 lb 4 oz |
| 1.25 kg | 2 lb 12 oz |
| 1.3 kg | 3 lb |
| 1.5 kg | 3 lb 5 oz |
| 1.6 kg | 3 lb 8 oz |
| 1.8 kg | 4 lb |
| 2.25 kg | 5 lb |
| 2.7 kg | 6 lb |

**MEASURES**

| Metric | Imperial |
|---|---|
| 2 mm | 1/16 in |
| 3 mm | ⅛ in |
| 5 mm | ¼ in |
| 8 mm | ⅜ in |
| 10 mm/1 cm | ½ in |
| 1.5 cm | ⅝ in |
| 2 cm | ¾ in |
| 2.5 cm | 1 in |
| 3 cm | 1¼ in |
| 4 cm | 1½ in |
| 4.5 cm | 1¾ in |
| 5 cm | 2 in |
| 5.5 cm | 2¼ in |
| 6 cm | 2½ in |
| 7 cm | 2¾ in |
| 7.5 cm | 3 in |
| 8 cm | 3¼ in |
| 9 cm | 3½ in |
| 9.5 cm | 3¾ in |
| 10 cm | 4 in |
| 11 cm | 4¼ in |
| 12 cm | 4½ in |
| 12.5 cm | 4¾ in |
| 13 cm | 5 in |
| 14 cm | 5½ in |
| 15 cm | 6 in |
| 16 cm | 6¼ in |
| 17 cm | 6½ in |
| 18 cm | 7 in |
| 19 cm | 7½ in |
| 20 cm | 8 in |
| 22 cm | 8½ in |
| 23 cm | 9 in |
| 24 cm | 9½ in |
| 25 cm | 10 in |
| 26 cm | 10½ in |
| 27 cm | 10¾ in |
| 28 cm | 11 in |
| 29 cm | 11½ in |
| 30 cm | 12 in |
| 31 cm | 12½ in |
| 33 cm | 13 in |
| 34 cm | 13½ in |
| 35 cm | 14 in |
| 37 cm | 14½ in |
| 38 cm | 15 in |
| 40 cm | 16 in |
| 43 cm | 17 in |
| 46 cm | 18 in |
| 48 cm | 19 in |
| 50 cm | 20 in |

# Soups & Appetizers

# SOUPS

Perhaps no dish is more inviting than a steaming bowl of homemade soup. Utterly comforting to eat and delightfully easy to prepare, most require little more than some initial chopping. Depending on richness, soup can play various roles in your weekly menus. A simple broth or puree makes an elegant first course; a hearty bean soup creates a meal on its own with crusty bread and a crisp salad. Garnishes are great – they add an extra blast of fragrance and color, making any soup more enticing. Add fresh herbs just before serving.

## KNOW YOUR SOUPS

**Bisque** A rich, creamy soup with a velvety texture, usually made with shellfish.

**Broth** A flavorful liquid made by simmering meat, fish, poultry and/or vegetables. Broth makes a light soup on its own and an excellent base for most other soups.

**Chowder** A hearty soup containing chunks of fish, shellfish, and/or vegetables. Clam chowder has been popular in New England since colonial times.

**Consommé** A clear soup, made by reducing stock and then filtering it meticulously. Good consommé has a heady aroma and strong flavor.

**Gumbo** A signature of Cajun cuisine, gumbo is a thick soup served over rice. It may contain a variety of vegetables, seafood, and meats, and may be thickened with okra or filé (made from sassafras leaves). The name gumbo comes from an African word for okra.

**Stock** A rich, clear liquid made by simmering poultry, meat, or fish bones in water with vegetables. The strained mixture is used as a base for soups, stews, and sauces.

## GARNISHING

• Stir chopped fresh parsley, dill, basil, or mint into sour cream or yogurt and dollop on a creamed soup.
• Toasted nuts or crunchy crumbled bacon are delicious sprinkled over Broccoli Soup (see page 16).
• Garlicky homemade croutons, grated Parmesan or Gruyère, pesto, and slices of fresh lemon or lime are other tasty options.
• As a pretty garnish for chilled soups, freeze ice cubes with tiny sprigs of fresh herbs or berries. Add just before serving.

## STORING

• Cool leftover soup; refrigerate in a sealed container for up to 3 days. Chilling can thicken soup, so add extra broth, water, cream, or milk when reheating.
• Most soups freeze well in airtight containers for up to 3 months. Place in a large, shallow container for quicker freezing; leave some headspace to allow for expansion.
• Don't add cream, yogurt, or eggs to soup bases before freezing; they'll curdle when soup is reheated.
• It's best to thaw frozen soup in the refrigerator before reheating. Freezing may diminish some flavors, so be sure to taste and adjust seasonings before serving, if needed.

## QUICK HOMEMADE SOUPS

Making soup from scratch can be a cinch. Choose your favorite from the chart, then just follow the steps below.

1 In 3-quart saucepan, heat 1 tablespoon vegetable oil, margarine, or butter over medium heat. Add 1 medium onion, finely chopped; cook 5 minutes, or until tender.

2 Add Flavoring for chosen soup; cook 30 seconds. Add 1 can (13¾ to 14½ ounces) chicken or vegetable broth, 1 cup water, and ¼ teaspoon salt; heat to boiling over high heat.

3 Now stir in Vegetables. Return the mixture to boiling. Reduce heat to medium and cook 10 to 20 minutes, until vegetables are very tender. In blender, blend in small batches until smooth. Season to taste. Makes 4 first-course servings.

### SOUP SELECTION

| SOUP | FLAVORING | VEGETABLES |
|------|-----------|------------|
| Spinach | 1 garlic clove, minced | 1 package (10 ounces) frozen spinach |
| Pea | 1 garlic clove, minced, and pinch dried mint | 1 package (10 ounces ) frozen peas |
| Carrot | ⅛ teaspoon ground nutmeg | 2 cups chopped carrots |
| Potato | ⅛ teaspoon ground nutmeg and ¼ teaspoon dried thyme | 2 cups chopped potatoes |
| Zucchini | 1 teaspoon curry powder | 2 cups chopped zucchini |

# PUREED SOUPS

Perfectly smooth, silky-textured soups make an elegant opener to almost any meal. Blenders produce the smoothest soups; to avoid burns, puree the cooked mixture in small batches. Removing the center part of the blender lid will prevent overflow and splatter. Hand-held immersion blenders also work well; cool the soup slightly before using one.

## WINTER SQUASH AND APPLE SOUP

◆◆◆◆◆◆◆◆◆◆◆◆◆◆

*Prep:* 35 minutes
*Cook:* 40 minutes
*Makes* 8 first-course servings

**2 medium Golden Delicious apples (about 12 ounces)**
**2 medium butternut squash (about 1¾ pounds each)**
**2 tablespoons vegetable oil**
**1 small onion, chopped**
**1 can (14½ ounces) vegetable broth**
**1 tablespoon chopped fresh thyme or ¼ teaspoon dried thyme**
**1 teaspoon salt**
**⅛ teaspoon coarsely ground black pepper**
**1 cup half-and-half or light cream**
**Chopped fresh thyme or parsley for garnish**

**1** Peel, quarter, and core each apple. Cut into ¾-inch chunks.

**2** With large chef's knife, cut each squash into 2 pieces and slice off peel. Remove seeds.

**3** Cut squash into ¾-inch chunks. In 4-quart saucepan, heat oil over medium heat; add onion and cook until tender.

**4** Stir in apples, squash, broth, 1 tablespoon thyme, salt, pepper, and *1½ cups water*; heat to boiling over high heat. Reduce heat to low; cover and simmer, stirring frequently, 20 to 25 minutes, until squash is tender.

**5** Spoon one-third of mixture into blender. Cover (with center part of blender lid removed) and blend at low speed until very smooth. Pour mixture into bowl. Repeat with remaining mixture.

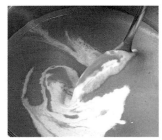

**6** Return pureed mixture to saucepan, stir in half-and-half, and heat through over medium heat, stirring occasionally (do not boil). Serve garnished with chopped fresh thyme.

EACH SERVING: ABOUT 175 CALORIES, 3g PROTEIN, 29g CARBOHYDRATE, 7g TOTAL FAT (3g SATURATED), 11mg CHOLESTEROL, 305mg SODIUM

## BROCCOLI SOUP

*Prep: 10 minutes    Cook: 30 minutes*
*Makes 8 first-course servings*

1 large bunch broccoli (1½ pounds)
1 tablespoon margarine or butter
1 medium onion, finely chopped
2 cans (13¾ to 14½ ounces each) chicken
  broth
½ teaspoon salt
¼ teaspoon ground black pepper
¼ teaspoon dried thyme
Pinch ground nutmeg
½ cup half-and-half or light cream

◆ Cut stems from broccoli; peel stems and thinly slice. Cut tops into flowerets. In 3-quart saucepan, melt margarine over medium heat. Add onion and cook, stirring often, 5 minutes, or until tender. Add broccoli stems and flowerets, broth, next 4 ingredients, and *2 cups water*. Heat to boiling over high heat; boil 15 minutes, or until broccoli stems are tender.

◆ Spoon small amount of broccoli mixture into blender; cover (with center part of blender lid removed) and blend at low speed until smooth. Pour mixture into bowl. Repeat with remaining broccoli mixture. Return mixture to saucepan. Stir in half-and-half and heat through over medium heat (do not boil).

**Each serving: About 80 calories, 4g protein, 8g carbohydrate, 4g total fat (2g saturated), 13mg cholesterol, 615mg sodium**

◆◆◆◆◆◆◆◆◆◆◆◆◆◆◆◆◆◆◆◆

### CREAM GARNISH

Drizzle 1 tablespoon crème fraîche or slightly thinned sour cream in ring onto soup. Draw tip of knife through ring at intervals, alternately moving toward the center, then toward the outside, until it forms a flower shape.

◆◆◆◆◆◆◆◆◆◆◆◆◆◆◆

## FRESH TOMATO AND BASIL SOUP

*Prep: 15 minutes    Cook: 25 minutes*
*Makes 4 first-course servings*

4 large ripe tomatoes (about 2 pounds)
1 medium bunch basil
2 tablespoons vegetable oil
1 large onion, chopped
1 small carrot, shredded
½ teaspoon sugar
1 can (13¾ to 14½ ounces) chicken broth
½ teaspoon salt
Sour cream (optional)

◆ Cut each tomato horizontally in half; squeeze out and discard seeds. Chop tomatoes. Reserve 4 small basil sprigs; chop enough remaining basil to equal ¼ cup.

◆ In 3-quart saucepan, heat oil over medium heat; add onion and carrot and cook, stirring occasionally, just until tender.

◆ Add chopped tomatoes and sugar; heat to boiling over high heat. Reduce heat to low; cover and simmer, stirring occasionally, 15 minutes, or until tomatoes are very soft.

◆ Spoon half of tomato mixture into blender; cover (with center part of blender lid removed) and blend at low speed until smooth. Pour mixture into bowl. Repeat with remaining tomato mixture. Return mixture to saucepan. Stir in chopped basil, broth, and salt and heat through over medium heat.

◆ Serve soup hot or cover and refrigerate to serve cold later. To serve, spoon soup into 4 soup bowls. Top each serving with a spoonful of sour cream, if you like. Garnish with basil sprigs.

**Each serving: About 155 calories, 4g protein, 19g carbohydrate, 9g total fat (2g saturated), 8mg cholesterol, 725mg sodium**

## ROASTED GARLIC AND POTATO SOUP

*Prep: 1 hour 5 minutes plus cooling*
*Cook: 30 minutes    Makes 6 first-course servings*

1 whole head garlic
3 tablespoons olive or vegetable oil
2 medium onions, diced
4 medium all-purpose potatoes (about
  1¼ pounds), peeled and diced
1 can (13¾ to 14½ ounces) chicken broth
1 cup half-and-half or light cream
1¼ teaspoons salt

◆ Preheat oven to 350°F. Remove any loose papery skin from garlic, leaving head intact. Place garlic in small baking dish; pour oil over garlic. Cover with foil and bake garlic 1 hour, or until soft. Cool garlic until easy to handle. Separate garlic head into cloves. Press soft, cooked garlic from each clove into small bowl; discard skin. Reserve 1 tablespoon oil from baking dish.

◆ In 4-quart saucepan, heat reserved oil over medium-high heat; add onions and cook, stirring often, 10 minutes, or until golden brown and tender.

◆ Add potatoes to saucepan with garlic, broth, and *3 cups water*; heat to boiling over high heat. Reduce heat to low; cover and simmer, stirring occasionally, about 10 minutes, until potatoes are tender.

◆ Spoon half of potato mixture into blender; cover (with center part of blender lid removed) and blend at low speed until smooth. Pour mixture into bowl. Repeat with remaining potato mixture. Return soup to saucepan; stir in half-and-half and salt. Heat soup to boiling over medium-high heat, stirring constantly. Serve hot or cover and refrigerate to serve cold later.

**Each serving: About 235 calories, 5g protein, 28g carbohydrate, 12g total fat (4g saturated), 20mg cholesterol, 755mg sodium**

# HEARTY VEGETABLE SOUPS

Chock-full of chunky vegetables and greens, as well as beans and grains, these long-simmered soups nourish body and soul. They're extremely simple, but substantial enough for supper – and so hearty, in fact, that you'll never miss the meat. There's a secret to thickening some of these soups: Puree a small amount of the soup, and then stir it back in.

## MUSHROOM-BARLEY SOUP

◆◆◆◆◆◆◆◆◆◆◆◆◆

*Prep: 20 minutes*
*Cook: 1 hour 15 minutes*
*Makes 6 main-dish servings*

**¾ cup pearl barley**
**1½ pounds mushrooms**
**5 medium carrots**
**2 tablespoons olive oil**
**3 medium celery stalks, sliced**
**1 large onion, coarsely chopped**
**2 tablespoons tomato paste**
**2 cans (13¾ to 14½ ounces each) beef broth**
**¼ cup dry sherry**
**Fresh oregano leaves for garnish**
**Crusty bread (optional)**

**1** In 3-quart saucepan, heat barley and *4 cups water* to boiling over high heat. Reduce heat to low. Cover; simmer 30 minutes. Drain.

**2** Meanwhile, cut mushrooms into thick slices. Cut carrots lengthwise in half, then crosswise into ¼-inch-thick slices.

**3** In 5-quart Dutch oven, heat olive oil over medium-high heat. Add celery and onion and cook, stirring occasionally, 8 to 10 minutes, until golden brown. Increase heat to high; add sliced mushrooms and cook, stirring occasionally, 10 to 12 minutes, until all liquid evaporates and mushrooms are lightly browned.

◆◆◆◆◆◆◆◆◆◆◆◆◆◆◆◆◆◆◆◆◆◆◆◆◆◆◆

### GARNISHING HEARTY SOUPS

Top steaming bowls of soup with one of the following for extra color, texture, or flavor: sour cream or yogurt; fresh herbs; crumbled bacon; thin strips of ham; chopped hard-cooked egg; shredded Gruyère; grated Parmesan; pesto tossed with chopped tomato; crumbled tortilla chips.

For crumbled bacon, cook bacon until crisp; break into tiny pieces to use as garnish.

**4** Reduce heat to medium-high; stir in tomato paste and cook, stirring, 2 minutes. Add beef broth, carrots, sherry, barley, and *4 cups water*; heat to boiling over high heat. Reduce heat to low; cover and simmer 20 to 25 minutes, until carrots and barley are tender. Garnish and serve hot, with crusty bread, if you like.

Pesto tossed with chopped tomato

Chopped hard-cooked egg

Chopped fresh parsley

◆◆◆◆◆◆◆◆◆◆◆◆◆◆◆◆◆◆◆◆◆◆◆◆◆◆

**EACH SERVING: ABOUT 220 CALORIES, 8g PROTEIN, 34g CARBOHYDRATE, 6g TOTAL FAT (1g SATURATED), 0mg CHOLESTEROL, 575mg SODIUM**

## LENTIL-VEGETABLE SOUP

*Prep:* 20 minutes    *Cook:* 40 minutes
*Makes* 4 main-dish servings

2 cans (13¾ to 14½ ounces each) reduced-sodium chicken or vegetable broth
½ cup lentils
2 tablespoons vegetable oil
2 medium carrots, cut into ½-inch thick slices
1 medium onion, coarsely chopped
1 medium zucchini, cut into ½-inch pieces
1 medium yellow straightneck squash, cut into ½-inch pieces
1 garlic clove, minced
½ medium head escarole, coarsely chopped
1 can (32 ounces) tomatoes
¼ cup seasoned dried bread crumbs

◆ In 4-quart saucepan, heat broth and lentils to boiling over high heat. Reduce heat to low; cover and simmer 20 minutes, or until lentils are almost tender.

◆ Meanwhile, in 12-inch skillet, heat oil over medium-high heat; add carrots and onion and cook about 5 minutes, until lightly browned. Add zucchini, yellow squash, and garlic; cook about 5 minutes, until lightly browned. Stir in escarole; cook about 2 minutes, until tender.

◆ To lentil mixture, add tomatoes with their juice, bread crumbs, vegetables in skillet, and *1 cup water*; heat to boiling over high heat, breaking up tomatoes with back of spoon. Reduce heat to low; cover and simmer 5 minutes.

Each serving: About 300 calories, 13g protein, 43g carbohydrate, 9g total fat (1g saturated), 0mg cholesterol, 675mg sodium

## MINESTRONE WITH PESTO

*Prep:* 30 minutes plus soaking and cooking beans    *Cook:* 1 hour
*Makes* 6 main-dish servings

2 tablespoons olive oil
3 medium carrots, sliced
2 medium celery stalks, thinly sliced
1 large onion, diced
2 ounces sliced pancetta or bacon, diced
3 medium all-purpose potatoes (about 1 pound), peeled and cut into ½-inch cubes
2 medium zucchini, diced
½ (2-pound) head savoy cabbage, thinly sliced
1 large garlic clove, minced
2 cans (13¾ to 14½ ounces each) reduced-sodium chicken broth
1 can (14½ to 16 ounces) diced tomatoes
1⅓ cups dry Great Northern beans, soaked (see page 108) and cooked
½ cup Pesto (see page 102)

◆ In 5-quart Dutch oven, heat oil over medium-high heat. Add carrots, celery, onion, and pancetta; cook, stirring occasionally, 10 minutes, or until onion begins to brown. Add potatoes, zucchini, cabbage, and garlic; cook, stirring, until cabbage wilts. Add broth, tomatoes with their juice, and *1 cup water*; heat to boiling over high heat. Reduce heat to low; cover and simmer 30 minutes, or until vegetables are tender.

◆ In blender or food processor with knife blade attached, blend ½ cup cooked beans with 1 cup soup until pureed. Stir bean puree and remaining cooked beans into soup; heat to boiling over high heat. Reduce heat to low; cover and simmer 10 minutes. Serve hot with Pesto.

Each serving: About 450 calories, 19g protein, 54g carbohydrate, 19g total fat (4g saturated), 10mg cholesterol, 510mg sodium

## BORSCHT

*Prep:* 25 minutes    *Cook:* 1 hour 15 minutes
*Makes* 4 main-dish servings

2 tablespoons margarine or butter
¼ (2-pound) head green cabbage, sliced
2 medium carrots, sliced
2 medium celery stalks, sliced
1 medium onion, diced
1 pound beets, peeled and cut into matchstick-thin sticks
1 can (14½ to 16 ounces) tomatoes in puree
2 cans (13¾ to 14½ ounces each) beef broth
1 tablespoon sugar
¼ teaspoon salt
⅛ teaspoon ground black pepper
Celery leaves for garnish
Pumpernickel bread (optional)

◆ In 5-quart Dutch oven, melt margarine over medium heat. Add cabbage, carrots, celery, and onion; cover and cook, stirring frequently, until tender and browned. Add beets, tomatoes with their puree, broth, sugar, salt, pepper, and *1½ cups water*; heat to boiling over high heat. Reduce heat to low; cover and simmer, stirring, 45 minutes, or until all vegetables are tender.

◆ Spoon 2 cups soup into blender; cover (with center part of blender lid removed) and blend at low speed until smooth. Return mixture to Dutch oven; heat through. Garnish and serve hot with pumpernickel bread, if you like. Or, cover and refrigerate to serve cold later.

Each serving: About 220 calories, 7g protein, 37g carbohydrate, 7g total fat (1g saturated), 0mg cholesterol, 1465mg sodium

# CORN CHOWDER

*Prep:* 20 minutes
*Cook:* 25 minutes
*Makes* 4 main-dish servings

1 tablespoon margarine or butter
1 medium onion, finely chopped
1 red pepper, finely chopped
3 medium all-purpose potatoes (about 1 pound), peeled and cut into ½-inch chunks
1 can (13¾ to 14½ ounces) chicken broth
⅛ teaspoon dried thyme
¾ teaspoon salt
Ground black pepper
4 medium ears corn, husks and silk removed
1 cup half-and-half or light cream
3 slices bacon, cooked and crumbled

◆ In 4-quart saucepan, melt margarine over medium heat. Add onion and red pepper and cook, stirring often, 5 minutes, or until vegetables are tender.

◆ Add potatoes, chicken broth, thyme, salt, ⅛ teaspoon pepper, and *1 cup water.* Heat to boiling; boil 10 minutes, or until potatoes are fork-tender.

◆ Meanwhile, cut corn kernels from cobs (you should have about 2 cups). With back of knife, scrape cobs to release milk. Add corn kernels and their milk to pan and cook 5 minutes.

◆ Stir in half-and-half; heat through (do not boil). Spoon soup into bowls; sprinkle with crumbled bacon and a little black pepper.

**Each serving:** About 380 calories, 11g protein, 59g carbohydrate, 14g total fat (6g saturated), 34mg cholesterol, 975mg sodium

# GARDEN VEGETABLE CHOWDER

*Prep:* 20 minutes
*Cook:* 30 minutes
*Makes* 4 main-dish servings

1 tablespoon margarine or butter
2 medium leeks (about 6 ounces each), white and light green parts, each cut lengthwise in half and sliced ¼ inch thick
2 medium carrots, sliced ¼ inch thick
1 medium celery stalk, sliced ¼ inch thick
3 medium red potatoes (about 1 pound), cut into ½-inch chunks
1 can (13¾ to 14½ ounces) chicken or vegetable broth
⅛ teaspoon dried thyme
¾ teaspoon salt
⅛ teaspoon ground black pepper
2 ounces green or wax beans, cut into ½-inch pieces
1 medium zucchini (about 10 ounces), cut into ½-inch chunks
1 cup half-and-half or light cream
1 tablespoon chopped fresh dill

◆ In 3-quart saucepan, melt margarine over medium heat. Stir in leeks, carrots, and celery. Cover and cook, stirring occasionally, 10 minutes, or until vegetables are tender.

◆ Stir in potatoes, next 4 ingredients, and *1 cup water.* Heat to boiling over high heat; boil, uncovered, 5 minutes. Stir in green beans; cook 5 minutes. Stir in zucchini and cook 5 minutes longer. Stir in half-and-half and heat through (do not boil). Remove from heat; stir in dill.

**Each serving:** About 285 calories, 7g protein, 42g carbohydrate, 11g total fat (5g saturated), 30mg cholesterol, 925mg sodium

# NEW ENGLAND-STYLE COD CHOWDER

*Prep:* 20 minutes
*Cook:* 30 minutes
*Makes* 5 main-dish servings

4 slices bacon
3 medium carrots, each cut lengthwise in half, then crosswise into slices
1 large fennel bulb (about 1 pound), diced, or 3 medium celery stalks, diced
1 medium onion, diced
3 medium all-purpose potatoes (about 1 pound), peeled and cut into ½-inch chunks
3 bottles (8 ounces each) clam juice
1 can (13¾ to 14½ ounces) chicken broth
1 bay leaf
1 piece cod fillet (about 1 pound), cut into 1½-inch pieces
1 cup half-and-half or light cream
Chopped fresh parsley for garnish

◆ In 5-quart Dutch oven or saucepot, cook bacon over medium heat until browned. Transfer bacon to paper towels to drain; crumble.

◆ Discard all but 2 tablespoons bacon drippings from Dutch oven. Add carrots, fennel, and onion and cook, stirring occasionally, 6 to 8 minutes, until lightly browned. Add potatoes, clam juice, chicken broth, and bay leaf; heat to boiling over high heat. Reduce heat to low; cover and simmer 10 to 15 minutes, until vegetables are tender.

◆ Add cod; cover and cook 3 to 5 minutes, until fish is opaque throughout. Stir in half-and-half; heat through (do not boil). Discard bay leaf. Serve soup hot, topped with crumbled bacon and chopped parsley.

**Each serving:** About 320 calories, 24g protein, 35g carbohydrate, 10g total fat (5g saturated), 68mg cholesterol, 850mg sodium

# APPETIZERS

Whether you're throwing a big cocktail party or an intimate dinner for a few friends, appetizers should entice the eye and spark the taste buds. Beyond that, just a few simple rules apply: The flavors, textures, and colors of the foods should complement each other – and the courses that will follow. There should always be a light option, such as fresh salsa or raw vegetables. Need inspiration? Check out what's in season and plentiful at the market.

## PLANNING FOR A PARTY

• To create a festive feel, serve a variety of colorful appetizers in assorted shapes.
• Make it easy on yourself: Prepare as many appetizers in advance as possible. When appropriate, make separate components ahead of time, such as a stuffed-vegetable filling, and then refrigerate for later assembly.
• Make only 1 or 2 hot appetizers, which demand last-minute attention, and serve some that require no work at all, like a cheese plate, nuts, grapes, or assorted salamis.
• If you're passing around an hors d'oeuvres platter, fill it with bite-size morsels that can be easily and neatly eaten.
• Arrange back-up platters; cover with plastic wrap and refrigerate to replenish your table when supplies dwindle.
• How much should you prepare? Figure on roughly 10 to 12 small hors d'oeuvres per guest if no meal follows. Otherwise, allow about 4 to 5 per guest.
• For maximum flavor, remove cold appetizers from the refrigerator about 30 minutes before serving.

## STOCKING UP

• Prepare vegetables for crudités up to 1 day ahead. Cook any vegetables that need to be blanched (lightly cooked) as directed and rinse with cold running water, and cut up raw vegetables. Wrap in damp paper towels, seal in plastic bags, and refrigerate.
• Most pâtés and terrines are best made 1 or 2 days ahead; wrap tightly in plastic wrap or foil and refrigerate.
• Freeze pastry appetizers (such as the phyllo-wrapped ones on pages 23 and 24), raw or baked, up to 1 month ahead. Bake uncooked pastries straight from the freezer as the recipe directs; warm cooked ones in a 350°F oven for about 10 minutes.

## SERVING WITH STYLE

Choose interesting serving dishes and garnishes that complement the food. Here are a few eye-catching ideas:
• Serve crudités on a tray or in a large basket lined with plastic wrap and a bed of arugula, red cabbage, purple kale, spinach, or other leafy salad greens.
• Serve cheese on a platter decorated with bunches of fresh herbs, such as thyme or rosemary.
• Serve an assortment of crackers (e.g., sesame, herb, wheat) and breads in wicker baskets lined with colorful napkins.
• Use nontoxic flowers and leaves (see page 74) as a lovely garnish. Flowers are even available at some supermarkets; see your florist for lemon leaves and the like.
• For party food that will be served on a buffet, use broad, flat dishes to create the most dramatic presentation.

## ALMOST-INSTANT APPETIZERS

When unexpected guests drop in, don't panic. These quick appetizers can be made in a flash from pantry staples:
**White bean and tuna dip** In a blender or food processor with the knife blade attached, whirl a can of tuna, drained, with a can of white kidney beans (cannellini), rinsed and drained, a little olive oil, lemon juice, and some coarsely chopped flat-leaf parsley and garlic until smooth.
**Stuffed dates** Break off chunks of good Parmesan cheese; use to stuff large pitted dates.
**French-style radishes** Set out radishes with stems still attached and provide small bowls of softened butter and coarse salt for dipping.
**Quick quesadillas** Sandwich shredded cheese and chopped green onions or salsa between flour tortillas. Heat in a skillet, turning once, until just beginning to brown on both sides. To serve, cut into wedges.
**Super salsa** Liven up bottled salsa with chopped fresh cilantro, or swirl in some sour cream.
**Herbed nuts** Toss walnuts or pecans with a little melted margarine or butter, crushed dried rosemary, and salt. Spread nuts on a cookie sheet and bake at 350°F for 10 minutes, or until toasted.
**Quick dips** In a blender, combine mayonnaise and sour cream with prepared pesto, drained jarred roasted red peppers, or dried tomatoes (rehydrated in boiling water if dry-packed, then drained) and process until smooth.
**Mediterranean mezze platter** Assemble bowls of store-bought hummus, eggplant dip, and olives; serve with wedges of pita bread, cucumber sticks, and carrots.
**Pizza pronto** Top a large Italian bread shell with one of the following, bake at 450°F for 10 minutes, and cut into small squares: olive oil and crushed dried rosemary; chopped marinated dried tomatoes and mozzarella or goat cheese; crumbled cooked bacon and Cheddar cheese.

# CRUDITÉS AND DIPS

Crudités – bite-size whole or cut-up vegetables, raw or lightly cooked – are usually served with a dip or sauce. For the prettiest effect, choose a colorful variety of vegetables. Ideal for parties or buffets, most crudités can be prepared up to one day in advance. To store, wrap vegetables separately in damp paper towels, place in plastic bags, and refrigerate.

## CRUDITÉS BASKET

◆◆◆◆◆◆◆◆◆◆◆◆

*Prep: 45 minutes*
*Cook: 8 to 10 minutes*
*Makes 12 appetizer servings*

**Moroccan Spice Bean Dip (shown above top right) and Parmesan Dip (shown above far right), or other dips of your choice (see page 22)**
**1 bunch broccoli**
**8 ounces snow peas or sugar snap peas**
**2 pounds asparagus**
**3 bunches baby carrots with tops**
**1 bunch small radishes with tops**
**2 large red peppers**
**2 large yellow peppers**
**2 heads Belgian endive**
**1 large head radicchio**
**2 large heads red leaf or romaine lettuce**

1 Prepare dips; cover and refrigerate until ready to use. Cut tough stems from broccoli. Cut broccoli into 2" by 1" pieces. Remove stem and strings along both edges of each pea pod. Bend base of asparagus stalks; ends will break off where stalks are tough. Discard ends; trim scales if stalks are gritty.

◆◆◆◆◆◆◆◆◆◆◆◆

**USING BROCCOLI STEMS**

Use broccoli stems as well as flowerets for crudités. Peel any stems that seem tough with a vegetable peeler; cut into sticks.

◆◆◆◆◆◆◆◆◆◆◆◆

2 Peel carrots; trim stems. Trim radish stems. Cut peppers into ½-inch strips. Separate leaves of endive, radicchio, and lettuce.

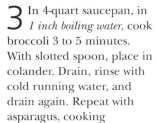

3 In 4-quart saucepan, in *1 inch boiling water*, cook broccoli 3 to 5 minutes. With slotted spoon, place in colander. Drain, rinse with cold running water, and drain again. Repeat with asparagus, cooking 3 minutes, then with snow peas, cooking 1 minute.

4 Line a large shallow basket with plastic wrap or foil. Arrange radicchio and lettuce leaves in basket. Arrange prepared vegetables on top; serve with dips.

**EACH SERVING WITHOUT DIP: ABOUT 75 CALORIES, 4g PROTEIN, 16g CARBOHYDRATE, 1g TOTAL FAT (0g SATURATED), 0mg CHOLESTEROL, 45mg SODIUM**

## MOROCCAN SPICE BEAN DIP

*Prep:* 10 minutes    *Makes* about 1⅔ cups

1 teaspoon paprika
¼ teaspoon fennel seeds, crushed
¼ teaspoon ground ginger
¼ teaspoon ground cumin
⅛ teaspoon ground red pepper (cayenne)
Pinch ground cinnamon
1 can (15 to 19 ounces) garbanzo beans, rinsed and drained
2 tablespoons olive oil
1 tablespoon fresh lemon juice
½ teaspoon salt
¼ teaspoon ground black pepper

◆ In 1-quart saucepan, heat first 6 ingredients over medium-low heat, stirring, 1 to 2 minutes, until very fragrant. Remove from heat.

◆ In food processor with knife blade attached, combine garbanzo beans, olive oil, lemon juice, salt, black pepper, toasted spices, and ¼ *cup water*; blend until smooth. Transfer to small serving bowl.

**Each tablespoon: About 25 calories, 1g protein, 3g carbohydrate, 1g total fat (0g saturated), 0mg cholesterol, 100mg sodium**

## PARMESAN DIP

*Prep:* 10 minutes plus chilling
*Makes* about 1¼ cups

⅔ cup sour cream
⅓ cup mayonnaise
¼ cup freshly grated Parmesan cheese
1 tablespoon fresh lemon juice
3 anchovy fillets, mashed
½ teaspoon coarsely ground black pepper

In small bowl, with fork or wire whisk, mix all ingredients. Cover and refrigerate about 2 hours for flavors to blend.

**Each tablespoon: About 50 calories, 1g protein, 1g carbohydrate, 5g total fat (2g saturated), 7mg cholesterol, 70mg sodium**

## GUACAMOLE

*Prep:* 15 minutes    *Makes* about 1½ cups

2 ripe avocados
2 tablespoons minced onion
2 tablespoons chopped fresh cilantro
1 tablespoon fresh lime juice
2 serrano or jalapeño chiles, seeded and minced
½ teaspoon salt
¼ teaspoon ground black pepper
1 plum tomato, finely chopped

◆ Cut each avocado in half; remove seeds. With spoon, scoop flesh from peel into medium bowl.

◆ Add next 6 ingredients. With potato masher, coarsely mash avocados. Stir in tomato. Transfer to small serving bowl.

**Each tablespoon: About 30 calories, 0g protein, 2g carbohydrate, 3g total fat (0g saturated), 0mg cholesterol, 45mg sodium**

## PUMPKIN AND ROASTED GARLIC DIP

*Prep:* 10 minutes plus cooling
*Bake:* 45 minutes    *Makes* about 2 cups

1 whole head garlic
1 can (16 ounces) solid-pack pumpkin (not pumpkin-pie mix)
2 tablespoons olive oil
1½ teaspoons salt
1 tablespoon chopped fresh parsley

◆ Preheat oven to 450°F. Discard papery outer layer from garlic; do not separate cloves. Wrap garlic in foil.

◆ Roast garlic 45 minutes, or until tender. Remove from oven; cool.

◆ When cool, squeeze garlic from skin. In food processor with knife blade attached, puree garlic, pumpkin, oil, and salt. Stir in parsley. Transfer to small serving bowl.

**Each tablespoon: About 15 calories, 0g protein, 2g carbohydrate, 1g total fat (0g saturated), 0mg cholesterol, 100mg sodium**

## ROASTED EGGPLANT DIP

*Prep:* 15 minutes plus draining    *Roast:* 1 hour
*Makes* about 2 cups

2 small eggplants (1 pound each)
2 garlic cloves, cut into thin slivers
2 tablespoons olive oil
4 teaspoons fresh lemon juice
1 teaspoon salt
¼ teaspoon ground black pepper
2 tablespoons chopped fresh parsley
2 tablespoons chopped fresh mint

◆ Preheat oven to 400°F. Cut slits all over eggplants; insert garlic. Place eggplants on jelly-roll pan and roast 1 hour, or until collapsed. Remove from oven; cool.

◆ When cool, cut each eggplant in half. With spoon, scoop flesh from skin into colander set over bowl; discard skin. Let drain 10 minutes.

◆ Transfer eggplant to food processor with knife blade attached. Add oil, lemon juice, salt, and pepper and blend, pulsing processor on and off, until coarsely chopped.

◆ Add herbs; pulse to combine. Transfer to small serving bowl.

**Each tablespoon: About 15 calories, 0g protein, 2g carbohydrate, 1g total fat (0g saturated), 0mg cholesterol, 70mg sodium**

## HONEY-MUSTARD DIP

*Prep:* 10 minutes    *Makes* about ⅔ cup

¼ cup Dijon mustard
¼ cup honey
1 tablespoon soy sauce
1 tablespoon minced green onion
2 teaspoons minced, peeled fresh ginger

In small bowl, with fork or wire whisk, mix all ingredients.

**Each tablespoon: About 30 calories, 0g protein, 7g carbohydrate, 0g total fat, 0mg cholesterol, 235mg sodium**

# Phyllo-wrapped Appetizers

Phyllo can be layered and wrapped around fillings of all sorts – keep it covered while you work to prevent it from drying out. Freeze these phyllo appetizers, unbaked, up to 1 month, and bake from frozen, allowing a little more baking time.

## Mini spring rolls

◆◆◆◆◆◆◆◆◆◆◆◆◆

*Prep: 40 minutes*
*Bake: 15 minutes*
*Makes 36*

**Shrimp and Vegetable Filling (see right)**
**12 sheets (about 16" by 12" each) fresh or frozen (thawed) phyllo (about 8 ounces)**
**4 tablespoons margarine or butter, melted**
**Soy sauce for serving**

**1** Grease two 15½" by 10½" jelly-roll pans. Prepare filling; set aside. Arrange phyllo sheets in one stack. Cut crosswise into 3 strips. Place strips on waxed paper; cover with plastic wrap.

**3** Roll strip with filling one-third of the way up, then fold left and right sides over and continue rolling to end.

**2** Place 1 strip phyllo on work surface. Brush top lightly with some melted margarine. Drain any liquid from filling. Place 1 scant tablespoon filling in center at end of strip.

**4** Place roll, seam-side down, in jelly-roll pan; brush lightly with melted margarine. Repeat with remaining phyllo strips, filling, and melted margarine, placing rolls about 1 inch apart in pans. If not serving right away, cover with foil and refrigerate. Preheat oven to 375°F. Bake spring rolls 15 minutes, or until golden. Serve hot with soy sauce.

## SHRIMP AND VEGETABLE FILLING

◆◆◆◆◆◆◆◆◆

**1 tablespoon cornstarch**
**1 tablespoon dry sherry**
**1 tablespoon soy sauce**
**¼ teaspoon sugar**
**4 tablespoons vegetable oil**
**2 cups packed, finely sliced napa cabbage (Chinese cabbage)**
**¼ cup chopped green onions**
**½ cup chopped mushrooms**
**½ pound medium shrimp, shelled and deveined, chopped**
**½ teaspoon grated, peeled fresh ginger**
**½ cup bean sprouts, chopped**
**½ cup chopped, drained, canned bamboo shoots**
**4 ounces cooked ham, chopped**

**1** In cup, mix first 4 ingredients, set aside. In 4-quart saucepan, heat 2 tablespoons oil over high heat. Add napa cabbage, green onions, and mushrooms and cook, stirring frequently, about 1 minute, just until tender-crisp. With slotted spoon, transfer to large bowl.

**2** In same saucepan, heat 2 more tablespoons oil over high heat. Add shrimp and ginger; cook, stirring constantly, 30 seconds, or until shrimp turn opaque throughout. Pour in cornstarch mixture and stir until thickened. Add shrimp mixture to bowl with vegetables. With paper towels, pat bean sprouts and bamboo shoots dry; add to vegetables with ham and mix.

EACH PIECE: ABOUT 55 CALORIES, 2g PROTEIN, 4g CARBOHYDRATE, 3g TOTAL FAT (1g SATURATED), 11mg CHOLESTEROL, 120mg SODIUM

## GREEK CHEESE BUNDLES

*Prep: 40 minutes    Bake: 15 to 20 minutes*

*Makes 50*

| | |
|---|---|
| 4 ounces feta cheese, crumbled (about 1 cup) | 1 large egg |
| ½ cup part-skim ricotta cheese | 8 sheets (about 16" by 12" each) fresh or frozen (thawed) phyllo (about 5 ounces) |
| 2 tablespoons chopped fresh parsley | |
| ¼ teaspoon coarsely ground black pepper | 4 tablespoons margarine or butter, melted |

◆ Grease two 15½" by 10½" jelly-roll pans. In medium bowl, with fork, mix first 5 ingredients. Arrange phyllo sheets in one stack. Cut lengthwise into 5 strips; cut each strip crosswise into 5 rectangles. Place cut phyllo on waxed paper; cover with plastic wrap to prevent phyllo from drying out.

◆ Place 2 rectangles of phyllo on top of each other on work surface; brush top lightly with melted margarine. Place 2 more rectangles crosswise on top of first 2 rectangles; brush lightly with more margarine. Place 1 rounded teaspoon filling in center; crimp phyllo around filling to form a bundle. Repeat with remaining phyllo, margarine, and filling.

◆ Place bundles, crimped-side up, in jelly-roll pans. Brush with melted margarine. If not serving right away, cover and refrigerate. Preheat oven to 400°F. Bake cheese bundles 15 to 20 minutes, until golden. Serve hot.

**Each piece: About 25 calories, 1g protein, 2g carbohydrate, 2g total fat (1g saturated), 7mg cholesterol, 50mg sodium**

## MUSHROOM TRIANGLES

*Prep: 45 minutes    Bake: 10 to 12 minutes*

*Makes 35*

| | |
|---|---|
| 2 tablespoons vegetable oil | ¼ teaspoon dried thyme |
| 2 pounds mushrooms, minced | 7 sheets (about 16" by 12" each) fresh or frozen (thawed) phyllo (about 5 ounces) |
| 1 large onion, minced | |
| 1 teaspoon salt | |
| 2 tablespoons freshly grated Parmesan cheese | 3 tablespoons margarine or butter, melted |

◆ In nonstick 12-inch skillet, heat oil over medium-high heat; add mushrooms, onion, and salt and cook about 15 minutes, until mushrooms and onion are golden and all liquid has evaporated. Remove skillet from heat; stir in Parmesan cheese and thyme.

◆ Arrange phyllo sheets in one stack. Cut stack lengthwise into 5 strips. Place cut phyllo on waxed paper; cover with plastic wrap to prevent phyllo from drying out.

◆ Place 1 phyllo strip on work surface; brush top lightly with melted margarine. Place about 2 teaspoons mushroom mixture at end of strip. Fold one corner of strip diagonally over filling so that short edge meets long edge of strip, forming a right angle. Continue folding over at right angles to form a triangular-shaped package.

◆ Repeat with remaining phyllo strips and mushroom mixture, brushing each strip with some melted margarine. Place triangles, seam-side down, in ungreased 15½" by 10½" jelly-roll pan; brush with remaining margarine. If not serving right away, cover and refrigerate. Preheat oven to 425°F. Bake triangles 10 to 12 minutes, until golden. Serve hot.

**Each piece: About 35 calories, 1g protein, 4g carbohydrate, 2g total fat (0g saturated), 0mg cholesterol, 100mg sodium**

◆◆◆◆◆◆◆◆◆◆◆◆◆◆◆◆◆◆◆◆◆◆◆◆◆◆

### DECORATIVE TOUCHES FOR PHYLLO

If you like, for the Mushroom Triangles above, when you reach the last fold at the end of the phyllo strip, place a tiny sprig of fresh thyme, flat-leaf parsley, or other herb on the phyllo, and then fold the phyllo over to complete the triangular-shaped package. The herb will lend a pleasantly subtle fragrance and flavor.

◆◆◆◆◆◆◆◆◆◆◆◆◆◆◆◆◆◆◆◆◆◆◆◆◆◆

# VEGETABLE
# DISHES

# VEGETABLES

With hundreds of varieties to choose from, and countless ways to prepare them, there is a vegetable for practically every taste and occasion. Supermarkets offer myriad new and exotic vegetables alongside the basic broccoli, while farmers' markets bring top-notch local produce at its peak, in season, into the cities. Many of these markets offer heirloom produce – revivals of old-fashioned native varieties, particularly tomatoes, potatoes, and beans, that are generally more flavorful than their mass-market cousins.

## BUYING AND STORING

As a rule, buy vegetables in season – you'll get them at their peak of flavor and freshness and prices will be lower too. In general, choose firm, brightly colored vegetables without blemishes or wilted leaves. Smaller vegetables tend to be sweeter and more tender. Avoid buying packaged vegetables if you can, because the quality is harder to check.

Most vegetables stay freshest if they're stored in the coldest part of the refrigerator – usually the bottom shelf or the crisper drawer – in loosely sealed paper or plastic bags. Don't wrap them airtight, because condensation can form on the surface and speed deterioration. Store potatoes, onions, garlic, and winter squash in a cool, dark, well-ventilated place. For most vegetables, the sooner you use them, the more flavorful and nutritious they'll be.

## PREPARATION

• Shake or brush off loose dirt before washing, then use a soft vegetable brush for scrubbing. Lukewarm water is good for removing sand and grit from leafy vegetables and zucchini.
• Wash vegetables just before you use them.
• Peel off only a thin layer of skin, or don't peel at all, to cut the loss of vitamins, minerals, and fiber.
• Vegetables such as artichokes and celery root discolor quickly when cut. To reduce discoloration, use a stainless steel knife and rub the cut portions with a lemon half. Or, immediately place prepared vegetables in a bowl of acidulated water (combine 1 quart water with 3 tablespoons lemon juice).
• To revive limp cut vegetables or slightly wilted greens, soak them in ice water for about 15 minutes. Avoid soaking vegetables in water for longer than necessary, as it leaches out nutrients and creates waterlogged vegetables.

## COOKING SUCCESS

• Most vegetables should be cooked as briefly as possible for the brightest color, best texture, and freshest flavor. Unless the recipe directs otherwise, cook in the minimum amount of lightly salted water so you don't drain away nutrients.
• Most vegetables can be cooked in the microwave. The short cooking time means that they retain their color and texture, as well as more of their nutrients.
• If you're cooking vegetables to serve cold or reheat later, after steaming or boiling, drain and then immediately rinse under cold running water to halt the cooking.
• Don't discard vegetable cooking water; it's full of nutrients. Save to use in sauces, soups, stocks, and stews.

## THE RIGHT CUT

A sharp knife is essential for cutting vegetables. For speedy slicing, you can use an adjustable-blade slicer (see page 55) or a food processor.

Cut vegetables into same-sized pieces for even cooking and a more attractive finished dish.

Dice – small, even cubes

Julienne – fine strips the size of a matchstick

Chop – small, irregular-shaped pieces

### ORGANIC VEGETABLES

Concern about chemicals in food has led to the wider availability of organic produce, with California leading the field. Produced without the use of chemical fertilizers and pesticides, these vegetables are not only healthful, but can be more flavorful as well. Production is labor-intensive and yields relatively low, however, so organic vegetables are more expensive than their supermarket counterparts. At present there are no consistent regulations guiding the standards of growers. If in doubt, ask what standards are being met – a reputable supplier will be happy to answer your questions.

## CABBAGE FAMILY

**Broccoli and broccoli rabe (rapini, broccoli di rape)** Choose broccoli with firm, tightly closed buds (either dark green or purplish green) and no sign of yellowing or flowering. The stems should be firm; if they seem tough, peel away the outer layer with a vegetable peeler. Broccoli rabe has leafy stalks with clusters of tiny broccoli-like buds; the flavor is pleasantly bitter. Look for sturdy stalks and fresh, dark-green leaves.

**Brussels sprouts** Buy bright green, firm, tight heads. Small are best; large sprouts can be bitter. If boiling or steaming, cut an "x" in the base of each sprout first for even cooking.

**Cauliflower and broccoflower** When buying either cauliflower or broccoflower (a pale-green cross between broccoli and cauliflower with a mild flavor), choose firm heads that feel heavy for their size. Check that flowerets are tightly packed and unblemished; leaves should look fresh and green. The size of the head has no bearing on quality.

**Chinese cabbage** Resembling lettuce more than cabbage, napa (or simply "Chinese cabbage") has an elongated shape and pale green leaves that curl at the tips – look for crisp, firm leaves and a freshly cut stalk end. Bok choy has wide white or pale green stalks gathered in a loose head flowing to large green leaves. Choose bok choy with crisp, firm, stalks and moist, deep green leaves.

**Head cabbage (green, red, savoy)** Of these cabbages, savoy has the most mellow flavor. Buy heads that feel heavy for their size with fresh, unwilted leaves free of browning.

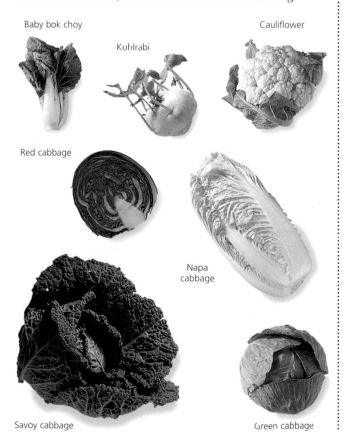

Baby bok choy

Kohlrabi

Cauliflower

Red cabbage

Napa cabbage

Savoy cabbage

Green cabbage

**Kohlrabi** This pale green or purple bulb has leafy shoots at the top; the bulb tastes like turnip, while the leaves have a spinach flavor. Choose small, heavy bulbs with dark green leaves; larger bulbs can be woody. Always peel before using.

## LEAFY GREENS

Vitamin-rich leafy greens can be young and tender and eaten raw, or mature and strong-flavored and better cooked. Greens cook down substantially; a pound yields only ½ cup cooked. Look for crisp, unblemished, brightly colored greens; small leaves with thin stems are the most tender. To store, wash greens in several changes of water and pat dry with paper towels. Line a zip-tight plastic bag with a damp paper towel, loosely fill with greens, and use within 3 days.
• Mild-flavored greens include spinach, lettuce, and Swiss chard, with stalks that taste like celery and leaves that taste like spinach. Spinach is great in salads; chard is best cooked.
• For a moderately strong flavor, choose beet greens, collards, Belgian endive, and escarole.
• Pungent greens include chicory (curly endive), kale, dandelion greens, mustard greens, and turnip greens. Except when very young and tender, these greens are bitter raw, but are delicious sautéed with garlic and olive oil, or added (at the end of cooking time) to soups and stews.

## ARTICHOKES, ASPARAGUS, CELERY, AND FENNEL

**Artichokes** Choose globe artichokes that feel heavy for their size, with compact heads and tightly closed green leaves. Heavily browned artichokes are old, but a little brown at the ends of the leaves (from frost) is fine. For baby artichokes, look for compact heads with soft leaves and soft stalks.

**Asparagus** Look for brightly colored, firm spears with tight buds; choose even-sized spears for uniform cooking. White asparagus is more expensive. Peeling is optional; if you do peel, remove only the tough peel at the stem end. You can also remove the scales with a paring knife, if you like. To store, trim ends and stand spears upright, loosely covered, in a tall glass with 1 inch of water in the bottom.

**Celery** A head of celery should look moist and crisp. Look for tight, compact heads with unblemished stalks and fresh leaves. In general, a darker color indicates a stronger taste. If you like, use a vegetable peeler to remove the outer strings.

**Fennel (sometimes labeled anise)** All parts of fennel are edible, from the bulb to the celery-like stalks and feathery leaves (add to salads or use as a garnish). Fennel can be eaten raw (slice it thin and add to salads or crudités platters) or cooked. Slow-cooking fennel by roasting or braising brings out its sweetness and tames the licorice flavor. Look for compact, uncracked, whitish-green bulbs free of discoloration; the leaves should look fresh and green. Bulbs that are spreading at the top indicate an older, tougher vegetable.

## BEANS, CORN, OKRA, AND PEAS

**Beans** The beans with edible pods include green beans, yellow wax beans, Italian green beans, and haricots verts, a slender French variety (see page 50). Beans should have a good color and firm, unblemished pods that snap crisply when bent (though haricots verts tend to be less crisp).

**Corn** Always cook corn soon after purchase, before the natural sugars turn to starch and reduce sweetness. Look for green, healthy husks that fit the cob tightly. The silk should be moist and fresh-looking – dry silk indicates old corn. Kernels should be plump and milky and grow in tight rows right to the tip. Pass on corn that's sold husked, since it deteriorates faster – shuck just before cooking.

**Okra** Buy small, bright green pods that are firm, not limp. Avoid large pods, which can be fibrous or tough. Okra becomes slippery when cooked and acts as a thickener for sauced dishes. Don't cook okra in a cast-iron or aluminum pot – these metals can cause okra to discolor.

**Edible-pod peas** These crisp treats are eaten pod and all. Snow peas have flat, almost translucent pods, while sugar snap peas have plumper, rounder pods. For either variety, look for firm, crisp pods with a good green color. Sugar snaps should be plump but not bursting at the seam.

**Peas** Choose fresh peas with plump, firm, bright green pods. The sugars in peas turn to starch soon after picking, so buy and cook as fresh as possible. Shell just before using. A pound of peas in the pod yields about 1 cup shelled peas.

## ROOT VEGETABLES

**Beets** Loved for their sweetness, beets have the highest sugar content of any vegetable (however, they're very low in calories). Choose firm, unblemished, small to medium-sized beets. If possible, buy bunches with the green tops on, which can be cooked like spinach. The leaves should look fresh and healthy.

Turnips

**Carrots and parsnips** Buy firm, smooth, slender roots without cracks or blemishes. Small parsnips have the sweetest flavor; large parsnips may have a woody center. Baby carrots look great on a plate, but mature, dark orange carrots actually have the sweetest taste and most vitamins.

Beets

**Celery root (celeriac)** This aromatic knobby root tastes like a cross between celery and parsley. Small, firm roots have the best texture;

Parsnips

---

Carrots          Rutabaga          Celery root

for easy peeling, look for a minimum of rootlets and knobs. Celery root can be shredded and dressed for salad; it's also delicious cooked in soups or purees.

**Radish** Look for smooth radishes that feel firm, not spongy. They vary in color (white, red, purple, black), shape (round, oval, elongated), and flavor (from peppery-hot to mild).

**Rutabaga** Choose firm, heavy rutabagas with smooth skin. When cooked, their yellow flesh takes on a creamy texture.

**Sunchokes (Jerusalem artichokes)** Look for small, firm sunchokes free of soft or green-tinged spots (see page 54).

**Turnips** Buy small turnips that feel heavy for their size, with smooth, unbruised skins. Large turnips can be woody.

## POTATOES

Potatoes vary in their starch content, which makes a difference to the texture of the finished dish. Russet, or baking, potatoes have a fluffy, mealy texture that makes them good for frying and baking. Waxy potatoes – all-purpose round reds, round whites, and long whites – have less starch and hold their shape when cooked. They're ideal for boiling and salads. Tiny fingerlings are perfect steamed whole, while yellow-fleshed potatoes have a creamy texture.

Sweet potatoes can be yellow or orange. The yellow-fleshed variety is drier and less sweet than the orange-fleshed sweet potato, which is often incorrectly called a yam. (True yams are ivory-fleshed tropical tubers available in Latin markets.)

Sweet potato

Whatever the variety, choose dry, smooth potatoes without sprouts. Pass on potatoes with a greenish cast (the result of prolonged exposure to light) because they'll taste bitter. Store potatoes in a cool, dark, well-ventilated place – not the refrigerator. Older potatoes will keep for about 2 weeks; new and sweet potatoes will keep for about a week.

Red potato

Peeling or not is a matter of choice, but do cut off any green areas or sprouts.

Baking potato          Round white

# ONION FAMILY

These vegetables range from "dry" ones with papery outer skins, such as onions and garlic, to "green" varieties that have a bulb at one end, such as green and spring onions. Dry onions are categorized either as storage onions, which are firm, compact, available year-round, and strong-flavored (freeze for 20 minutes before chopping for fewer tears), or sweet onions, like Vidalia and Walla Walla. Sweet onions, ripe in spring and summer, have a higher water and sugar content and are more fragile. Of all the onion family, leeks alone need thorough cleaning: Slit lengthwise from top to bottom and rinse well, fanning the leaves to remove all grit.

Choose dry onions that feel heavy for their size with dry, papery skins. Avoid any with sprouts or soft spots. Green onions should have clean white bulbs and fresh-looking tops. Store dry onions, preferably in a single layer, in a cool, dry, dark, airy place. Refrigerate green onions up to 2 weeks. (For more information on garlic, see page 99.)

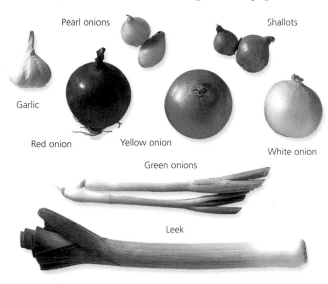

Pearl onions

Shallots

Garlic

Red onion     Yellow onion

White onion

Green onions

Leek

# SQUASH

Squash are divided into two groups, summer and winter, but most are available year-round. Summer squash have tender flesh and seeds and soft edible skins. Winter squash have hard, thick skins and seeds and firm flesh. When buying summer squash, choose small ones that feel firm, not flabby. Winter squash should have hard, blemish-free skin. For either type, look for dry, well-shaped squash with good color; a squash should feel heavy for its size. Store summer squash in the refrigerator and winter squash in a cool, dry spot.

## SUMMER SQUASH

**Pattypan** This small, pretty, bowl-shaped squash has a scalloped edge; it can be white, yellow, or pale green. The whimsical shape of this quick-cooking squash makes it perfect for grilling or, if large, for stuffing.

**Yellow squash and zucchini** Yellow squash comes as crookneck (with a curved neck) and straightneck. Besides regular zucchini, there are yellow and gray zucchini. Both vegetables can be eaten raw or cooked. Younger varieties tend to have the sweetest flavor (look for baby yellow squash and zucchini, which have a particularly sweet taste and crisp texture and look pretty on crudités platters or in stir-fries). Avoid fat, overgrown squash – they tend to have a bland flavor, large seeds, and a spongy texture.

## WINTER SQUASH

**Acorn** This round, deeply ridged squash has a dark green skin, sometimes with an orange blotch, and a sweet orange flesh. There is also an orange-skinned variety. It is often stuffed with savory fillings or simply sliced and baked.

**Butternut** With one end shaped like a bulb, this large tan squash has deep orange flesh that's moist and sweet. It's used in soups and pies as well as served on its own.

**Chayote** Also called mirliton, this pear-shaped, pale green squash has a large center seed and a slight apple taste. Although it's a winter squash, prepare as you would zucchini.

**Hubbard** A very large greenish-gray squash, Hubbard is often sold in cut pieces. The flesh is dry but sweet, delicious roasted with herbs and root vegetables.

**Pumpkin** Jack-o'-lantern pumpkins have stringy flesh, which should be strained after cooking; pie pumpkins, with more flesh and fewer fibers, make better eating. Cut in half or into wedges, remove seeds, and bake as you would other squash. Buy blemish-free, heavy pumpkins.

**Spaghetti** This watermelon-shaped squash has yellow-gold flesh that separates into spaghetti-like strands when cooked. Look for pale yellow skin; if greenish, the squash is underripe.

Yellow zucchini

Pattypan squash

Acorn squash

Baby pumpkin

Spaghetti squash

## MUSHROOMS

Fresh or dried, mushrooms come in great variety (see page 63). Buy plump, firm, unblemished fresh mushrooms with an even color. To store, refrigerate in a loosely closed paper bag (so they can breathe), loosely covered with a damp paper towel. Avoid storing in plastic bags – they'll become too moist, acquire a slimy texture, and deteriorate faster. Clean mushrooms just before using with a soft brush or a swipe of a damp cloth. Never subject mushrooms to a long rinsing or soak them in water – they'll absorb water and become soggy.

Dried mushrooms are available in many varieties. They have a more concentrated flavor and will add a woody depth to soups, stews, and sauces. Soak dried mushrooms in warm water for 20 minutes before using. Be sure to use the flavorful soaking liquid in your recipe (strain it first).

**White (button)** This common cultivated mushroom can also be cream or brown-colored. White mushrooms have a mild flavor, with caps that range from ½ to 3 inches in diameter.

**Portobello** A dark brown mushroom measuring as much as 6 inches in diameter. Portobellos have open caps with exposed gills and are prized for their rich flavor and meaty texture. The woody stems can be used in stocks.

**Cremini** A brown, full-flavored variation of the button mushroom. Portobellos are the mature form of cremini.

**Shiitake** A brown Asian mushroom with a flat cap and a rich, meaty flavor. The stems are usually too tough to eat.

**Oyster** A delicate-tasting Asian variety with a soft cream or gray color, large, ruffled top, and a short, fat stem.

**Morel** A golden-brown mushroom with a honeycombed, elongated cap and unusual spongy texture. Morels are available in specialty food stores; they have a hearty, woodsy flavor and tender texture when cooked.

**Porcini** Also called cèpes, these delicious mushrooms are pale brown and range in size from an ounce to a pound. They have a meaty texture and strong, woodsy flavor. They are expensive and rarely available fresh in the U.S. Dried porcini are widely available, however, and even a small quantity will add a lot of flavor to a dish.

**Chanterelle** A trumpet-shaped mushroom that ranges in color from bright yellow to orange. Chanterelles have a delicate, nutty flavor and chewy texture. When buying, avoid any that are broken or shrivelled. Cook gently and briefly.

## EGGPLANT

This vegetable comes in many guises – including the ubiquitous pear-shaped Western eggplant, small baby Italian or long, slender Japanese eggplant, and elegant creamy-white varieties (see page 66). Choose eggplants that feel heavy for their size with smooth, glossy, taut skins free of soft or brown spots. Avoid hard eggplants, which are underripe. Unlike many vegetables, eggplant will not suffer if it's overcooked – it will simply have a softer texture. Peeling is optional; the skin is edible and adds a beautiful color to dishes.

## PEPPERS AND CHILES

Although peppers are classed as fruits, sweet bell peppers are used as a vegetable, while chiles, the hot peppers, are used more as a seasoning. As sweet peppers ripen, they become even sweeter. Red peppers are simply green peppers that have been left on the vine to ripen. The sweetest pepper is the pimiento, which is sold canned or jarred.

Chiles vary widely in flavor and hotness, from mild to burning. As a broad rule, the smaller the chile, the hotter it is. Tiny Thai chiles, habaneros, and Scotch bonnets are searingly hot; jalapeños and serranos are less so. Large poblanos are quite mild. Capsaicin is the compound that gives chiles their heat, and most of the capsaicin is in the seeds and veins. To tame the fire, remove the seeds and veins, but take care – the oils released can irritate the skin. If you have sensitive skin, wear rubber gloves when preparing chiles, and wash your hands well when you are finished.

Choose sweet peppers and chiles with a bright color for their variety and firm, smooth skins. Pass on blemished or bruised peppers. Some chiles are also sold dried; soak them in hot water for about 30 minutes before using.

Jalapeño
Serrano
Habanero
Scotch bonnet
Thai

## TOMATOES

Tomatoes come in many forms (see page 70) and vary in sweetness and acidity. Cherry tomatoes, red or yellow, are reliably sweet all year round. Yellow tomatoes are lower in acid than red varieties. Plum tomatoes have thick, meaty walls – they're ideal for cooked sauces.

Select firm (but not hard), heavy tomatoes with deeply colored, unblemished skins. Don't store tomatoes in the refrigerator, because cold kills their flavor; the only time to refrigerate a tomato is when it's overripe. Otherwise, store them at room temperature, but out of direct sunlight, where they can turn mushy. Unripe tomatoes can be placed in a paper bag with an apple to speed ripening.

Canned tomatoes are preferable to fresh in cooking when good-quality fresh tomatoes are unavailable.

# CABBAGE FAMILY

The cabbage family includes green, red, savoy, and napa varieties, plus broccoli, Brussels sprouts, and cauliflower. A lesser-known member is kohlrabi, which resembles a knobby pale green beet and is a cross between cabbage and turnip. Best known for being nutritious and economical, these underrated vegetables are tasty both raw and cooked. The freshest vegetables have the mildest, most delicate flavor; with long storage or overcooking, they develop stronger "cabbage-y" flavor and odor. Red cabbage, with its sturdier structure, demands slightly longer cooking than green.

## VEGETARIAN STUFFED CABBAGE

◆◆◆◆◆◆◆◆◆◆◆◆◆◆◆◆◆◆◆◆◆◆◆◆◆◆◆◆◆

*Prep:* 50 minutes    *Cook:* 1 hour
*Makes* 6 main-dish servings

1 medium head savoy cabbage (3 pounds), tough outer leaves discarded
2 tablespoons vegetable oil
1 red pepper, finely chopped
1 yellow pepper, finely chopped
2 medium onions, finely chopped
1 tablespoon seasoned rice vinegar
1 garlic clove, minced
2 tablespoons soy sauce

2 tablespoons minced, peeled fresh ginger
½ cup regular long-grain rice, cooked as label directs
1 can (15 to 19 ounces) white kidney beans (cannellini), rinsed and drained
1 can (8 ounces) sliced water chestnuts, drained and finely chopped
1 can (28 ounces) tomatoes
French bread (optional)

1 Remove 2 large cabbage leaves; set aside. Cut out core and center of cabbage, leaving a 1-inch shell. Discard core and dice 2 cups cabbage from center leaves.

2 In nonstick 12-inch skillet, heat 1 tablespoon oil over medium-high heat. Add peppers and half of onions; cook, stirring often, 8 to 10 minutes, until tender.

3 Add diced cabbage, rice vinegar, garlic, 1 tablespoon soy sauce, and 1 tablespoon ginger; cook 5 minutes. Remove from heat; stir in rice, beans, and water chestnuts.

4 Fill cabbage shell with vegetable mixture, packing mixture firmly but gently. Cover opening with reserved cabbage leaves, overlapping slightly; tie with string. In 8-quart Dutch oven, heat remaining 1 tablespoon oil over medium heat. Add remaining onions and cook 5 minutes, or until tender. Add remaining 1 tablespoon ginger; cook 30 seconds.

5 Add tomatoes with their juice, remaining 1 tablespoon soy sauce, and *1 cup water*, breaking up tomatoes with back of spoon. Place stuffed cabbage, core-end down, in tomato sauce and heat to boiling over high heat. Reduce heat to low; cover and simmer 1 hour, basting cabbage occasionally. To serve, place cabbage in deep platter; discard string. Spoon sauce around cabbage. Cut into wedges. Serve with French bread, if you like.

EACH SERVING: ABOUT 295 CALORIES, 12g PROTEIN, 54g CARBOHYDRATE, 5g TOTAL FAT (1g SATURATED), 0mg CHOLESTEROL, 885mg SODIUM

## KOHLRABI AND CARROTS WITH DILL

*Prep: 25 minutes    Cook: 25 minutes*
*Makes 6 accompaniment servings*

6 medium kohlrabi (about 2 pounds), peeled
1 bag (16 ounces) carrots
2 tablespoons vegetable oil
4 tablespoons margarine or butter
2 teaspoons all-purpose flour
1 chicken-flavor bouillon cube or envelope
1 tablespoon chopped fresh dill or ½ teaspoon dillweed

Cut each kohlrabi into ½-inch-thick slices; cut each slice into ½-inch-wide sticks. Cut each carrot crosswise into 3 pieces; cut each piece lengthwise into quarters. In 12-inch skillet, heat oil over medium-high heat; add vegetables and cook, stirring often, about 15 minutes, until browned. Add *⅓ cup water*; reduce heat to low. Cover and cook 10 minutes, or until vegetables are tender-crisp and liquid evaporates. Meanwhile, in 1-quart saucepan, melt margarine over low heat; stir in flour and cook 1 minute. Add bouillon; gradually stir in *½ cup water*; cook, stirring constantly, until mixture thickens slightly and boils. Pour sauce over vegetables and sprinkle with dill; gently toss to coat well.

**Each serving: About 185 calories, 4g protein, 18g carbohydrate, 12g total fat (2g saturated), 0mg cholesterol, 295mg sodium**

## RED CABBAGE WITH APPLES

*Prep: 15 minutes    Cook: 25 minutes*
*Makes 8 accompaniment servings*

2 tablespoons olive oil
1 medium head red cabbage (about 2½ pounds), quartered, cored, and coarsely sliced
2 Golden Delicious apples, peeled, cored, and chopped
1 tablespoon sugar
2 tablespoons red wine vinegar
2 teaspoons salt
Chopped fresh parsley for garnish

In 12-inch skillet, heat olive oil over high heat. Add cabbage and apples; toss to coat. Stir in sugar, vinegar, and salt. Reduce heat to medium; cook, stirring occasionally, about 20 minutes, until cabbage is tender. To serve, sprinkle with parsley.

**Each serving: About 90 calories, 2g protein, 15g carbohydrate, 4g total fat (1g saturated), 0mg cholesterol, 550mg sodium**

## SAUTÉED CABBAGE AND FRESH PEAS

*Prep: 25 minutes    Cook: 15 to 20 minutes*
*Makes 6 accompaniment servings*

3 tablespoons vegetable oil
1 medium onion, chopped
1 medium head green cabbage (about 2½ pounds), quartered, cored, and cut into ¾-inch-wide slices
2 pounds fresh peas, shelled (2 cups), or 1 package (10 ounces) frozen peas
1¼ teaspoons salt
¼ teaspoon crushed red pepper
1 tablespoon chopped fresh thyme or parsley

◆ In 5-quart Dutch oven, heat oil over medium heat; add onion and cook, stirring occasionally, 5 minutes, or until tender and golden.

◆ Stir in cabbage, peas, salt, crushed red pepper, and *2 tablespoons water*. Increase heat to high and cook, stirring frequently, 10 to 12 minutes, until cabbage is tender-crisp. To serve, sprinkle with thyme.

**Each serving: About 135 calories, 4g protein, 16g carbohydrate, 7g total fat (1g saturated), 0mg cholesterol, 480mg sodium**

## CABBAGE AND ONION WITH CARAWAY

*Prep: 10 minutes    Cook: 15 to 20 minutes*
*Makes 6 accompaniment servings*

1 medium head green cabbage (about 2½ pounds)
2 tablespoons vegetable oil
1 large onion, diced
1 teaspoon salt
¾ teaspoon caraway seeds, crushed
¼ teaspoon ground black pepper

◆ Carefully remove several large cabbage leaves and use to line serving platter, if you like. Set platter aside.

◆ Cut cabbage into quarters; cut out core. Coarsely slice cabbage and discard tough ribs.

◆ In 5-quart Dutch oven, heat 2 tablespoons oil over medium heat; add onion and cook, stirring occasionally, 5 minutes, or until tender and golden.

◆ Stir in cabbage, salt, caraway seeds, and pepper. Increase heat to high and cook, stirring frequently, 10 to 12 minutes, until cabbage is tender-crisp. To serve, spoon cabbage mixture onto platter lined with cabbage leaves.

**Each serving: About 100 calories, 3g protein, 13g carbohydrate, 5g total fat (1g saturated), 0mg cholesterol, 390mg sodium**

## SAUTÉED BRUSSELS SPROUTS

*Prep: 15 minutes    Cook: 5 minutes*
*Makes 6 accompaniment servings*

2 containers (10 ounces each)   ½ teaspoon salt
  Brussels sprouts, trimmed
3 tablespoons margarine or
  butter

Thinly slice Brussels sprouts. In 12-inch skillet, melt margarine over high heat. Add sliced Brussels sprouts; sprinkle with salt and cook, stirring, 5 minutes, or until sprouts are tender-crisp and beginning to brown.

**Each serving: About 90 calories, 3g protein, 9g carbohydrate, 6g total fat (1g saturated), 0mg cholesterol, 265mg sodium**

## CURRIED CAULIFLOWER WITH POTATOES AND PEAS

*Prep: 15 minutes    Cook: 30 minutes*
*Makes 8 accompaniment servings*

1 tablespoon vegetable oil   ¼ teaspoon ground cumin
1 large onion, finely chopped   1 teaspoon salt
2 all-purpose potatoes, peeled   1 small head cauliflower
  and cut into ½-inch pieces    (2 pounds), cut into small
1 tablespoon minced, peeled    flowerets
  fresh ginger   1 cup frozen peas
2 garlic cloves, minced   ¼ cup chopped fresh cilantro
1 teaspoon curry powder

In 10-inch skillet, heat oil over medium heat. Add onion and cook 5 minutes, or until tender. Add potatoes and next 4 ingredients; cook, stirring, 2 minutes. Stir in salt and *1½ cups water*; heat to boiling over high heat. Reduce heat to medium; cover and cook 10 minutes. Stir in cauliflower; cover and cook 10 minutes longer, or until tender. Stir in peas and cook, uncovered, until most of liquid evaporates. To serve, stir in cilantro.

**Each serving: About 120 calories, 5g protein, 21g carbohydrate, 2g total fat (0g saturated), 0mg cholesterol, 295mg sodium**

## BRUSSELS SPROUTS WITH BACON

*Prep: 15 minutes    Cook: 15 minutes*
*Makes 10 accompaniment servings*

3 containers (10 ounces each)   ½ teaspoon salt
  Brussels sprouts, trimmed   ¼ teaspoon coarsely ground
6 slices bacon    black pepper
1 tablespoon olive oil   ¼ cup pine nuts (pignoli),
2 garlic cloves, minced    toasted

◆ In 4-quart saucepan, heat *1 inch water* to boiling over high heat. Add Brussels sprouts; heat to boiling. Reduce heat to low; cover and simmer 5 minutes, or until sprouts are tender-crisp. Drain.

◆ In nonstick 12-inch skillet, cook bacon over medium-low heat until browned. Transfer bacon to paper towels to drain; crumble.

◆ Spoon off all but 1 tablespoon bacon fat from skillet. Heat bacon fat and olive oil over medium-high heat. Add Brussels sprouts, garlic, salt, and pepper. Cook, stirring frequently, about 5 minutes, until sprouts are browned. To serve, sprinkle with pine nuts and crumbled bacon.

**Each serving: About 85 calories, 4g protein, 9g carbohydrate, 5g total fat (1g saturated), 3mg cholesterol, 185mg sodium**

◆ ◆ ◆ ◆ ◆ ◆ ◆ ◆ ◆ ◆ ◆ ◆ ◆ ◆ ◆ ◆ ◆ ◆ ◆ ◆ ◆

### PREPARING BRUSSELS SPROUTS

First, remove any yellow or wilted leaves, then trim the stem. If boiling the sprouts, use a small knife to make an X-shaped cut in the stem end for faster and more uniform cooking.

◆ ◆ ◆ ◆ ◆ ◆ ◆ ◆ ◆ ◆ ◆ ◆ ◆ ◆ ◆ ◆ ◆ ◆ ◆ ◆ ◆

## VEGETABLES VINAIGRETTE

*Prep: 20 minutes    Cook: 25 to 30 minutes*
*Makes 8 accompaniment servings*

⅓ cup olive or vegetable oil
¼ cup Dijon mustard with
 seeds
¼ cup white wine vinegar
¾ teaspoon salt
1 large head cauliflower
 (3 pounds), cut into 2½" by
 ¾" pieces

1 large bunch broccoli, cut
 into 2½" by ¾" pieces
1 bag (16 ounces) carrots,
 cut into ¼-inch-thick
 diagonal slices

◆ In large bowl, with fork or wire whisk, mix oil, mustard, vinegar, and salt until blended; set aside.

◆ In 8-quart saucepot, heat *1 inch water* to boiling over high heat. Add cauliflower; heat to boiling. Reduce heat to low; cover and simmer 5 to 7 minutes, until tender-crisp. With slotted spoon, transfer cauliflower to colander; rinse with cold running water.

◆ In water remaining in saucepot, heat broccoli to boiling over high heat. Reduce heat to low; cover and simmer 5 to 7 minutes, until tender-crisp. With slotted spoon, transfer to colander with cauliflower; rinse with cold running water.

◆ In water remaining in saucepot (adding more *water* if necessary to equal 1 inch), heat carrots to boiling over high heat. Reduce heat to low; cover and simmer 5 minutes, or until tender-crisp. Transfer to colander with cauliflower and broccoli; rinse with cold running water.

◆ Add drained vegetables to bowl with vinaigrette; toss until coated with vinaigrette. Serve vegetables warm; or, cover and refrigerate to serve cold later.

**Each serving: About 180 calories, 7g protein, 19g carbohydrate, 10g total fat (1g saturated), 0mg cholesterol, 455mg sodium**

## WARM BROCCOLI AND POTATO SALAD

*Prep: 15 minutes    Cook: 25 minutes*
*Makes 8 accompaniment servings*

6 slices bacon, cut into ½-inch
 pieces
3 medium red potatoes, cut
 into ¼-inch-thick slices
1 medium onion, chopped
3 tablespoons red wine vinegar

2 teaspoons sugar
1½ teaspoons salt
¼ teaspoon crushed red
 pepper
1 large bunch broccoli, cut
 into 3" by 1" pieces

◆ In 12-inch skillet, cook bacon over medium-low heat until browned; drain on paper towels. Spoon off all but 3 tablespoons fat from skillet. Increase heat to medium. Add potatoes and onion; cook, turning potatoes occasionally, about 10 minutes, until browned. Add ½ cup water; reduce heat to medium-low. Cover and cook 5 minutes longer, until potatoes are tender. Stir in vinegar and next 3 ingredients; cook, stirring, until liquid boils and thickens slightly.

◆ Meanwhile, in 5-quart saucepot, in *1 inch boiling water*, heat broccoli to boiling over high heat. Reduce heat to low; cover and simmer, stirring occasionally, 8 to 10 minutes, until tender-crisp. Drain broccoli. Stir broccoli and bacon into potato mixture until broccoli is coated with dressing.

**Each serving: About 110 calories, 5g protein, 18g carbohydrate, 3g total fat (1g saturated), 4mg cholesterol, 505mg sodium**

## BROCCOLI AND RED-PEPPER AMANDINE

*Prep: 10 minutes    Cook: 15 minutes*
*Makes 5 accompaniment servings*

2 tablespoons olive or
 vegetable oil
1 red pepper, cut into ½-inch-
 wide strips
1 large bunch broccoli, cut
 into 2½" by 2" pieces

½ teaspoon salt
1 tablespoon fresh lemon
 juice
2 tablespoons sliced almonds,
 toasted

◆ In 12-inch skillet, heat 1 tablespoon oil over medium-high heat; add red pepper and cook until tender-crisp and browned. With slotted spoon, transfer to plate.

◆ In same skillet, heat remaining 1 tablespoon oil; add broccoli and cook, stirring constantly, until coated with oil. Add salt and *3 tablespoons water*. Reduce heat to medium; cover and cook 2 minutes. Uncover; stir-fry 5 minutes longer, or until broccoli is tender-crisp. Stir in red pepper. Spoon mixture onto platter. Sprinkle with lemon juice and almonds.

**Each serving: About 110 calories, 5g protein, 9g carbohydrate, 7g total fat (1g saturated), 0mg cholesterol, 250mg sodium**

# LEAFY GREENS

Packed with flavor and nutrients, leafy greens range in texture and taste from tender and mild to assertive, resilient, and slightly peppery or bitter – depending on type, age, and growing conditions. Spinach is especially delicate and versatile, but you can mix and match most leafy greens for variety (tougher or stronger-flavored greens will need longer cooking). For speed, use prewashed fresh spinach or frozen spinach. Always squeeze excess moisture from cooked or thawed spinach to avoid a watery dish.

## SPINACH AND RICOTTA DUMPLINGS

◆◆◆◆◆◆◆◆◆◆◆◆

*Prep: 50 minutes*
*Bake: 15 to 20 minutes*
*Makes 4 main-dish servings*

**2 bunches (10 to 12 ounces each) spinach or 2 packages (10 ounces each) frozen chopped spinach, thawed and squeezed dry**
**1 container (8 ounces) ricotta cheese**
**2 large eggs**
**¼ teaspoon ground black pepper**
**1 cup freshly grated Parmesan cheese**
**½ cup plus 2 tablespoons all-purpose flour**
**2 tablespoons margarine or butter**
**2 cups milk**

1 If using fresh spinach, remove tough stems; wash spinach well. In 5-quart Dutch oven, cook spinach with water clinging to leaves over high heat, stirring, until wilted. Drain. Squeeze dry; coarsely chop. Prepare dumplings: In large bowl, mix spinach, ricotta, eggs, pepper, ½ cup Parmesan, and ½ cup flour. With floured hands, shape spinach mixture into 2" by 1" ovals.

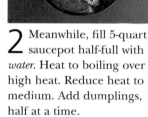

2 Meanwhile, fill 5-quart saucepot half-full with *water*. Heat to boiling over high heat. Reduce heat to medium. Add dumplings, half at a time.

3 Cook dumplings in simmering water, gently stirring occasionally, 3 to 5 minutes, until they float to the top. With slotted spoon, transfer dumplings to paper towels to drain. Preheat oven to 350°F.

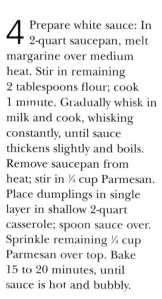

4 Prepare white sauce: In 2-quart saucepan, melt margarine over medium heat. Stir in remaining 2 tablespoons flour; cook 1 minute. Gradually whisk in milk and cook, whisking constantly, until sauce thickens slightly and boils. Remove saucepan from heat; stir in ¼ cup Parmesan. Place dumplings in single layer in shallow 2-quart casserole; spoon sauce over. Sprinkle remaining ¼ cup Parmesan over top. Bake 15 to 20 minutes, until sauce is hot and bubbly.

EACH SERVING: ABOUT 475 CALORIES, 30g PROTEIN, 27g CARBOHYDRATE, 28g TOTAL FAT (14g SATURATED), 171mg CHOLESTEROL, 785mg SODIUM

## ITALIAN SPINACH WITH GARBANZO BEANS AND RAISINS

*Prep: 15 minutes    Cook: 6 minutes*
*Makes 4 accompaniment servings*

1 tablespoon olive oil
1 garlic clove, crushed with side of knife
¼ teaspoon crushed red pepper
1 can (15 to 19 ounces) garbanzo beans, rinsed and drained
2 bunches (10 to 12 ounces each) spinach, washed and dried very well
¼ cup golden raisins
½ teaspoon salt

In 5-quart Dutch oven, heat oil with garlic over medium heat until garlic is golden; discard garlic. Add crushed red pepper to oil and cook 15 seconds. Stir in garbanzo beans and cook, stirring, 2 minutes, or until hot. Increase heat to high. Add spinach, raisins, and salt. Cook, stirring, 2 to 3 minutes, just until spinach wilts.

**Each serving: About 200 calories, 9g protein, 31g carbohydrate, 6g total fat (1g saturated), 0mg cholesterol, 805mg sodium**

## INDIAN CREAMED SPINACH

*Prep: 20 minutes    Cook: 12 minutes*
*Makes 4 accompaniment servings*

1 tablespoon margarine or butter
1 medium onion, finely chopped
2 teaspoons minced, peeled fresh ginger
2 garlic cloves, minced
½ teaspoon ground coriander
½ teaspoon ground cumin
⅛ teaspoon ground red pepper (cayenne)
2 bunches (10 to 12 ounces each) spinach, washed and dried very well
½ teaspoon salt
¼ cup heavy or whipping cream

◆ In 5-quart Dutch oven, melt margarine over medium heat. Add onion and cook, stirring often, 5 minutes, or until tender. Add ginger, garlic, coriander, cumin, and ground red pepper and cook, stirring, 1 minute.

◆ Increase heat to high. Add spinach and salt; cook, stirring, 2 to 3 minutes, just until spinach wilts. Stir in cream and boil 2 minutes, until thickened.

**Each serving: About 130 calories, 5g protein, 10g carbohydrate, 9g total fat (4g saturated), 20mg cholesterol, 420mg sodium**

## BAKED SPINACH AND RICE BALLS

*Prep: 45 minutes    Bake: 25 to 30 minutes*
*Makes 4 main-dish servings*

½ cup regular long-grain rice
2 bunches (10 to 12 ounces each) spinach or 2 packages (10 ounces each) frozen chopped spinach, thawed and squeezed dry
3 tablespoons olive or vegetable oil
2 large onions, diced
¼ teaspoon salt
Ground black pepper
½ cup freshly grated Parmesan cheese
¼ cup plain dried bread crumbs
1 large egg
1 large carrot, diced
½ teaspoon dried basil
1 can (14½ to 16 ounces) tomatoes
1 can (13¾ to 14½ ounces) vegetable or beef broth
2 teaspoons sugar

◆ In 1-quart saucepan, prepare rice as label directs. Meanwhile, if using fresh spinach, remove tough stems; wash spinach. Dry well; chop.

◆ In 12-inch skillet, heat 2 tablespoons oil over medium-high heat; add half of onions with salt and ½ teaspoon pepper and cook, stirring often, until tender and golden.

◆ Stir in spinach and cook, stirring, just until spinach wilts; remove skillet from heat. Stir in Parmesan cheese, bread crumbs, egg, and cooked rice until blended. Shape mixture into 12 balls; set aside.

◆ Preheat oven to 375°F. In 3-quart saucepan, heat remaining 1 tablespoon oil over medium-high heat; add carrot, basil, ¼ teaspoon pepper, and remaining onion and cook, stirring often, until onion and carrot are tender.

◆ Add tomatoes with their juice, broth, and sugar, breaking up tomatoes with back of spoon. Heat mixture to boiling over high heat and pour into shallow 2-quart baking dish.

◆ Arrange the spinach balls in sauce in baking dish. Bake 25 to 30 minutes, until sauce is hot and bubbly and spinach balls are heated through.

**Each serving: About 400 calories, 16g protein, 50g carbohydrate, 17g total fat (4g saturated), 63mg cholesterol, 765mg sodium**

## SPINACH WITH MUSHROOMS AND BACON

*Prep: 20 minutes   Cook: 15 minutes*
*Makes 4 accompaniment servings*

3 slices bacon
1 tablespoon olive oil
2 garlic cloves, crushed with
  side of knife
8 ounces mushrooms, cut into
  ¼-inch-thick slices
⅛ teaspoon ground black
  pepper

Salt
2 bunches (10 to 12 ounces
  each) spinach, washed and
  dried very well
1 tablespoon red wine vinegar
  (optional)

◆ In 5-quart Dutch oven, cook bacon over medium-low heat until browned; transfer to paper towels to drain. Discard drippings from Dutch oven.

◆ In same Dutch oven, heat oil with garlic over medium heat until garlic is golden; discard garlic. Add mushrooms, pepper, and ¼ teaspoon salt to oil; cook about 5 minutes, until mushrooms are tender and liquid has evaporated.

◆ Increase heat to high. Add spinach to Dutch oven, sprinkle with ¼ teaspoon salt, and cook, stirring, 2 to 3 minutes, just until spinach wilts. Stir in vinegar, if using. To serve, crumble bacon on top.

**Each serving: About 105 calories, 7g protein, 8g carbohydrate, 6g total fat (1g saturated), 4mg cholesterol, 455mg sodium**

## ESCAROLE PIE

*Prep: 50 minutes plus chilling and standing   Bake: 40 to 45 minutes*
*Makes 6 main-dish servings*

Pastry for 2-crust pie or
  1 package (10 to 11 ounces)
  piecrust mix, prepared as
  label directs
3 tablespoons olive oil
1 large onion, finely chopped
2 garlic cloves, minced
2 large heads escarole (about
  2½ pounds), cut into bite-
  size pieces

½ cup plus 2 tablespoons
  freshly grated Parmesan
  cheese
½ teaspoon crushed red
  pepper
½ teaspoon salt
2 tablespoons seasoned dried
  bread crumbs

◆ Prepare Pastry for 2-crust pie. Shape dough into 2 balls, one slightly larger. Wrap and chill 30 minutes, or overnight.

◆ Meanwhile, in 8-quart Dutch oven, heat 2 tablespoons oil over medium heat; add onion and garlic and cook 10 to 15 minutes, until onion is very tender. Increase heat to high. Stir in escarole; cook about 10 minutes, stirring often, just until escarole is tender. Drain well, pressing out excess liquid.

◆ Return escarole to Dutch oven; stir in ½ cup Parmesan, red pepper, salt, and remaining 1 tablespoon oil. Set aside.

◆ Preheat oven to 375°F. On lightly floured surface, with floured rolling pin, roll larger ball of dough 1½ inches larger all around than inverted 9-inch pie plate; use to line pie plate. Sprinkle crumbs over crust; top with escarole filling.

◆ Roll smaller ball of dough into 10-inch round. Cut several slits in dough; place over filling. Trim edge, leaving ½-inch overhang; fold overhang under and press gently all around rim to make stand-up edge. Sprinkle crust with remaining 2 tablespoons Parmesan. Bake 40 to 45 minutes, until crust is golden. Let pie stand 10 minutes; cut into wedges.

**Each serving: About 540 calories, 15g protein, 45g carbohydrate, 35g total fat (8g saturated), 8mg cholesterol, 945mg sodium**

## BRAISED ENDIVE

*Prep: 5 minutes   Cook: 15 to 25 minutes*
*Makes 6 accompaniment servings*

6 large heads Belgian endive
2 tablespoons vegetable oil
2 tablespoons margarine or
  butter

1 teaspoon sugar
½ teaspoon salt
Fresh basil or parsley leaves
  for garnish

◆ Cut each endive lengthwise in half. In 12-inch skillet, heat oil and margarine over medium-high heat; arrange endive, cut-side down, in 1 layer in skillet. Cook, uncovered, 5 to 10 minutes, until cut sides are lightly browned.

◆ Turn endive cut-side up. Reduce heat to low; add ¼ *cup water*. Sprinkle endive with sugar and salt; cover and cook 10 to 15 minutes longer, until tender. Transfer endive to warm large platter; garnish with basil.

**Each serving: About 85 calories, 1g protein, 3g carbohydrate, 8g total fat (2g saturated), 0mg cholesterol, 235mg sodium**

## STIR-FRYING GREENS

One of the best ways to prepare leafy green vegetables is to stir-fry them – just enough to wilt them while retaining their bright color. Some of the tougher or more bitter greens, such as collard and mustard greens, should be blanched (cooked briefly in boiling water first) to mellow and tenderize them. See below for instructions on how to prepare, blanch, and stir-fry some of the most common varieties of greens. If you like, use a combination. The cooking times are short; be sure to keep an eye on the greens so they don't overcook.

Enhance the flavor and texture of stir-fried greens with any of the following easy additions:

**Flavorful oil** Drizzle cooked greens with extra-virgin olive oil, walnut oil, or a few drops of Asian sesame oil.

**Extra dimension** Stir in a little soy sauce, lemon juice, vinegar, or oyster sauce at the end of cooking.

**Extra spice** Add grated fresh ginger, mustard seeds, or cumin seeds with the crushed red pepper.

**Crunchy toppings** Sprinkle cooked greens with toasted sesame seeds, almonds, walnuts, or pine nuts.

**Preparation and blanching**
Prepare 1 pound greens (see chart, right); discard discolored leaves, if any. To blanch, if recommended, add greens to 6 quarts boiling water; cook as directed and drain.

**Stir-frying** In 12-inch skillet or wok, heat 1 tablespoon olive oil over high heat. Add 2 garlic cloves, crushed with side of knife; cook, stirring frequently, until golden. Add ⅛ teaspoon crushed red pepper; cook 30 seconds. Add prepared greens (pan may splatter if greens are wet); sprinkle with ¼ teaspoon salt and cook, stirring. Discard garlic, if desired.

### PREPARING AND STIR-FRYING GREENS

| TYPE OF GREENS | PREPARE | BLANCH | STIR-FRY |
|---|---|---|---|
| Beet greens | Wash; chop stems | No | 5 minutes |
| Bok choy (pak choi; pak choy; Chinese mustard cabbage) | Wash; thinly slice stems; cut leaves into 1-inch slices | No | 5 minutes |
| Broccoli rabe (rape; rapini) | Wash; trim thick stems | Yes, for 5 minutes | 5 minutes |
| Chicory (curly endive) | Wash; tear leaves | No | 5 minutes |
| Collard greens | Wash; discard stems; cut leaves into 1-inch slices | Yes, for 3 minutes | 5 minutes |
| Dandelion greens | Wash | Yes, for 3 minutes | 5 minutes |
| Escarole | Wash; tear leaves | No | 5 minutes |
| Kale | Wash; discard stems; tear leaves | Yes, for 5 minutes | 5 minutes |
| Mustard greens | Wash | Yes, for 5 minutes | 5 minutes |
| Napa cabbage (Chinese cabbage; celery cabbage) | Wash; thinly slice | No | 3 minutes |
| Spinach | Wash very well | No | 3 minutes |
| Swiss chard (chard) | Wash; thinly slice stems; cut leaves into 1-inch slices | No | 3 minutes |
| Watercress | Wash | No | 3 minutes |

# ARTICHOKES

With just a little more work than is required for most vegetables, fresh artichokes offer high rewards both in great taste and presentation.

## STUFFED ARTICHOKES, CAESAR-STYLE

◆◆◆◆◆◆◆◆◆◆◆◆◆

*Prep:* 1 hour
*Bake:* 15 to 20 minutes
*Makes* 4 main-dish servings

**4 large artichokes**
**4 slices firm white bread, torn**
   **into ¼-inch crumbs**
**2 tablespoons olive oil**
**1 large garlic clove, minced**
**4 anchovy fillets, chopped**
**½ cup pine nuts (pignoli),**
   **lightly toasted, or walnuts,**
   **toasted and chopped**
**⅓ cup freshly grated Parmesan**
   **cheese**
**2 tablespoons chopped fresh**
   **parsley**
**1 tablespoon fresh lemon juice**
**¼ teaspoon salt**
**¾ cup chicken broth**
**Flat-leaf parsley for garnish**

**1** Prepare and cook artichokes (see below). Preheat oven to 400°F. Bake bread crumbs in jelly-roll pan 5 minutes, or until golden. In 1-quart saucepan, heat oil over medium heat. Add garlic; cook 1 minute. Add anchovies; cook until almost dissolved and garlic is golden. Dice artichoke stems. In bowl, mix stems, crumbs, garlic mixture, pine nuts, next 4 ingredients, and ¼ cup chicken broth.

**2** Pour remaining ½ cup chicken broth into shallow baking dish large enough to hold all artichokes (about 13" by 9"). Place artichokes in dish.

**3** Spoon crumb mixture between artichoke leaves and into center cavities. Bake 15 to 20 minutes, until artichokes are hot. Served garnished with parsley.

### PREPARING AND COOKING ARTICHOKES

**1** With sharp knife, cut 1 inch straight across top of each artichoke. Cut off stem; with vegetable peeler, peel stem. Reserve.

**2** Pull loose dark green outer leaves from artichoke bottom. With kitchen shears, trim thorny tips of leaves.

**3** Spread artichoke open; carefully cut around choke with small knife. Scrape out fuzzy center portion with spoon; discard.

**4** Rinse artichoke well. In 5-quart saucepot, heat 1 tablespoon fresh lemon juice and 1 inch water to boiling over high heat. Add artichoke, stem-end down, with stem; heat to boiling. Reduce heat to low; cover and simmer 30 to 40 minutes, until knife inserted in center of artichoke goes through bottom easily. Drain.

**EACH SERVING: ABOUT 335 CALORIES, 16g PROTEIN, 33g CARBOHYDRATE, 19g TOTAL FAT (4g SATURATED), 14mg CHOLESTEROL, 915mg SODIUM**

## BRAISED BABY ARTICHOKES WITH OLIVES

*Prep: 20 minutes    Cook: 15 minutes*
*Makes 8 first-course servings*

| | |
|---|---|
| 16 baby artichokes (about 2 pounds) | ½ teaspoon salt |
| ¼ cup olive oil | ⅓ cup oil-cured or Kalamata olives, pitted and coarsely chopped |
| 3 medium garlic cloves, sliced | |
| ½ teaspoon coarsely ground black pepper | Lemon wedges for garnish |

◆ Trim baby artichokes: Bend back outer green leaves and snap off at base until leaves are half-green (at the top) and half-yellow (at the bottom). Cut off stems and across top of each artichoke at point where yellow meets green. Cut each artichoke lengthwise in half.

◆ In 12-inch skillet, heat *1 inch water* to boiling over high heat. Add artichokes and cook 5 minutes; drain.

◆ Dry skillet. In same skillet, heat olive oil over medium-high heat. Add garlic and cook, stirring, until lightly browned. Add artichokes; cook 2 minutes, until lightly browned. Stir in pepper, salt, and *1 cup water*; cover and cook about 5 minutes longer, until knife inserted in bottom of artichoke goes through easily. Stir in olives; heat through. Spoon into bowl; garnish with lemon wedges.

**Each serving: About 100 calories, 2g protein, 6g carbohydrate, 8g total fat (1g saturated), 0mg cholesterol, 280mg sodium**

## ARTICHOKES WITH ROASTED RED PEPPER AND BASIL SAUCE

*Prep: 25 minutes    Cook: 35 to 45 minutes*
*Makes 8 first-course or accompaniment servings*

| | |
|---|---|
| 4 medium artichokes | 1 tablespoon fresh lemon juice |
| ¾ cup light mayonnaise | |
| 1 jar (7 ounces) roasted red peppers, drained | ½ cup chopped fresh basil or parsley |
| 1 teaspoon sugar | Shredded fresh basil for garnish |
| ¾ teaspoon salt | |
| ½ teaspoon hot-pepper sauce | |

◆ Prepare and cook artichokes (see page 39), but omit Step 3. Meanwhile, in food processor with knife blade attached or in blender at medium speed, blend mayonnaise, roasted red peppers, sugar, salt, hot-pepper sauce, and lemon juice until smooth. Spoon red-pepper sauce into bowl; stir in chopped basil. Cover and refrigerate.

◆ Cut each artichoke into 4 wedges. Cut out and discard fuzzy centers. Serve artichokes warm or cover and refrigerate to serve cold later. To serve, arrange artichoke

wedges around bowl of red-pepper sauce on platter; garnish sauce with shredded basil. Let each person dip artichoke leaves and hearts in sauce.

**Each serving: About 110 calories, 2g protein, 10g carbohydrate, 6g total fat (1g saturated), 8mg cholesterol, 300mg sodium**

## COUSCOUS-STUFFED ARTICHOKES

*Prep: 1 hour    Bake: 15 to 20 minutes*
*Makes 4 main-dish servings*

| | |
|---|---|
| 4 large artichokes | 1 cup couscous (Moroccan pasta) |
| 3 tablespoons olive oil | |
| 2 medium carrots, diced | 1½ cups chicken broth |
| 2 garlic cloves, minced | ½ teaspoon salt |
| ¼ cup chopped fresh mint | ¼ teaspoon coarsely ground black pepper |
| 3 tablespoons chopped fresh parsley | |
| | 1 lemon, cut into wedges |

◆ Prepare and cook artichokes (see page 39). Meanwhile, preheat oven to 400°F. In nonstick 10-inch skillet, heat 1 tablespoon olive oil over medium heat. Add carrots and cook about 10 minutes, until tender. Stir in garlic; cook 1 minute longer. Transfer carrots and garlic to medium bowl. Dice artichoke stems; add to carrot mixture with mint and parsley.

◆ Prepare couscous as label directs but use 1 cup chicken broth in place of water. When couscous is done, stir in salt, pepper, carrot mixture, and remaining 2 tablespoons oil.

◆ Pour remaining ½ cup chicken broth into shallow baking dish large enough to hold all artichokes (about 13" by 9"); place artichokes in dish. Spoon couscous mixture between artichoke leaves and into center cavities. Bake 15 to 20 minutes, until artichokes are heated through. Serve with lemon wedges.

**Each serving: About 375 calories, 13g protein, 61g carbohydrate, 12g total fat (2g saturated), 7mg cholesterol, 830mg sodium**

# FENNEL AND CELERY

Cool, crunchy raw celery is a popular staple on crudité platters, but many people are not aware that cooking transforms it into an elegant side dish. Paired with parsnips, toasted walnuts, and a hint of brown butter, for example, it makes a delicate winter sauté. A relative of celery, fennel shares its crisp texture but offers a distinctive, sweet anise flavor. While fennel is delicious raw, simply sliced thin and drizzled with vinaigrette, cooked fennel has a more subtle flavor and melting texture. Roast it in olive oil to accompany roasted chicken or fish, or slice and layer it into a cheese-rich gratin. When purchasing either vegetable, choose firm, crisp varieties with fresh-looking leaves.

## BRAISED FENNEL WITH TWO CHEESES

◆◆◆◆◆◆◆◆◆◆◆◆◆◆◆◆◆◆◆◆◆◆◆◆◆◆◆

*Prep: 15 minutes　Cook: 45 minutes plus broiling*
*Makes 6 accompaniment servings*

**3 small fennel bulbs**
　**(8 ounces each)**
**1 can (13¾ to 14½ ounces)**
　**chicken broth**
**6 ounces mozzarella cheese,**
　**shredded (1½ cups)**

**2 tablespoons freshly grated**
　**Parmesan cheese**
**1 tablespoon chopped fresh**
　**parsley**

1 Rinse fennel bulbs with cold running water; cut off root end and stalks from bulbs. Slice each bulb lengthwise in half. In deep 12-inch skillet, heat chicken broth and *1½ cups water* to boiling over high heat. Add fennel; heat to boiling.

2 Reduce heat to low; cover and simmer 35 minutes, turning bulbs once, or until fennel is fork-tender; drain. Preheat broiler. Place fennel, cut-side up, in shallow broiler-safe 1½-quart casserole. In small bowl, mix mozzarella and Parmesan cheeses and parsley.

3 Sprinkle cheese mixture evenly over fennel in casserole. Place casserole in broiler at closest position to heat source. Broil 1 to 2 minutes, until cheese topping is golden and bubbly and fennel is heated through.

### BRAISED CELERY WITH GRUYÈRE

Substitute 2 bunches celery for fennel; trim stalks from bases of celery. Cut each stalk in half to give 5- to 6-inch lengths. Proceed as directed, but simmer only 20 minutes in Step 2 and use 4 ounces Gruyère or Swiss cheese, shredded (about 1 cup), instead of mozzarella.

Each serving: About 125 calories, 8g protein, 7g carbohydrate, 8g total fat (4g saturated), 28mg cholesterol, 530mg sodium

EACH SERVING: ABOUT 135 CALORIES, 8g PROTEIN, 10g CARBOHYDRATE, 8g TOTAL FAT (4g SATURATED), 29mg CHOLESTEROL, 490mg SODIUM

## ROASTED FENNEL

*Prep: 5 minutes    Roast: 1 hour*
*Makes 6 accompaniment servings*

| | |
|---|---|
| 3 large fennel bulbs | ½ teaspoon salt |
| (1¼ pounds each) | ¼ teaspoon ground black |
| 1 tablespoon olive oil | pepper |

◆ Preheat oven to 425°F. Trim fennel bulbs and cut each into 6 wedges. Place fennel in jelly-roll pan and toss with olive oil, salt, and pepper to coat evenly.

◆ Roast fennel about 1 hour, or until browned at edges and tender when pierced with tip of knife.

**Each serving: About 110 calories, 4g protein, 21g carbohydrate, 3g total fat (0g saturated), 0mg cholesterol, 325mg sodium**

## CELERY AND PARSNIPS IN BROWN BUTTER

*Prep: 20 minutes    Cook: 25 to 30 minutes*
*Makes 5 accompaniment servings*

| | |
|---|---|
| 2 tablespoons coarsely | 6 stalks celery, cut into |
| chopped walnuts | 3-inch-long matchstick-thin |
| 1 tablespoon vegetable oil | strips |
| 8 ounces parsnips, | ¼ teaspoon salt |
| peeled and cut into | 2 tablespoons butter |
| 3-inch-long matchstick-thin | |
| strips | |

◆ In 10-inch skillet, toast walnuts over medium heat until lightly browned; transfer to small bowl. Wipe skillet clean with paper towels.

◆ In same skillet, heat oil over medium heat; add parsnips, celery, and salt and cook about 20 minutes, stirring frequently, until vegetables are tender.

◆ Transfer vegetables to warm platter; keep warm. In same skillet, melt butter; cook until butter turns golden, stirring (if butter gets dark, it will be bitter). Add walnuts; toss to coat. Spoon mixture over vegetables.

**Each serving: About 120 calories, 2g protein, 11g carbohydrate, 9g total fat (3g saturated), 12mg cholesterol, 200mg sodium**

## FENNEL AND POTATO GRATIN

*Prep: 20 minutes    Bake: 1 hour 20 minutes*
*Makes 8 accompaniment servings*

| | |
|---|---|
| 1 large fennel bulb | ¼ teaspoon ground black |
| (1¼ pounds), trimmed, | pepper |
| cored, and very thinly sliced | 1 cup heavy or whipping |
| (about 3½ cups) | cream |
| 1½ pounds all-purpose | 1 garlic clove, crushed with |
| potatoes, peeled and very | side of knife |
| thinly sliced (about | Pinch ground nutmeg |
| 3½ cups) | ¼ cup freshly grated |
| 1 teaspoon salt | Parmesan cheese |

Preheat oven to 400°F. In large bowl, toss fennel with potatoes, salt, and pepper. Spread evenly in shallow 2-quart baking dish. Cover tightly with foil and bake 1 hour. In 1-quart saucepan, combine cream, garlic, and nutmeg; heat to boiling over high heat. Discard garlic. Pour cream mixture over fennel mixture. Sprinkle with Parmesan. Bake, uncovered, 20 minutes longer, or until golden.

**Each serving: About 215 calories, 4g protein, 23g carbohydrate, 12g total fat (7g saturated), 43mg cholesterol, 375mg sodium**

◆◆◆◆◆◆◆◆◆◆◆◆◆◆◆◆◆◆◆◆◆◆◆◆◆

### PREPARING FENNEL

Also known as anise, sweet anise, and finocchio, fennel is a vegetable valued for all its parts: bulb, leaves, stalks, and seeds. The bulb is the part most often eaten, but young fennel stalks can be served as crudités. The feathery leaves can be added to salads or used as a stuffing for fish; they also make an attractive garnish.

1 To prepare fennel, rinse the bulb in cold water. With a large chef's knife, trim root end.

2 Cut off stalks and feathery leaves, reserving them for other uses, if you like. Remove any bruised or discolored outer stalks, then halve or quarter, cut out core, if you like, and slice bulb as recipe directs.

◆◆◆◆◆◆◆◆◆◆◆◆◆◆◆◆◆◆◆◆◆◆◆◆◆

# ASPARAGUS

Asparagus are at their best cooked simply and briefly, just until the spears are slightly limp. When buying, look for stalks with tips that are dry, tight, and purplish in color. The thickness of the spear makes no difference in the taste, but do select spears of uniform size so they cook evenly.

## ASPARAGUS WITH PARMESAN VINAIGRETTE

◆◆◆◆◆◆◆◆◆◆◆◆◆◆

*Prep:* 20 minutes
*Cook:* 10 to 15 minutes
*Makes* 8 accompaniment servings

**3 pounds asparagus**
**½ cup olive or vegetable oil**
**¼ cup red wine vinegar**
**1 tablespoon Dijon mustard**
**1 teaspoon salt**
**3 tablespoons freshly grated Parmesan cheese**
**2 ounces prosciutto or cooked ham, chopped (about ¼ cup)**

**1** Hold base of each asparagus stalk firmly and bend stalk; end will break off at spot where it becomes too tough to eat. Discard ends; trim scales if stalks are gritty.

**2** In deep 12-inch skillet, in *1 inch boiling water,* heat asparagus to boiling over high heat. Reduce heat to medium-low; simmer 5 to 10 minutes, just until tender; drain well.

**3** In 13" by 9" glass baking dish, prepare vinaigrette: With wire whisk or fork, mix oil, vinegar, mustard, salt, and 2 tablespoons Parmesan cheese.

### PREPARING ASPARAGUS

Asparagus may need only minimal trimming, but if the end of the stalk looks tough and woody, simply bend the stalk to snap the end off. Rinse the asparagus thoroughly under cold running water. You can trim the scales with a paring knife or vegetable peeler, if you like, though this is not really necessary – do so only if the stalks seem gritty.

Asparagus may be peeled for an elegant presentation or if the skin is thick and tough, but we prefer to leave them unpeeled; the outside of the stalk is rich in vitamin C, folic acid, and thiamine, which are lost in peeling. Store asparagus upright in 1 inch water, loosely covered, in the refrigerator.

**4** Add asparagus to vinaigrette; turn to coat. Serve at room temperature or cover and refrigerate, turning occasionally, 2 hours. To serve, spoon asparagus and vinaigrette onto serving platter. Sprinkle with prosciutto and remaining 1 tablespoon Parmesan cheese.

EACH SERVING: ABOUT 180 CALORIES, 7g PROTEIN, 7g CARBOHYDRATE, 15g TOTAL FAT (2g SATURATED), 4mg CHOLESTEROL, 460mg SODIUM

## ASPARAGUS GRATIN

*Prep: 25 minutes    Cook: 10 to 15 minutes plus broiling*
*Makes 6 accompaniment servings*

| | |
|---|---|
| 2 tablespoons plus<br>  2 teaspoons olive oil | ¼ cup freshly grated<br>  Parmesan cheese |
| 1 large shallot, finely chopped | 1 tablespoon chopped fresh<br>  parsley |
| 2 slices firm white bread | |
| 2 pounds asparagus, tough<br>  ends removed | 1 tablespoon fresh lemon<br>  juice |
| Salt | |

◆ Preheat oven to 400°F. In 1-quart saucepan, heat 2 tablespoons olive oil over medium-low heat. Add shallot; cook about 6 minutes, until golden. Remove from heat.

◆ In blender, process bread to fine crumbs; or tear bread into small crumbs. Spread crumbs in jelly-roll pan; bake 3 to 6 minutes, until golden. Set aside.

◆ In 12-inch skillet, in *1 inch boiling water*, heat asparagus and ½ teaspoon salt to boiling over high heat. Reduce heat to medium-low and simmer, uncovered, 5 to 10 minutes, just until asparagus are tender; drain. Place asparagus in shallow, broiler-safe dish; drizzle with remaining 2 teaspoons oil.

### GRATIN DISHES

Designed for broiling, or baking at high temperatures, a gratin dish is shallow so food heats through quickly and achieves the maximum browned top.

◆ Preheat broiler. In medium bowl, toss bread crumbs with Parmesan cheese, parsley, lemon juice, shallot, and ¼ teaspoon salt. Sprinkle bread-crumb mixture over asparagus. Place dish in broiler 5 inches from heat source; broil about 3 minutes, until crumbs are lightly browned.

**Each serving: About 130 calories, 6g protein, 11g carbohydrate, 8g total fat (2g saturated), 3mg cholesterol, 265mg sodium**

## CHILLED ASPARAGUS WITH WATERCRESS MAYONNAISE

*Prep: 20 minutes plus chilling    Cook: 10 to 15 minutes*
*Makes 6 accompaniment servings*

| | |
|---|---|
| 2 pounds asparagus, tough<br>  ends removed | 2 tablespoons capers, drained<br>  and minced |
| 1 bunch watercress | 1 tablespoon fresh lemon<br>  juice |
| ½ cup mayonnaise | |
| 2 tablespoons milk | Lemon slices for garnish |

◆ In 12-inch skillet, in *1 inch boiling water*, heat asparagus to boiling over high heat. Reduce heat to medium-low and simmer, uncovered, 5 to 10 minutes, just until asparagus are tender; drain. Place on serving platter; cover and refrigerate 2 hours, or until chilled.

◆ Prepare watercress mayonnaise: Chop ¾ cup watercress; reserve remaining watercress for garnish. In medium bowl, combine chopped watercress, mayonnaise, milk, capers, and lemon juice; spoon over chilled asparagus. Garnish with lemon slices and reserved watercress.

**Each serving: About 170 calories, 4g protein, 7g carbohydrate, 15g total fat (2g saturated), 11mg cholesterol, 235mg sodium**

## SESAME STIR-FRIED ASPARAGUS

*Prep: 5 minutes    Cook: 10 minutes*
*Makes 4 accompaniment servings*

| | |
|---|---|
| 1 tablespoon sesame seeds | 1 pound thin asparagus, tough<br>  ends removed and cut<br>  diagonally into 1-inch pieces |
| 1 tablespoon vegetable oil | |
| ½ teaspoon Asian sesame<br>  oil | ¼ teaspoon salt |

In 10-inch skillet, toast sesame seeds over medium heat, shaking pan frequently, 5 minutes, or until fragrant and pale golden. Remove from skillet. In same skillet, heat vegetable oil and sesame oil over high heat until very hot. Add asparagus; sprinkle with salt and cook, stirring constantly, 5 minutes, or until tender-crisp. To serve, sprinkle with sesame seeds.

**Each serving: About 70 calories, 3g protein, 5g carbohydrate, 5g total fat (1g saturated) 0mg cholesterol, 145mg sodium**

# CORN

Sweet corn on the cob is a perennial summer delight. For added flavor, tuck a fragrant herb sprig such as rosemary or sage right into the husk and grill the cob for a sweet, roasted flavor. Another appealing idea? Cut the fresh kernels from the cob and transform them into a quick sauté with chives, a savory corn pudding with a comforting texture, or an innovative succotash flavored with smoked Gouda. For the sweetest corn, cook it as soon as possible after buying, before its sugar content turns to starch. New hybrids of supersweet corn retain their sugars longer and can be stored for several days in the refrigerator.

**1** Pull husks back from each ear of corn; cut off corn cobs and remove silk, leaving husks intact. In large bowl, soak husks and string in *water* to cover 20 minutes.

**2** Meanwhile, cut 3 cups corn kernels from cobs; place in another large bowl (reserve remaining corn for another day). Stir in remaining ingredients.

## ROASTED SUCCOTASH IN CORN HUSKS

◆◆◆◆◆◆◆◆◆◆◆◆◆◆◆◆◆◆◆◆◆◆◆◆◆◆◆◆

*Prep: 30 minutes   Roast: 35 minutes*
*Makes 6 accompaniment servings*

6 large ears corn with husks
6 pieces (10 inches each) string
1 package (10 ounces) frozen baby lima beans, thawed
1 large tomato, diced
4 ounces smoked Gouda cheese, shredded (1 cup)
3 tablespoons margarine or butter, melted
1 teaspoon sugar
½ teaspoon lemon-pepper seasoning salt
½ teaspoon salt

**3** Preheat oven to 425°F. Remove husks and string from water. Shake excess water from husks. Carefully place about 1 cup succotash mixture in each husk.

**4** Bring husks together, being sure to enclose succotash filling completely; tie open end of each husk tightly with string; cut off loose ends of string.

**5** Place filled corn husks in jelly-roll pan; roast 35 minutes, or until corn is tender and succotash is heated through. To serve, place filled corn husks on platter; remove string.

EACH SERVING: ABOUT 325 CALORIES, 13g PROTEIN, 47g CARBOHYDRATE, 12g TOTAL FAT (5g SATURATED), 22mg CHOLESTEROL, 535mg SODIUM

## CREAMY CORN PUDDING

*Prep: 30 minutes    Bake: 1 hour 15 minutes*
*Makes 8 accompaniment servings*

2 medium ears corn, husks
  and silk removed, or
  1 package (10 ounces)
  frozen whole-kernel corn,
  thawed
2 tablespoons margarine or
  butter
1 small onion, minced

¼ cup all-purpose flour
1 teaspoon salt
¼ teaspoon coarsely ground
  black pepper
2 cups half-and-half or light
  cream
1 cup milk
4 large eggs

◆ Preheat oven to 325°F. Cut corn kernels from cobs. In
2-quart saucepan, melt margarine over medium heat. Add
onion and cook, stirring occasionally, about 10 minutes,
until tender and golden brown.

◆ Stir in flour, salt, and pepper until blended. Gradually
stir in half-and-half and milk and cook, stirring constantly,
until mixture thickens slightly and boils. Remove saucepan
from heat; stir in corn.

◆ In deep 2-quart casserole or soufflé dish, beat eggs
slightly. Gradually beat in corn mixture. Set casserole in
larger baking pan; place pan on oven rack. Pour *boiling
water* into pan to come halfway up side of casserole. Bake
pudding 1¼ hours, or until knife inserted in center comes
out clean.

**Each serving: About 210 calories, 8g protein, 16g carbohydrate,
13g total fat (6g saturated), 133mg cholesterol, 375mg sodium**

## GRILLED SWEET CORN

*Prep: 25 minutes plus soaking    Grill: 30 to 40 minutes*
*Makes 8 accompaniment servings*

8 medium ears corn
  with husks
8 teaspoons
  olive oil

Several sprigs each basil,
  rosemary, sage, and/or
  thyme

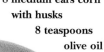

◆ Prepare outdoor grill. In 8-quart
saucepot or bowl, place corn with
husks and *cold water* to cover; let
soak 15 minutes. (Soaking keeps
husks from burning on grill.)

◆ Drain corn well. Gently pull back
husks to about three-fourths way down;
remove silk.

◆ With pastry brush, brush each ear of
corn with 1 teaspoon olive oil. Tuck several
sprigs of herbs into each ear.

◆ Rewrap corn with husks, removing 1 strip of husk from
each ear of corn and tying tops of husks together with strip
of extra husk.

◆ Place corn on grill over medium heat; grill, turning corn
occasionally, 30 to 40 minutes, until tender when pierced
with tip of sharp knife.

**Each serving: About 155 calories, 4g protein, 28g carbohydrate,
5g total fat (1g saturated), 0mg cholesterol, 5mg sodium**

## SAUTÉED FRESH CORN

*Prep: 10 minutes    Cook: 5 minutes*
*Makes 4 accompaniment servings*

6 medium ears corn, husks
  and silk removed
2 tablespoons margarine or
  butter
½ teaspoon salt

¼ teaspoon coarsely ground
  black pepper
¼ cup chopped fresh chives or
  thinly sliced green onions

Cut corn kernels from cobs. In 10-inch skillet, melt
margarine over medium-high heat. Add corn, salt, and
pepper and cook, stirring frequently, 4 minutes, or until
corn is tender. Remove from heat; stir in chives.

**Each serving: About 225 calories, 6g protein, 42g carbohydrate,
7g total fat (1g saturated) 0mg cholesterol, 340mg sodium**

### MAKE YOUR OWN HERB BRUSH

If you have an abundance of garden herbs, try making a
fragrant herb brush, which can be used for brushing oil or
melted margarine or butter over grilled or broiled fish,
meat or poultry, garlic bread, or focaccia, as well as corn on
the cob. Or, use to dab vinaigrette over salads and steamed
vegetables. Choose herbs such as rosemary, sage, and thyme
for your herb brush.

1 Tie a small bouquet of
herb sprigs together at
the stem end with a piece of
string or another sprig.

2 Dip in olive oil or melted
margarine or butter and
brush over grilled corn on
the cob or other food.

# PEAS, SNAP PEAS, AND SNOW PEAS

Tender peas and snow peas are very easy to overcook; it's almost impossible to undercook them. Fresh green peas from a garden or farmstand are a spring and summer treat and well worth the extra time and effort of shelling; eat them as soon as possible after picking or buying, because, like corn, their sugars quickly convert to starch. Frozen peas are often sweeter than "fresh" peas that have been off the vine for some time. Both flat snow peas and plump sugar snap peas are meant to be eaten whole, pod and all – simply pull off the tough string first.

## SWEET SUMMER PEAS

◆◆◆◆◆◆◆◆◆◆◆◆◆◆◆◆◆◆◆◆◆◆◆◆◆◆◆

*Prep: 25 minutes    Cook: 8 to 10 minutes*
*Makes 6 accompaniment servings*

2½ pounds fresh peas or
  2 packages (10 ounces each)
  frozen peas, thawed
¼ cup mayonnaise
1 tablespoon chopped fresh
  parsley
1 tablespoon tarragon vinegar

¾ teaspoon salt
⅛ teaspoon ground black
  pepper
1 bunch or 1 bag (6 ounces)
  radishes, finely chopped
Lettuce leaves

**1** If using fresh peas, shell them (you should have about 2½ cups shelled peas). In 3-quart saucepan, heat *¾ cup water* to boiling over high heat; add fresh peas and heat to boiling.

**2** Reduce heat to low; cover saucepan and simmer 3 to 5 minutes, just until peas are tender. Drain peas in a colander; rinse with cold running water until cool. Set aside.

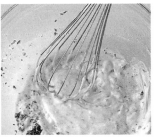

**3** Prepare dressing: In large bowl, with wire whisk or fork, mix mayonnaise, parsley, tarragon vinegar, salt, and pepper until mixture is smooth and well combined.

**4** Add fresh or frozen thawed peas and radishes to dressing; toss to coat. Cover and refrigerate if not serving right away. To serve, line bowl with lettuce; spoon salad over lettuce.

### HOMEMADE TARRAGON VINEGAR

Wash 4-cup-capacity bottle with cork in hot soapy water. Put bottle in large pot, and cork in small pan, and fill with water. Heat to boiling over high heat. Boil gently 5 minutes; drain. Place 3 or 4 sprigs tarragon in bottle; push in with skewer if necessary. In nonreactive saucepan, heat 4 cups white wine vinegar to boiling over high heat. Pour through funnel into bottle. Cork; let stand in cool, dark place 2 weeks.

Strain through fine sieve into glass measuring cup. Discard tarragon sprigs. Return vinegar to bottle; add fresh tarragon. Vinegar can be stored up to 3 months at cool room temperature; if stored in a warm place, it may ferment and develop an off flavor. If the cork pops, discard the vinegar.

EACH SERVING: ABOUT 110 CALORIES, 3g PROTEIN, 9g CARBOHYDRATE, 8g TOTAL FAT (1g SATURATED), 5mg CHOLESTEROL, 370mg SODIUM

## SNAP PEAS AND YELLOW PEPPERS

*Prep: 20 minutes    Cook: 15 minutes*
*Makes 6 accompaniment servings*

1 tablespoon plus 2 teaspoons olive or vegetable oil
1 large yellow pepper, cut into 2" by ¾" pieces
2 large celery stalks, cut diagonally into ¼-inch-thick slices
Salt
Coarsely ground black pepper
1 pound sugar snap peas or snow peas, strings removed

◆ In nonstick 12-inch skillet, heat 1 tablespoon oil over medium-high heat; add yellow pepper, celery, ¾ teaspoon salt, and ¼ teaspoon black pepper and cook, stirring frequently, about 10 minutes, until vegetables are tender and lightly browned.

◆ Transfer pepper mixture to bowl. In same skillet, heat remaining 2 teaspoons oil; add sugar snap peas, ½ teaspoon salt, and ¼ teaspoon black pepper and cook, stirring frequently, about 4 minutes, until peas are tender-crisp. Stir in pepper mixture until well combined.

◆ Spoon vegetable mixture onto platter. If not serving right away, cover and refrigerate to serve cold later.

**Each serving: About 75 calories, 3g protein, 8g carbohydrate, 4g total fat (1g saturated), 0mg cholesterol, 460mg sodium**

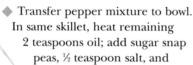

### PREPARING SNOW AND SNAP PEAS

Rinse snow peas well. To remove the string, pull off the tip of the pod, keeping the string intact. Pull the string along the length of the pod. With sugar snap peas, the string runs along both sides of the pod.

## MIXED PEA POD STIR-FRY

*Prep: 15 minutes    Cook: 8 minutes*
*Makes 4 accompaniment servings*

8 ounces green beans, ends trimmed
1 teaspoon salt
2 teaspoons vegetable oil
4 ounces snow peas, strings removed
4 ounces sugar snap peas, strings removed
1 garlic clove, minced
1 tablespoon soy sauce

◆ In 12-inch skillet, in *1 inch boiling water*, heat green beans and salt to boiling over high heat. Reduce heat to low. Simmer, uncovered, 3 minutes; drain in colander. Wipe skillet dry.

◆ In same skillet, heat oil over high heat until hot. Add green beans and cook, stirring often, 1 minute, or until beginning to brown.

◆ Add snow peas, sugar snap peas, and garlic; cook, stirring, 2 to 3 minutes, until peas are tender-crisp. Remove from heat and stir in soy sauce.

**Each serving; About 60 calories, 3g protein, 8g carbohydrate, 2g total fat (0g saturated), 0mg cholesterol, 295mg sodium**

## SAUTÉED PEAS WITH GREEN ONIONS

*Prep: 30 minutes    Cook: 15 minutes*
*Makes 6 accompaniment servings*

4 pounds fresh peas, shelled (about 4 cups), or 1 bag (20 ounces) frozen peas, thawed
2 tablespoons margarine or butter
1 bunch green onions, cut into ¼-inch pieces (½ cup)
½ teaspoon salt
¼ teaspoon ground black pepper
¼ cup chopped fresh mint

◆ If using fresh peas, in 4-quart saucepan, heat *1 cup water* to boiling over high heat; add peas and heat to boiling. Reduce heat to low; cover and simmer 3 minutes, or just until peas are tender. Drain; set aside.

◆ In 10-inch skillet, melt margarine over medium heat. Add green onions and cook 2 minutes, or until tender. Add fresh or frozen thawed peas, salt, and pepper and cook, stirring often, 3 minutes longer, or until peas are hot. Remove from heat; stir in mint. Spoon into warm serving bowl.

**Each serving; About 110 calories, 5g protein, 14g carbohydrate, 4g total fat (1g saturated), 0mg cholesterol, 305mg sodium**

# GREEN BEANS

Green beans take well to simple preparations – roasted in a very hot oven, blanched and then stir-fried with Asian seasonings, or sautéed in a little olive oil. Whatever variety you choose, buy firm, straight, slender beans without blemishes. To test for freshness, try breaking one in half: If it bends, the bean is past its prime; if it snaps easily, the bean should be tender and sweet.

## ROASTED GREEN BEANS WITH DILL VINAIGRETTE

◆◆◆◆◆◆◆◆◆◆◆◆

*Prep: 20 minutes*
*Roast: 20 to 30 minutes*
*Makes 8 accompaniment servings*

**2 pounds green beans, ends trimmed**
**3 tablespoons olive oil**
**Salt**
**2 tablespoons white wine vinegar**
**1½ teaspoons Dijon mustard**
**½ teaspoon sugar**
**½ teaspoon coarsely ground black pepper**
**2 tablespoons chopped fresh dill**

**1** Preheat oven to 450°F. In 17" by 11½" roasting pan, combine green beans, 1 tablespoon olive oil, and ½ teaspoon salt; toss until beans are coated with oil.

**2** Roast green beans, uncovered, 20 to 30 minutes, until tender and slightly browned, stirring twice during roasting for even cooking. Meanwhile, prepare vinaigrette: In small bowl, with wire whisk or fork, mix vinegar, mustard, sugar, pepper, and ¼ teaspoon salt.

### DILL

A member of the parsley family, dill is both an herb and a spice. Fresh dill has feathery green leaves and a slightly lemony anise flavor. It's a favorite for yogurt-based dips, cream sauces, soups, and salads, especially fish and cucumber salads. It loses its flavor quickly on heating, so when used in hot dishes it should be added towards the end of cooking time. (Dried dill, usually known as dillweed, does not have quite the same flavor.) Dill seeds are more pungent and are good in pickles, breads, and vegetable dishes.

**3** Slowly whisk in remaining 2 tablespoons olive oil; whisk in dill. When beans are done, in large bowl, toss beans with vinaigrette. Serve warm or at room temperature.

**EACH SERVING: ABOUT 75 CALORIES, 1g PROTEIN, 7g CARBOHYDRATE, 5g TOTAL FAT (1g SATURATED), 0mg CHOLESTEROL, 240mg SODIUM**

## ROMAN-STYLE GREEN BEANS

*Prep:* 15 minutes   *Cook:* 20 to 25 minutes
*Makes* 8 accompaniment servings

**2 pounds green beans, ends trimmed**
**4 ounces sliced pancetta or bacon, cut into ½-inch strips**
**1 tablespoon olive oil**
**½ teaspoon salt**
**¼ cup pine nuts (pignoli), toasted**

◆ In 5-quart saucepot in *1 inch boiling water*, heat beans to boiling over high heat. Reduce heat to low. Simmer, uncovered, 5 to 10 minutes, until beans are tender-crisp; drain. Wipe saucepot dry.

◆ In same saucepot, cook pancetta, stirring frequently, over medium heat until golden. With slotted spoon, transfer pancetta to paper towels to drain. Set aside.

◆ To drippings in saucepot, add olive oil; heat over medium-high heat until hot. Add green beans with salt and cook, stirring frequently, until beans are lightly browned and tender.

◆ Spoon green beans onto warm large platter; sprinkle with pancetta and toasted pine nuts.

**Each serving: About 90 calories, 6g protein, 7g carbohydrate, 5g total fat (1g saturated), 8mg cholesterol, 365mg sodium**

## GREEN BEANS WITH HAZELNUTS

*Prep:* 20 minutes   *Cook:* 10 to 15 minutes
*Makes* 6 accompaniment servings

**1½ pounds green beans, ends trimmed**
**Salt**
**2 tablespoons margarine or butter**
**½ cup hazelnuts, toasted and skinned**
**1 teaspoon grated lemon peel**
**¼ teaspoon ground black pepper**

◆ In 5-quart saucepot, in *1 inch boiling water*, heat beans and 2 teaspoons salt to boiling over high heat.

◆ Reduce heat to low and simmer, uncovered, 5 to 10 minutes, until tender-crisp; drain. Wipe saucepot dry.

◆ In same saucepot, melt margarine over medium heat. Add hazelnuts and cook, stirring, 3 minutes, or just until margarine begins to brown.

◆ Stir in lemon peel, pepper, beans and ¼ teaspoon salt and cook, stirring, 5 minutes.

**Each serving; About 120 calories, 3g protein, 8g carbohydrate, 10g total fat (1g saturated), 0mg cholesterol, 140mg sodium**

## SESAME GREEN BEANS

*Prep:* 15 minutes   *Cook:* 10 to 15 minutes
*Makes* 8 accompaniment servings

**2 pounds green beans, ends trimmed**
**1 tablespoon sesame seeds**
**2 tablespoons soy sauce**
**2 teaspoons Asian sesame oil**
**1 tablespoon minced, peeled fresh ginger or ¾ teaspoon ground ginger**

◆ In 5-quart saucepot, in *1 inch boiling water*, heat beans to boiling over high heat. Reduce heat to low; simmer, uncovered, 5 to 10 minutes, until beans are tender-crisp.

◆ Meanwhile, in small saucepan, toast sesame seeds over medium heat, stirring and shaking pan frequently, until golden brown.

◆ Drain beans. Wipe saucepot dry. Return beans to saucepot. Stir in soy sauce, sesame oil, and ginger; heat through.

◆ Sprinkle beans with toasted sesame seeds. Serve beans warm or cover and refrigerate to serve cold later.

**Each serving: About 45 calories, 2g protein, 7g carbohydrate, 2g total fat (0g saturated), 0mg cholesterol, 270mg sodium**

---

### BEANS

Regular green beans are widely available; Italian green beans may be easier to come by at farmers' markets. Haricots verts, a slender, tender but expensive French bean, are increasingly available at large supermarkets and specialty markets. Feel free to substitute a different bean in a favorite recipe. Just remember that thicker beans will take longer to cook than thinner beans.

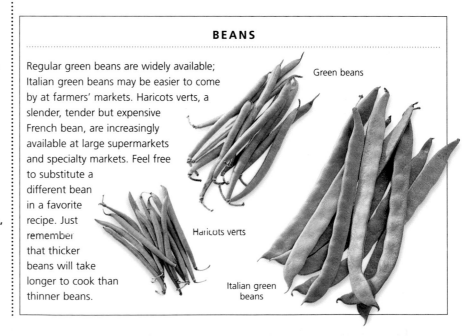

Green beans

Haricots verts

Italian green beans

# ROOT VEGETABLES

Many of nature's edible gifts come from beneath the ground. Besides potatoes, which fall into their own category, carrots are perhaps the favorite root. But beets, turnips, parsnips, celery root (celeriac), rutabagas, and sunchokes (Jerusalem artichokes) are equally delicious – sweet and earthy – whether mashed, baked, roasted, or candied.

## HARVEST CASSEROLE

◆◆◆◆◆◆◆◆◆◆◆◆

*Prep: 40 minutes*
*Bake: 1 hour*
*Makes 8 accompaniment servings*

**5 tablespoons margarine or butter**
**1 jumbo onion (about 1 pound), cut into ¼-inch-thick slices**
**2 garlic cloves, minced**
**6 medium carrots (about 1 pound), peeled and thinly sliced**
**6 medium parsnips (about 1 pound), peeled and thinly sliced**
**1 small rutabaga (about 1 pound), peeled, cut into quarters, and thinly sliced**
**3 tablespoons all-purpose flour**
**1½ teaspoons salt**
**¼ teaspoon coarsely ground black pepper**
**¼ teaspoon ground nutmeg**
**2½ cups milk**
**¼ cup freshly grated Parmesan cheese**
**Chopped fresh parsley for garnish**

**1** Preheat oven to 375°F. In nonstick 10-inch skillet, melt 3 tablespoons margarine over medium heat. Add onion and garlic; cook 15 to 20 minutes, stirring often, until golden.

### RUTABAGA

A cross between a cabbage and a turnip, rutabagas have yellow-orange flesh and a thick skin, which is often waxed to prevent drying out. They will keep for up to 2 weeks in the refrigerator, and can be prepared as for turnips.

**2** In shallow 2½-quart casserole, toss carrots, parsnips, rutabaga, and onion mixture until well combined. Cover casserole and bake 45 minutes, or until vegetables are fork-tender.

**3** Meanwhile, in 2-quart saucepan, melt remaining 2 tablespoons margarine over medium heat. Stir in flour and next 3 ingredients; cook, stirring, 1 minute.

**4** Gradually stir milk into flour mixture in saucepan; cook, stirring constantly, until sauce thickens slightly and boils.

**5** Stir sauce into vegetables. Sprinkle grated Parmesan cheese evenly on top. Bake casserole, uncovered, 15 minutes longer, or until sauce is bubbly and top is golden brown. To serve, sprinkle with parsley.

**EACH SERVING: ABOUT 245 CALORIES, 7g PROTEIN, 32g CARBOHYDRATE, 11g TOTAL FAT (4g SATURATED), 13mg CHOLESTEROL, 615mg SODIUM**

## CELERY ROOT RÉMOULADE

*Prep: 20 minutes plus chilling*
*Makes 6 accompaniment servings*

2 tablespoons fresh lemon
   juice
1½ pounds celery root
   (celeriac)
½ cup mayonnaise

2 tablespoons Dijon mustard
1 tablespoon minced fresh
   parsley
¼ teaspoon ground black
   pepper

◆ Place lemon juice in large bowl. Peel celery root. With adjustable-blade slicer or mandoline, or very sharp knife, cut celery root into ⅛-inch-thick matchstick strips. As you cut it, add celery root to lemon juice in bowl and toss to coat to prevent browning.

◆ In small bowl, mix mayonnaise, mustard, parsley, and pepper until well combined. Add to celery root and toss to coat. Cover and refrigerate at least 1 hour, or overnight.

**Each serving; About 160 calories, 2g protein, 6g carbohydrate, 15g total fat (2g saturated), 11mg cholesterol, 340mg sodium**

## MASHED ROOT VEGETABLES

*Prep: 15 minutes   Cook: 25 minutes*
*Makes 8 accompaniment servings*

2 pounds carrots, celery root
   (celeriac), parsnips, white
   turnips, and/or rutabaga
1 pound all-purpose potatoes
Salt

3 tablespoons margarine or
   butter
Pinch ground nutmeg
¼ teaspoon ground black
   pepper

◆ Peel root vegetables and potatoes and cut into 1-inch pieces. In 4-quart saucepan, combine root vegetables, potatoes, 2 teaspoons salt, and *water* to cover; heat to boiling over high heat. Reduce heat to low; cover and simmer 15 minutes, or until vegetables are tender. Drain; return to saucepan.

◆ Add margarine, nutmeg, pepper, and ½ teaspoon salt and mash with potato masher until smooth.

**Each serving; About 135 calories, 2g protein, 23g carbohydrate, 5g total fat (1g saturated), 0mg cholesterol, 250mg sodium**

## VEGETABLE COBBLER

*Prep: 30 minutes   Bake: 1 hour 15 minutes*
*Makes 6 main-dish servings*

1 medium butternut squash
   (about 2 pounds), peeled,
   seeded, and cut into 1½-inch
   chunks
3 large red potatoes (about
   1 pound), cut into 1½-inch
   chunks
3 medium parsnips (about
   ½ pound), peeled and cut
   into 1-inch pieces
1 medium red onion, cut into
   6 wedges
2 tablespoons olive oil
¼ teaspoon salt

½ teaspoon dried tarragon
1 can (13¾ to 14½ ounces)
   chicken or vegetable broth
½ teaspoon grated lemon peel
1 small bunch (about
   ¾ pound) broccoli, cut into
   2" by 1" pieces
½ cup plus ⅔ cup milk
1 tablespoon cornstarch
1¾ cups all-purpose baking
   mix
½ cup yellow cornmeal
¾ teaspoon coarsely ground
   black pepper

◆ Preheat oven to 450°F. In shallow 3- to 4-quart casserole or 13" by 9" glass baking dish, toss first 7 ingredients together until vegetables are well coated with oil. Bake, uncovered, 1 hour, or until vegetables are fork-tender and lightly browned, stirring once.

◆ Meanwhile, after vegetables have cooked about 45 minutes, in 3-quart saucepan, heat broth and lemon peel to boiling over high heat. Add broccoli; heat to boiling. Reduce heat to low; cover and simmer broccoli 1 minute.

◆ In cup, mix ½ cup milk with cornstarch; stir into broccoli mixture. Cook, stirring constantly, until mixture thickens slightly and boils; boil 1 minute.

◆ Pour broccoli mixture over vegetables; stir until brown bits are loosened from bottom of casserole.

◆ In medium bowl, mix baking mix, cornmeal, pepper, and remaining ⅔ cup milk until just combined. Drop 12 heaping spoonfuls of biscuit dough on top of vegetable mixture. Bake cobbler, uncovered, 15 minutes longer, or until biscuits are browned.

**Each serving: About 450 calories, 11g protein, 79g carbohydrate, 12g total fat (2g saturated), 12mg cholesterol, 840mg sodium**

## CARROTS AND PARSNIPS AU GRATIN

*Prep:* 45 minutes    *Bake:* 20 minutes
*Makes* 8 accompaniment servings

1 bag (16 ounces) carrots, peeled and cut diagonally into ¼-inch-thick slices
1 pound parsnips, peeled and cut diagonally into ¼-inch-thick slices
2 tablespoons margarine or butter
1 small onion, minced
½ cup mayonnaise
2 tablespoons prepared white horseradish
¼ teaspoon salt
⅛ teaspoon ground black pepper
1 slice firm white bread, torn into ¼-inch crumbs

◆ In 12-inch skillet, in *1½ inches boiling water*, heat carrots and parsnips to boiling over high heat. Reduce heat to low; cover and simmer 20 minutes, or until vegetables are tender. Drain, reserving ¼ cup cooking liquid. Transfer vegetables to 1½-quart casserole.

◆ Preheat oven to 350°F. In 1-quart saucepan, melt 1 tablespoon margarine over medium heat; add onion and cook, stirring occasionally, until tender. Remove from heat.

◆ Stir in mayonnaise, horseradish, salt, pepper, and reserved cooking liquid. Gently fold sauce into vegetables.

◆ In small skillet, melt remaining 1 tablespoon margarine over low heat. Stir in bread crumbs; mix until coated with margarine and scatter over casserole. Bake 20 minutes, or until crumbs are browned and vegetables are hot.

**Each serving: About 210 calories, 2g protein, 21g carbohydrate, 14g total fat (2g saturated), 8mg cholesterol, 260mg sodium**

## ROASTED CARROTS AND PARSNIPS

*Prep:* 15 minutes    *Roast:* 1 hour
*Makes* 8 accompaniment servings

1 bag (16 ounces) carrots, peeled and cut into 2-inch pieces
1 pound parsnips, peeled and cut into 2-inch pieces
8 ounces large shallots, peeled
1 tablespoon olive oil
⅛ teaspoon dried thyme
½ teaspoon salt
¼ teaspoon ground black pepper

Preheat oven to 425°F. In 14" by 10" roasting pan, toss carrots, parsnips, and shallots with olive oil, thyme, salt, and pepper until evenly coated. Roast 1 hour, or until vegetables are tender when pierced with knife.

**Each serving; About 105 calories, 2g protein, 22g carbohydrate, 2g total fat (0g saturated), 0mg cholesterol, 160mg sodium**

## MAPLE-GLAZED CARROTS WITH PISTACHIOS

*Prep:* 30 minutes    *Cook:* 30 to 40 minutes
*Makes* 10 accompaniment servings

8 bunches (4 pounds) baby carrots, peeled or scrubbed, or 3 bags (16 ounces each) carrots, peeled and cut into 3" by ½" sticks
4 tablespoons margarine or butter, cut up
1 teaspoon salt
½ cup maple syrup
½ cup pistachios, chopped and toasted

◆ In 12-inch skillet, heat *1 inch water* to boiling over high heat. Add carrots; heat to boiling. Reduce heat to low; cover and simmer 8 to 10 minutes, until tender-crisp. Drain.

◆ Wipe skillet dry. Return carrots to skillet; add margarine and salt and cook, uncovered, over medium-high heat, gently stirring occasionally, 10 to 15 minutes, until carrots are glazed and golden.

◆ Add maple syrup; heat to boiling. Boil 2 minutes, stirring frequently, until carrots are lightly coated with glaze. Transfer to bowl; sprinkle with pistachios.

**Each serving: About 175 calories, 3g protein, 25g carbohydrate, 8g total fat (1g saturated), 0mg cholesterol, 315mg sodium**

### PARSNIPS

Available all year round, parsnips are at their peak in winter. Their creamy texture lends itself beautifully to cold-weather favorites such as smooth mashes, purees, and soups, while their sweet nutty flavor makes them excellent in stews or roasted as an accompaniment. When buying, look for firm, smooth, medium-size parsnips without cracks. Large, older parsnips have a stronger flavor than younger ones; they may also have a woody core, which should be removed before cooking.

# BEETS WITH BASIL VINAIGRETTE

*Prep: 30 minutes plus cooling    Cook: 45 minutes*
*Makes 8 accompaniment servings*

| | |
|---|---|
| 6 pounds beets with tops (about 12 medium beets) | 2 teaspoons sugar |
| 3 tablespoons cider vinegar | 1 teaspoon salt |
| 2 tablespoons olive or vegetable oil | ¼ cup chopped fresh basil |
| | ½ small onion, cut into paper-thin slices |

◆ Trim stems and leaves from beets; reserve several leaves for garnish. With vegetable brush, scrub beets. In 5-quart saucepot, heat beets with *water* to cover to boiling over high heat. Reduce heat to low; cover and simmer 30 minutes, or until beets are tender when pierced with knife.

◆ Drain beets; cool until easy to handle. Peel beets and cut into bite-size chunks.

◆ In large bowl, with fork or wire whisk, mix vinegar, oil, sugar, and salt. Add basil, onion, and beets; toss to combine. Serve at room temperature or cover and refrigerate to serve cold later.

◆ To serve, line platter with reserved beet leaves; spoon beets on top.

**Each serving: About 125 calories, 3g protein, 21g carbohydrate, 4g total fat (0g saturated), 0mg cholesterol, 410mg sodium**

# ROASTED BEETS WITH CARDAMOM SPICE BUTTER

*Prep: 20 minutes plus cooling    Roast: 1 hour to 1 hour 30 minutes*
*Makes 4 accompaniment servings*

| | |
|---|---|
| 3 pounds beets with tops (about 6 medium beets) | Pinch ground cloves |
| ½ teaspoon ground cardamom | 1 tablespoon margarine or butter |
| ¼ teaspoon ground cumin | ¼ teaspoon salt |

◆ Preheat oven to 425°F. Trim stems and leaves from beets. With vegetable brush, scrub beets.

◆ Place beets in 14" by 10" roasting pan; cover tightly with foil. Roast 1 to 1½ hours, until tender when pierced with knife. Cool until easy to handle. Peel beets; cut into wedges.

◆ In 3-quart saucepan, heat cardamom, cumin, and cloves over low heat, shaking pan occasionally, 2 minutes, or until very fragrant. Add margarine and heat until bubbling. Add beets and salt; increase heat to medium and cook, stirring often, 5 minutes, or until hot.

**Each serving: About 115 calories, 3g protein, 20g carbohydrate, 3g total fat (1g saturated), 0mg cholesterol, 310mg sodium.**

# CANDIED TURNIPS

*Prep: 10 minutes    Cook: 20 minutes*
*Makes 6 accompaniment servings*

| | |
|---|---|
| 1½ pounds turnips, peeled and cut into 1-inch wedges | 2 tablespoons margarine or butter |
| 1 teaspoon salt | ⅛ cup sugar |

◆ In 12-inch skillet, combine turnips with salt and *water* to cover; heat to boiling over high heat.

◆ Reduce heat to low; cover and simmer 7 to 10 minutes, just until turnips are tender when pierced with knife. Drain.

◆ Wipe skillet dry. In same skillet, melt margarine over high heat. Add sugar and cook, stirring occasionally, about 2 minutes, until amber in color. Add turnips and cook, stirring often, 5 minutes, or until well coated.

**Each serving: About 95 calories, 1g protein, 16g carbohydrate, 4g total fat (1g saturated), 0mg cholesterol, 455mg sodium**

# ROASTED SUNCHOKES

*Prep: 15 minutes    Roast: 1 hour*
*Makes 8 accompaniment servings*

| | |
|---|---|
| 2 pounds sunchokes (Jerusalem artichokes) | ¼ teaspoon ground black pepper |
| 1 tablespoon olive oil | Chopped fresh parsley for garnish |
| 1 teaspoon salt | |

◆ Preheat oven to 425°F. With vegetable brush, scrub sunchokes. In 14" by 10" roasting pan, toss sunchokes with oil, salt, and pepper.

◆ Roast 1 hour, until sunchokes are tender when pierced with knife. To serve, sprinkle with parsley.

**Each serving: About 100 calories, 2g protein, 20g carbohydrate, 2g total fat (0g saturated), 0mg cholesterol, 270mg sodium**

---

### SUNCHOKES (JERUSALEM ARTICHOKES)

Neither an artichoke nor from Jerusalem, this brown-skinned tuber is a member of the sunflower family. Crisp, nutty, and slightly sweet in taste, sunchokes are equally good served raw in a salad or cooked. Peel them or simply scrub the skin well before using. When shopping, choose firm, unblemished tubers free of soft spots and green-tinged portions.

# POTATOES

Mashed, roasted, fried, or baked, potatoes are a supremely satisfying side dish in any guise. They can also be a tempting main course: Stuff a baked potato with a hearty filling, or create a rich potato pancake accented with artichokes.

## TWO-POTATOES ANNA

◆◆◆◆◆◆◆◆◆◆◆◆◆

*Prep:* 45 minutes
*Bake:* 25 minutes
*Makes* 10 accompaniment servings

**6 medium all-purpose potatoes (about 2 pounds)**
**4 medium sweet potatoes (about 2 pounds)**
**¼ cup vegetable oil**
**1 large onion, chopped**
**4 tablespoons margarine or butter**
**Salt**
**Ground black pepper**
**Parsley sprigs for garnish**

### ADJUSTABLE-BLADE SLICER

To slice, julienne, and waffle-cut vegetables easily, use an adjustable-blade slicer. These range from the classic all-metal mandoline to lightweight plastic models. Some have a selection of blades for different functions; the best are adjustable to paper-thinness. To protect your fingers, a safety shield holds the food in place as you slide it over the blade.

**1** Peel all-purpose and sweet potatoes. Using an adjustable-blade slicer or sharp knife, thinly slice potatoes, keeping sliced white and sweet potatoes in separate piles.

**2** In 10-inch cast-iron skillet with oven-safe handle (or wrap handle with double thickness of foil), heat oil over medium heat. Add onion; cook until tender. Transfer to bowl.

**3** In same skillet, arrange white potatoes, overlapping them slightly. Sprinkle with onion; dot with 2 tablespoons margarine. Sprinkle with ¾ teaspoon salt and ¼ teaspoon pepper.

**4** Arrange sweet-potato slices over white potatoes. Dot with remaining 2 tablespoons margarine; sprinkle with ¾ teaspoon salt and ¼ teaspoon pepper.

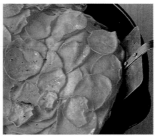

**5** Cook layered potato mixture over medium heat 15 minutes, or until bottom layer of potatoes is lightly browned. Meanwhile, preheat oven to 450°F.

**6** Place skillet on bottom rack in oven and bake 25 minutes, or until potatoes are tender when pierced with knife, pressing potatoes down with pancake turner occasionally. To serve, loosen edge of potatoes with pancake turner; carefully invert potatoes onto warm platter. Garnish with parsley sprigs; cut into wedges.

EACH SERVING: ABOUT 250 CALORIES, 3g PROTEIN, 37g CARBOHYDRATE, 10g TOTAL FAT (2g SATURATED), 0mg CHOLESTEROL, 385mg SODIUM

# ROASTED POTATOES WITH GARLIC

*Prep:* 20 minutes   *Roast:* 1 hour
*Makes* 10 accompaniment servings

4½ pounds medium red
  and/or all-purpose
  potatoes, unpeeled and
  each cut into quarters
2 medium red onions, each
  cut into 6 wedges
¼ cup olive oil

1 tablespoon chopped fresh
  thyme or 1 teaspoon dried
  thyme
1¼ teaspoons salt
½ teaspoon coarsely ground
  black pepper
2 garlic cloves, minced

Preheat oven to 425°F. In 17" by 11½" roasting pan, toss potatoes with remaining ingredients. Roast, turning occasionally with metal spatula, 1 hour, or until golden and fork-tender. Serve warm or at room temperature.

**Each serving: About 240 calories, 4g protein, 44g carbohydrate, 6g total fat (1g saturated), 0mg cholesterol, 275mg sodium**

# POTATO AND ARTICHOKE RÖSTI

*Prep:* 35 minutes   *Bake:* 20 to 25 minutes
*Makes* 4 main-dish servings

2½ pounds baking potatoes
  (about 4 large)
¾ teaspoon salt
¼ teaspoon coarsely ground
  black pepper
2 tablespoons olive oil

4 ounces Fontina or
  mozzarella cheese,
  shredded (1 cup)
1 jar (8¼ ounces) marinated
  artichoke hearts, rinsed,
  well drained, and sliced

◆ Preheat oven to 400°F. Peel and coarsely shred potatoes; pat dry. In large bowl, toss potatoes with salt and pepper.

◆ In nonstick 10-inch skillet with oven-safe handle (or wrap handle with double thickness of foil), heat 1 tablespoon oil over medium heat. Working quickly, add half the potatoes, patting with rubber spatula to cover skillet. Leaving ½-inch border, top potatoes with half the cheese, all the artichokes,

then remaining cheese. Cover with remaining potatoes, patting to edge of skillet. Cook 10 minutes, or until bottom is brown, shaking skillet occasionally to keep pancake moving freely. Carefully invert pancake onto large plate.

◆ Add remaining 1 tablespoon oil to skillet; slide pancake back into skillet. Cook 10 minutes, gently shaking skillet. Place in oven and bake 20 to 25 minutes, until potatoes are tender.

**Each serving: About 475 calories, 15g protein, 71g carbohydrate, 16g total fat (6g saturated), 33mg cholesterol, 700mg sodium**

# CLASSIC MASHED POTATOES

*Prep:* 20 minutes   *Cook:* 30 minutes
*Makes* 8 accompaniment servings

3 pounds all-purpose potatoes
4 tablespoons margarine or
  butter

1½ teaspoons salt
1 cup hot milk

Peel potatoes and cut into 1-inch chunks. In 3-quart saucepan, heat potatoes and enough *water* to cover to boiling over high heat. Reduce heat to low. Cover and simmer 15 minutes, or until fork-tender; drain. Return potatoes to pan. With potato masher, mash potatoes with margarine and salt. Gradually add milk; mash until smooth.

**Each serving: About 215 calories, 4g protein, 36g carbohydrate, 7g total fat (2g saturated), 4mg cholesterol, 490mg sodium**

## MASHED POTATOES PLUS

**Garlic and lemon** Prepare Classic Mashed Potatoes as above through draining. Meanwhile, in 1-quart saucepan, heat the margarine and salt with 2 cloves garlic, minced, over low heat 3 minutes. Add to potatoes; mash. Add milk as directed; stir in 2 tablespoons minced parsley and 1 teaspoon grated lemon peel.

**Each serving: About 215 calories, 4g protein, 36g carbohydrate, 7g total fat (2g saturated), 4mg cholesterol, 490mg sodium**

**Horseradish** Prepare Classic Mashed Potatoes as above, but add 2 tablespoons undrained prepared white horseradish with the milk.

**Each serving: About 215 calories, 4g protein, 36g carbohydrate, 7g total fat (2g saturated), 4mg cholesterol, 530mg sodium**

**Parsnip** Prepare Classic Mashed Potatoes as above, but substitute 1 pound parsnips, peeled and cut into 1-inch pieces, for 1 pound potatoes and use only ¾ cup milk.

**Each serving: About 210 calories, 4g protein, 35g carbohydrate, 7g total fat (2g saturated), 3mg cholesterol, 490mg sodium**

# DELUXE STUFFED BAKED POTATOES

*Prep: 15 to 25 minutes    Bake: 45 minutes*
*Makes 4 main-dish servings*

**4 large baking potatoes**
  **(12 ounces each)**

**Choice of Baked Potato**
  **Topping (see below)**

Preheat oven to 450°F. Pierce potatoes with a fork. Bake potatoes directly on oven rack 45 minutes, or until fork-tender. Meanwhile, prepare Baked Potato Topping. When potatoes are done, slash tops, press to open slightly, and spoon on topping.

**For nutritional values, see below.**

# CHUNKY HOME FRIES

*Prep: 5 minutes    Cook: 25 minutes*
*Makes 4 accompaniment servings*

**1½ pounds medium red**
  **potatoes**

**2 tablespoons olive oil**
  **½ teaspoon salt**

◆ Cut potatoes into 1½-inch chunks. In nonstick 12-inch skillet, heat oil over medium-high heat; add potatoes and salt and cook, turning occasionally, until golden brown.

◆ Reduce heat to medium; cover skillet and continue cooking potato chunks, turning once or twice, until potatoes are fork-tender.

**Each serving: About 205 calories, 3g protein, 34g carbohydrate, 7g total fat (1g saturated), 0mg cholesterol, 275mg sodium**

# OVEN FRIES

*Prep: 10 minutes    Bake: 45 minutes*
*Makes 4 accompaniment servings*

**3 medium baking potatoes or**
  **sweet potatoes (about**
  **1½ pounds), unpeeled**
**1 tablespoon vegetable oil**

**½ teaspoon salt**
**⅛ teaspoon ground black**
  **pepper**

◆ Preheat oven to 425°F. Cut each potato lengthwise into quarters, then cut each quarter lengthwise into 3 wedges.

◆ In 15½" by 10½" jelly-roll pan, toss potato wedges with oil, salt, and black pepper until evenly coated. Bake 45 minutes, or until potatoes are golden.

**Each serving: About 195 calories, 3g protein, 38g carbohydrate, 4g total fat (1g saturated), 0mg cholesterol, 280mg sodium**

## BAKED POTATO TOPPINGS (EACH TOPS 4 POTATOES)

**CHILI** Heat nonstick 12-inch skillet over medium-high heat. Add ¾ pound ground beef and 1 small onion, chopped; cook, stirring, until meat is browned and onion is tender. Stir in 3 tablespoons chili powder; cook 1 minute. Add 1 can (14½ ounces) chili-style chunky tomatoes, ¾ cup water, and 1 teaspoon sugar; cook 1 minute longer.

Each serving: About 435 calories, 11g protein, 96g carbohydrate, 3g total fat (1g saturated), 4mg cholesterol, 500mg sodium

**HAM AND EGG** In nonstick 12-inch skillet, melt 2 tablespoons margarine or butter over medium heat. Add 1 medium green pepper, diced, and 1 medium onion, diced; cook until tender and browned. Stir in 4 ounces ham, diced, and 6 large eggs, beaten with ¼ cup water and ¼ teaspoon each salt and coarsely ground black pepper; stir until eggs are cooked.

Each serving: About 595 calories, 24g protein, 92g carbohydrate, 15g total fat (4g saturated), 328mg cholesterol, 645mg sodium

**CHUNKY VEGETABLE** Cut 1 small eggplant, 1 medium zucchini, and 1 large red pepper into ½-inch pieces. In nonstick 12-inch skillet, heat 2 tablespoons olive oil over medium-high heat. Add vegetables; cook 15 minutes. Stir in 1 can (14½ ounces) Italian-style stewed tomatoes, ¼ cup water, 1 tablespoon balsamic vinegar, and 1 teaspoon salt; heat through.

Each serving: About 490 calories, 10g protein, 99g carbohydrate, 7g total fat (1g saturated), 0mg cholesterol, 760mg sodium

**SPINACH AND FETA** In 2-quart saucepan, melt 2 tablespoons margarine or butter over medium heat; stir in 2 tablespoons all-purpose flour. Add 1⅓ cups milk; heat to boiling, stirring. Add 10 ounces frozen chopped spinach, thawed, ¼ teaspoon each dillweed and ground black pepper, and 2 ounces crumbled feta; heat through. Top with 2 ounces feta.

Each serving: About 590 calories, 18g protein, 99g carbohydrate, 16g total fat (8g saturated), 39mg cholesterol, 520mg sodium

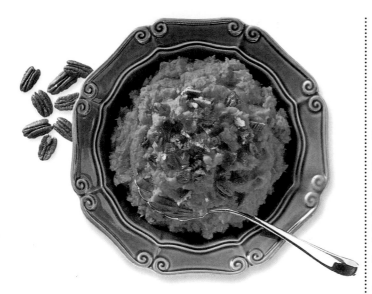

## PRALINE SWEET POTATOES

*Prep:* 15 minutes plus cooling   *Cook:* 35 to 40 minutes
**Makes** 10 accompaniment servings

**8 medium sweet potatoes
  (about 5 pounds), peeled
  and each cut crosswise into
  thirds
¼ cup sugar**

**1 cup pecans (about 4 ounces)
5 tablespoons margarine or
  butter
½ cup milk
1¼ teaspoons salt**

◆ In 8-quart saucepot, heat sweet potatoes and enough *water* to cover to boiling over high heat. Reduce heat to low; cover and simmer 20 to 25 minutes, until sweet potatoes are fork-tender. Drain; return to saucepot.

◆ Meanwhile, grease cookie sheet. In 1-quart saucepan, heat sugar and ¼ cup *water*, stirring gently, over low heat until sugar dissolves. Increase heat to medium and boil rapidly, without stirring, about 7 minutes, until syrup turns a light golden brown.

◆ Working quickly, stir in pecans and 2 tablespoons margarine until combined. Spread pecan mixture in a thin layer on cookie sheet; cool.

◆ To saucepot with sweet potatoes, add milk, salt, and remaining 3 tablespoons margarine. With potato masher, mash sweet potatoes until almost smooth. Heat mixture through over low heat.

◆ To serve, spoon mashed sweet potatoes into large bowl. Break pecan mixture into small pieces; sprinkle on top of sweet potatoes.

**Each serving: About 335 calories, 4g protein, 51g carbohydrate, 14g total fat (2g saturated), 2mg cholesterol, 360mg sodium**

## SWEET-POTATO CASSEROLE

*Prep:* 20 minutes   *Bake:* 60 to 70 minutes
**Makes** 8 accompaniment servings

**5 large sweet potatoes
  (4 pounds), peeled and cut
  into ¾-inch-thick slices
⅓ cup packed dark brown
  sugar
Salt**

**¼ teaspoon coarsely ground
  black pepper
4 tablespoons margarine or
  butter, cut into small pieces
½ cup coarsely chopped
  walnuts**

◆ Preheat oven to 400°F. In 13" by 9" ceramic or glass baking dish, arrange half of potato slices. Sprinkle with half of sugar, ¼ teaspoon salt, and all of pepper. Dot with half of margarine. Top with remaining potatoes. Sprinkle with remaining sugar and ¼ teaspoon salt; dot with remaining margarine.

◆ Cover with foil; bake 30 minutes. Uncover; sprinkle with walnuts and bake 30 to 40 minutes longer, until potatoes are tender, basting with syrup in dish 3 times during cooking.

**Each serving: About 300 calories, 4g protein, 52g carbohydrate, 9g total fat (1g saturated), 0mg cholesterol, 225mg sodium**

## TWO-POTATO CASSEROLE

*Prep:* 1 hour plus cooling   *Bake:* 45 minutes
**Makes** 8 accompaniment servings

**4 large baking potatoes
  (about 2 pounds), unpeeled
4 medium sweet potatoes
  (about 2 pounds), unpeeled
3 tablespoons margarine or
  butter
1 small onion, minced
3 tablespoons all-purpose flour**

**2 teaspoons salt
¼ teaspoon coarsely ground
  black pepper
2½ cups milk
2 packages (10 ounces each)
  frozen chopped spinach,
  thawed and squeezed dry**

◆ In 8-quart saucepot, heat baking and sweet potatoes and enough *water* to cover to boiling over high heat. Reduce heat to low; cover and simmer 20 to 30 minutes, just until potatoes are fork-tender but not soft. Drain and cool.

◆ Preheat oven to 375°F. In 2-quart saucepan, melt margarine over medium heat; add onion and cook until tender. Stir in flour, salt, and pepper. Gradually whisk in milk and cook, whisking, until sauce boils. Set aside.

◆ Peel all potatoes; cut into ¼-inch-thick slices. In greased deep 2-quart casserole, arrange half of potato slices. Top with all of spinach; pour half of sauce on top. Repeat with remaining potatoes and sauce. Cover and bake 30 minutes. Uncover; bake 15 minutes longer, or until top is browned.

**Each serving: About 335 calories, 9g protein, 61g carbohydrate, 7g total fat (3g saturated), 10mg cholesterol, 700mg sodium**

# ONION FAMILY

Leeks, garlic, and onions are the foundation of some irresistibly fragrant and appetizing side dishes. Leeks can be marinated in oil and herbs and then broiled to bring out their fresh, delicate onion flavor. Onions and garlic become sweet, succulent, and considerably milder in flavor when roasted or cooked with a bit of jelly or sugar in a skillet until they're nicely glazed. Try any of these recipes with roasted meats or poultry.

## BROILED LEEKS

◆◆◆◆◆◆◆◆◆◆◆◆◆◆◆◆◆◆◆◆◆◆◆◆◆◆◆◆◆◆◆◆

*Prep: 25 minutes plus marinating   Broil: 10 minutes*
*Makes 6 accompaniment servings*

6 large leeks
Salt
¼ cup olive or vegetable oil
2 tablespoons tarragon
   vinegar
1½ teaspoons minced fresh
   oregano

½ teaspoon sugar
½ teaspoon coarsely ground
   black pepper
Oregano or parsley sprigs for
   garnish

1 Cut off roots from base and trim tops of leeks. Cut each leek lengthwise in half to within 2 inches of root ends.

2 Separate leaves slightly; rinse leeks thoroughly with cold running water to wash away all sand and grit.

3 In 8-quart saucepot over high heat, in *2 inches boiling water*, heat leeks and 2 teaspoons salt to boiling over high heat. Reduce heat to low; cover and simmer 5 to 10 minutes, just until leeks are tender. Drain in a colander; shake to remove excess water.

4 Prepare marinade: In shallow glass or ceramic baking dish, with wire whisk or fork, combine oil, vinegar, minced oregano, sugar, black pepper, and ½ teaspoon salt. Add leeks to dish and turn to coat. Cover and refrigerate at least 2 hours, turning leeks occasionally.

5 Preheat broiler. Place leeks on rack in broiling pan, reserving marinade. Broil leeks 7 to 10 inches from heat source 10 minutes, or until hot and lightly browned, turning once and brushing with marinade.

6 Transfer leeks to large platter. Pour pan juices in broiling pan over leeks. Serve warm or cover with plastic wrap and refrigerate to serve cold later. Garnish with oregano sprigs.

EACH SERVING: ABOUT 130 CALORIES, 1g PROTEIN, 13g CARBOHYDRATE, 9g TOTAL FAT (1g SATURATED), 0mg CHOLESTEROL, 230mg SODIUM

## CARAMELIZED ONIONS

*Prep: 45 minutes plus cooling*
*Cook: 30 minutes*
*Makes 4 accompaniment servings*

1½ pounds small white onions
½ cup golden raisins
2 tablespoons sugar
2 tablespoons vegetable oil
½ teaspoon salt

◆ In deep 12-inch skillet, heat onions and *1 inch water* to boiling over high heat. Reduce heat to low; cover and simmer 15 minutes, or until onions are tender. Drain. Cool onions under cold running water; drain again.

◆ Peel onions, leaving a little of the root end on to help hold shape.

◆ Wipe skillet dry. In same skillet, cook onions, raisins, sugar, oil, and salt over medium-high heat, stirring and shaking skillet often, about 5 minutes, until onions are glazed and browned.

**Each serving: About 210 calories, 3g protein, 37g carbohydrate, 7g total fat (1g saturated), 0mg cholesterol, 275mg sodium**

## GLAZED PEARL ONIONS

*Prep: 45 minutes plus cooling     Cook: 25 minutes*
*Makes 6 accompaniment servings*

2 pounds pearl onions
3 tablespoons margarine or butter
2 tablespoons red currant jelly
2 teaspoons sugar
¼ teaspoon salt

◆ In deep 12-inch skillet, heat onions and *1 inch water* to boiling over high heat. Reduce heat to low; cover and simmer 5 to 10 minutes, until onions are tender. Drain. Cool onions under cold running water; drain again.

◆ Peel onions, leaving a little of the root end of each to help hold shape. Wipe skillet dry.

◆ In same skillet, cook onions and remaining ingredients over medium-high heat, stirring and shaking skillet often, about 5 minutes, until onions are glazed and browned.

**Each serving: About 130 calories, 2g protein, 19g carbohydrate, 6g total fat (1g saturated), 0mg cholesterol, 160mg sodium**

## OVEN-ROASTED ONIONS

*Prep: 10 minutes     Roast: 1 hour 20 minutes*
*Makes 12 accompaniment servings*

4 tablespoons olive or vegetable oil
4 jumbo red or white onions (about 1¼ pounds each), cut crosswise into ¾-inch-thick slices
Salt
2 tablespoons brown sugar
1 tablespoon cider vinegar

◆ Preheat oven to 400°F. Grease each of two 15½" by 10½" jelly-roll pans with 1 tablespoon oil. Place onion slices in single layer in jelly-roll pans.

◆ In cup, mix remaining 2 tablespoons oil with 1 teaspoon salt. Brush onion slices with half of oil mixture. Place jelly-roll pans on 2 oven racks and roast onions 45 minutes.

◆ With pancake turner, turn onion slices; brush with remaining oil mixture. Switch jelly-roll pans between upper and lower racks and roast onions 30 minutes longer.

◆ In cup, mix brown sugar, vinegar, and ½ teaspoon salt. Brush onion slices with brown-sugar mixture and roast 5 minutes longer, or until onions are tender and golden.

**Each serving: About 110 calories, 2g protein, 19g carbohydrate, 4g total fat (1g saturated), 0mg cholesterol, 275mg sodium**

## PAN-ROASTED GARLIC

*Prep: 15 minutes plus cooling     Cook: 30 minutes*
*Makes about 1 cup*

4 heads garlic (about ¾ pound), separated into cloves, unpeeled
1 tablespoon sugar
1 tablespoon vegetable oil
½ teaspoon salt

◆ In 3-quart saucepan, heat garlic cloves and *6 cups water* to boiling over high heat. Reduce heat to low; cover and simmer 15 minutes, or until garlic cloves are fork-tender. Drain. Cool garlic under cold running water; drain again.

◆ Peel garlic cloves. In 10-inch skillet, cook garlic, sugar, oil, and salt over medium-high heat, stirring and shaking skillet often, about 5 minutes, until garlic cloves are glazed and browned. Use pan-roasted garlic as a condiment to sprinkle over salads or cooked vegetables, serve alongside roasted meats and poultry, or spread like butter on bread.

**Each tablespoon: About 40 calories, 1g protein, 8g carbohydrate, 1g total fat (0g saturated), 0mg cholesterol, 70mg sodium**

# SQUASH

Squash are grouped into summer and winter varieties, although most are available year-round. Winter varieties (including butternut, acorn, and spaghetti squash) have hard skin and seeds, typically contain a firm, orange-colored flesh, and are equally good large or small. By contrast, soft-skinned summer squash, such as zucchini and yellow straightneck, have a creamy-white flesh and are most tender and flavorful when small. Cooking options for both are plentiful: Squash can be sliced and sautéed in garlic-flavored olive oil, shredded and fried for crisp, golden fritters, or halved and baked with a buttery pecan topping.

1 With coarse shredder, shred carrot, zucchini, and squash. Pat vegetables very dry with paper towels.

2 In medium bowl, mix shredded vegetables with flour, Parmesan cheese, salt, pepper, and egg.

## VEGETABLE FRITTERS

◆◆◆◆◆◆◆◆◆◆◆◆◆◆◆◆◆◆◆◆◆◆◆◆◆◆◆◆◆

*Prep: 20 minutes    Cook: 5 minutes per batch*
*Makes 4 accompaniment servings*

| | |
|---|---|
| 1 large carrot | ½ teaspoon salt |
| 1 medium zucchini (10 ounces) | ⅛ teaspoon ground black pepper |
| 1 medium yellow straightneck squash (10 ounces) | 1 large egg |
| ⅓ cup all-purpose flour | ½ cup vegetable oil |
| ⅓ cup freshly grated Parmesan cheese | |

3 In 10-inch skillet, heat oil over medium heat. Gently drop one-eighth of vegetable mixture at a time (¼ cup) into oil in skillet, flattening slightly to about 3-inch round.

4 Cook 3 fritters at a time, turning once, 5 minutes, until golden brown. With pancake turner, transfer to paper towels to drain. Keep warm in low oven while cooking remainder.

### MINI FRITTERS

Try tiny fritters with a basil dipping sauce. For sauce, in blender, process ⅔ cup sour cream, ⅔ cup loosely packed fresh basil, 1 teaspoon fresh lemon juice, and ¼ teaspoon each salt and black pepper until smooth. In Step 3, drop mixture into skillet 1 tablespoon at a time. Cook until golden, turning once. Makes about 32 mini-fritters.

Each fritter with 1 teaspoon sauce: About 40 calories, 1g protein, 2g carbohydrate, 3g total fat (2g saturated), 9mg cholesterol, 75mg sodium

EACH SERVING: ABOUT 245 CALORIES, 8g PROTEIN, 15g CARBOHYDRATE, 18g TOTAL FAT (4g SATURATED), 60mg CHOLESTEROL, 450mg SODIUM

## ACORN SQUASH WITH BROWN SUGAR–PECAN TOPPING

*Prep: 15 minutes    Bake: 45 minutes*
*Makes 4 accompaniment servings*

2 small acorn squash
  (1 pound each)
½ teaspoon salt
½ cup pecans or walnuts
  (about 2 ounces), chopped

¼ cup packed light brown
  sugar
2 tablespoons margarine or
  butter, melted

◆ Preheat oven to 375°F. Cut each acorn squash lengthwise in half; discard seeds. Cut squash crosswise into 1-inch slices. Place slices, in a single layer, in 15½" by 10½" jelly-roll pan; sprinkle with salt. Drizzle *2 tablespoons water* around squash. Cover pan tightly with foil. Bake 30 minutes.

◆ Meanwhile, in small bowl, stir nuts with brown sugar and margarine until combined. Spoon nut mixture evenly over squash. Bake, uncovered, 15 minutes longer.

**Each serving; About 320 calories, 4g protein, 49g carbohydrate, 15g total fat (2g saturated), 0mg cholesterol, 350g sodium**

## ZUCCHINI RIBBONS WITH MINT

*Prep: 10 minutes    Cook: 3 minutes*
*Makes 4 accompaniment servings*

4 very small zucchini (4 ounces
  each) or 2 medium zucchini
  (8 ounces each)
1 tablespoon olive oil
2 garlic cloves, crushed with
  side of knife

½ teaspoon salt
2 tablespoons chopped fresh
  mint
Mint sprig for garnish

◆ Trim ends from zucchini. With vegetable peeler or adjustable-blade slicer, shave zucchini lengthwise into long strips (if zucchini are wider than peeler, first cut each lengthwise in half). In 12-inch skillet, heat olive oil with garlic over medium heat until garlic is golden; discard garlic.

◆ Increase heat to high. Add zucchini and salt and cook, stirring, 2 minutes, or just until zucchini wilts. Remove from heat; stir in chopped mint. To serve, garnish with mint sprig.

**Each serving; About 50 calories, 1g protein, 4g carbohydrate, 4g total fat (0g saturated), 0mg cholesterol, 270mg sodium**

## ROSEMARY-ROASTED BUTTERNUT SQUASH

*Prep: 20 minutes    Roast: 35 minutes*
*Makes 10 accompaniment servings*

4 tablespoons margarine or
  butter
3 medium butternut squash
  (about 1¾ pounds each)
1 medium onion, diced

1¾ teaspoons salt
1¼ teaspoons dried rosemary,
  crushed
½ teaspoon coarsely ground
  black pepper

◆ Preheat oven to 400°F. Place margarine in 17" by 11½" roasting pan; place roasting pan in oven until margarine melts. Meanwhile, cut each squash lengthwise in half; discard seeds. Cut squash into 2-inch chunks. Cut peel from chunks.

◆ Remove roasting pan from oven. Add squash, onion, salt, rosemary, and pepper; toss to coat with margarine. Arrange squash in single layer; roast 35 minutes, or until tender.

**Each serving: About 145 calories, 2g protein, 27g carbohydrate, 5g total fat (1g saturated), 0mg cholesterol, 435mg sodium**

## THREE-SQUASH SAUTÉ

*Prep: 20 minutes    Cook: 45 minutes*
*Makes 6 accompaniment servings*

1 medium spaghetti squash
3 tablespoons olive oil
1 garlic clove, crushed with
  side of knife
1 small zucchini (6 ounces),
  cut into ½-inch pieces
1 small yellow straightneck
  squash (6 ounces), cut into
  ½-inch pieces

½ pint cherry tomatoes, each
  cut in half
2 tablespoons minced fresh
  basil
¾ teaspoon salt
¼ teaspoon ground black
  pepper
2 tablespoons pine nuts
  (pignoli), toasted

◆ Cut spaghetti squash lengthwise in half; discard seeds. In 8-quart Dutch oven, in *¾ inch boiling water*, heat squash, cut-side up, to boiling over high heat. Reduce heat to low; cover and simmer 30 minutes, or until tender.

◆ Remove spaghetti squash from Dutch oven; drain. With 2 forks, gently scrape squash lengthwise, lifting out pulp as it becomes free. Drain pulp thoroughly on paper towels. Discard squash skin.

◆ Wipe Dutch oven dry. In Dutch oven, heat oil over medium-high heat; add garlic and cook until lightly browned. Discard garlic. Stir in zucchini and yellow squash; cook until tender. Add spaghetti squash, cherry tomatoes, basil, salt, and pepper; heat through. Sprinkle with pine nuts.

**Each serving: About 110 calories, 2g protein, 9g carbohydrate, 9g total fat (1g saturated), 0mg cholesterol, 275mg sodium**

# MUSHROOMS

There's a world of mushrooms beyond the common cultivated white variety: Exotics such as shiitake and portobello, with their big, meaty flavor, and the delicate oyster mushroom are increasingly available.

### WARM MUSHROOM SALAD

◆◆◆◆◆◆◆◆◆◆◆◆◆

*Prep:* 20 minutes
*Cook:* 35 minutes
*Makes* 6 first-course or accompaniment servings

1 bunch arugula
8 ounces shiitake mushrooms
3 tablespoons vegetable oil
1 large red onion, cut into ½-inch-wide wedges
2½ pounds cremini and/or white mushrooms, each cut in half if large
2 tablespoons soy sauce
2 tablespoons red wine vinegar
¼ cup pine nuts (pignoli), toasted (optional)
Parsley sprigs for garnish

**1** Arrange arugula on platter; set aside. Cut and discard stems from shiitake mushrooms; cut shiitake caps into ½-inch-wide strips.

**2** In nonstick 12-inch skillet, heat 1 tablespoon oil over medium heat. Add onion and cook just until tender; with slotted spoon, transfer to medium bowl.

**3** In same skillet, heat 1 tablespoon oil over medium-high heat. Add half of all mushrooms; cook until liquid evaporates. Stir in 1 tablespoon soy sauce.

**4** Transfer mushrooms to bowl with onion. Repeat with remaining 1 tablespoon oil, remaining mushrooms, and remaining 1 tablespoon soy sauce. Add vinegar to mushroom mixture in bowl; toss to coat. Spoon mushroom mixture on top of arugula on platter. Sprinkle with pine nuts, if using; garnish with parsley.

---

## EXOTIC MUSHROOMS

These mushrooms generally have a more intense flavor than regular white button; use a selection to add interest to almost any mushroom recipe. Morels, porcini (cèpe in French), and shiitake are available fresh or dried. Don't throw away the soaking water from dried mushrooms – it is full of flavor and can be used in stocks, soups, and sauces.

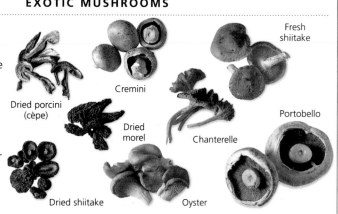

Fresh shiitake
Cremini
Dried porcini (cèpe)
Dried morel
Chanterelle
Portobello
Dried shiitake
Oyster

---

**EACH SERVING: ABOUT 150 CALORIES, 6g PROTEIN, 19g CARBOHYDRATE, 8g TOTAL FAT (1g SATURATED), 0mg CHOLESTEROL, 360mg SODIUM**

## MUSHROOM, ASPARAGUS, AND GRUYÈRE STRUDEL

*Prep: 40 minutes plus cooling    Bake: 25 minutes*
*Makes 6 main-dish servings*

| | |
|---|---|
| 12 ounces asparagus | 2 tablespoons plain dried |
| Salt | bread crumbs |
| 7 tablespoons margarine or | 12 sheets (about 16" by 12" |
| butter | each) fresh or frozen |
| 1 pound mushrooms, thinly | (thawed) phyllo (about |
| sliced | 8 ounces) |
| 2 teaspoons fresh lemon juice | 4 ounces Gruyère or Swiss |
| ⅓ cup walnuts (about | cheese, shredded (1 cup) |
| 1½ ounces), toasted and | |
| finely chopped | |

◆ Cut asparagus into 6-inch-long spears. In nonstick 12-inch skillet, heat *½ inch water* to boiling over medium-high heat. Add asparagus and ½ teaspoon salt; heat to boiling. Reduce heat to medium-low; cook 4 to 8 minutes, until asparagus are tender. Drain. Wipe skillet dry. In same skillet, melt 1 tablespoon margarine over medium-high heat. Add mushrooms and ½ teaspoon salt; cook until mushrooms are browned and liquid evaporates. Add lemon juice; cook 30 seconds. Transfer to plate; cool.

◆ Preheat oven to 375°F. Lightly grease cookie sheet. Melt remaining 6 tablespoons margarine. In small bowl, mix walnuts and bread crumbs. On work surface, place 1 phyllo sheet with a short side facing you; brush lightly with some melted margarine. Sprinkle all over with one-sixth of walnut mixture. Top with another phyllo sheet; brush with some margarine, being careful not to tear phyllo.

◆ Spoon one-sixth of cheese in a strip on phyllo 2 inches from edge facing you and leaving a 1½-inch border on both sides. Arrange one-sixth of asparagus on cheese; top with one-sixth of mushrooms. Fold bottom of phyllo over to enclose filling, then fold left and right sides in toward center. Roll up phyllo, jelly-roll fashion, forming a packet.

◆ Place packet, seam-side down, on cookie sheet. Brush lightly with some margarine. Repeat to make 5 more packets. Bake packets 25 minutes, or until slightly puffed and golden brown.

Each serving; About 375 calories, 13g protein, 28g carbohydrate, 25g total fat (7g saturated), 21mg cholesterol, 645mg sodium

## GRILLED PORTOBELLO MUSHROOM SALAD

*Prep: 15 minutes    Grill/broil: 8 to 9 minutes*
*Makes 4 first-course servings*

| | |
|---|---|
| 1 wedge Parmesan cheese | ¼ teaspoon salt |
| 2 bunches arugula | ⅛ teaspoon ground black |
| 2 tablespoons balsamic | pepper |
| vinegar | 1 pound portobello |
| 2 tablespoons olive oil | mushrooms, stems |
| 2 tablespoons minced shallots | discarded |
| 2 tablespoons chopped fresh | |
| parsley | |

◆ Prepare outdoor grill or preheat broiler. With vegetable peeler, shave ½ cup (about 1 ounce) curls from Parmesan cheese; set aside. Reserve remaining Parmesan for use another day. Arrange arugula on platter.

◆ Prepare dressing: In small bowl, mix vinegar, oil, shallots, parsley, salt, and pepper. Place mushrooms, top-side up, on grill or rack in broiling pan at position closest to heat source. Brush mushroom tops with 1 tablespoon dressing. Grill or broil 4 minutes. Turn mushrooms; brush with 1 more tablespoon dressing. Grill or broil 4 to 5 minutes longer, until tender.

◆ Slice mushrooms and arrange on arugula. Spoon remaining dressing over salad. Top with Parmesan curls.

Each serving; About 150 calories, 6g protein, 14g carbohydrate, 10g total fat (2g saturated), 6mg cholesterol, 280mg sodium

## SAUTÉED MIXED MUSHROOMS

*Prep: 15 minutes    Cook: 10 minutes*
*Makes 4 accompaniment servings*

| | |
|---|---|
| 2 tablespoons margarine or | 4 ounces oyster mushrooms, |
| butter | each cut in half if large |
| ¼ cup minced shallots | ⅛ teaspoon dried thyme |
| 8 ounces medium white | ¼ teaspoon salt |
| mushrooms, each cut into | ⅛ teaspoon ground black |
| quarters | pepper |
| 4 ounces shiitake mushrooms, | 1 small garlic clove, minced |
| stems discarded, cut into | 1 tablespoon chopped fresh |
| 1-inch wedges | parsley |

In 12-inch skillet, melt margarine over medium-high heat. Add shallots; cook, stirring, 1 minute. Stir in all mushrooms. Sprinkle with thyme, salt, and pepper and cook, stirring often, until mushrooms are tender and liquid evaporates. Stir in garlic and parsley; cook 1 minute longer.

Each serving; About 100 calories, 3g protein, 10g carbohydrate, 6g total fat (1g saturated), 0mg cholesterol, 205mg sodium

# EGGPLANT

Deep purple or creamy white, eggplant has a hearty, meaty texture and a neutral taste that readily absorbs the flavors of whatever ingredients are cooking along with it. Eggplant marries particularly well with strong flavors, such as garlic, olive oil, and balsamic vinegar. Be sure to purchase plump, shiny, unblemished eggplants that feel heavy for their size; light ones may be spongy.

## ITALIAN EGGPLANT WITH GARLIC

◆◆◆◆◆◆◆◆◆◆◆◆◆◆◆◆◆◆◆◆◆◆◆◆◆◆◆◆◆◆◆

*Prep:* 25 minutes    *Broil:* 40 minutes
*Makes* 10 accompaniment servings

½ cup olive oil
3 garlic cloves, sliced
¼ cup minced fresh basil
1½ teaspoons salt
½ teaspoon cracked black
  pepper

4 small eggplants (12 ounces
  each) or 10 baby eggplants
  (3 ounces each)
1 tablespoon grated lemon
  peel

1 In 1-quart saucepan, heat olive oil over medium heat; add garlic slices and cook, stirring occasionally, until lightly browned. Remove saucepan from heat; stir in minced basil, salt, and pepper.

2 Preheat broiler. Cut each eggplant lengthwise into ¾-inch-thick slices. Lightly score both sides of each slice in crisscross pattern. (If using baby eggplants, cut each lengthwise in half. Score cut sides only.)

3 Place half of eggplant slices in single layer on rack in broiling pan. Brush lightly with some olive-oil mixture from saucepan. (If using baby eggplant, place cut-side up. Brush cut sides with some olive-oil mixture, then turn cut-side down.) Broil eggplant 7 to 9 inches from heat source 10 minutes. Turn eggplant slices (or halves); lightly brush with some remaining olive-oil mixture, gently pressing garlic slices and minced basil into slits in eggplant.

4 Broil eggplant 10 minutes longer, or until fork-tender; transfer to platter. Repeat with remaining eggplant slices and olive-oil mixture. Sprinkle eggplant with lemon peel. Serve at room temperature or cover with plastic wrap and refrigerate to serve later.

EACH SERVING: ABOUT 135 CALORIES, 1g PROTEIN, 9g CARBOHYDRATE, 11g TOTAL FAT (1g SATURATED), 0mg CHOLESTEROL, 325mg SODIUM

# EGGPLANT LASAGNA

*Prep:* 50 minutes plus standing    *Bake:* 40 minutes
*Makes* 10 main-dish servings

| | |
|---|---|
| 2 medium eggplants (about 1½ pounds each), cut into ¼-inch-thick slices | 2 cans (28 ounces each) tomatoes |
| 5 tablespoons olive or vegetable oil | 12 lasagna noodles (about two-thirds 16-ounce package) |
| 1 small onion, chopped | ¼ cup freshly grated Parmesan cheese |
| 2 teaspoons sugar | 8 ounces mozzarella cheese, shredded (2 cups) |
| 1½ teaspoons salt | |
| 1 teaspoon dried basil | |

◆ Preheat broiler. Place half of eggplant slices on rack in broiling pan; using 2 tablespoons oil, brush on both sides. Place pan in broiler at closest position to heat source; broil 10 minutes, or until browned, turning once halfway through cooking. Transfer to plate. Repeat with remaining eggplant and 2 more tablespoons oil. Turn oven control to 375°F.

◆ While eggplants are broiling, prepare tomato sauce: In 4-quart saucepan, heat remaining 1 tablespoon oil over medium heat; add onion and cook until tender. Stir in sugar, salt, dried basil, and tomatoes with their juice; heat to boiling over high heat, breaking up tomatoes with back of spoon. Reduce heat to low; simmer, uncovered, 15 minutes, stirring occasionally.

◆ Meanwhile, prepare lasagna noodles as label directs; drain. In 13" by 9" glass or ceramic baking dish, spread 1 cup tomato sauce. Arrange half of noodles over sauce, overlapping to fit. Arrange half of eggplant slices over noodles; top with half of remaining sauce, then half of Parmesan, and half of mozzarella. Repeat with remaining noodles, eggplant, tomato sauce, Parmesan, and mozzarella.

◆ Bake lasagna 40 minutes, or until heated through. Remove from oven; let stand 10 minutes for easier serving.

**Each serving: About 325 calories, 12g protein, 41g carbohydrate, 14g total fat (5g saturated), 20mg cholesterol, 715mg sodium**

# SKILLET EGGPLANT STEW

*Prep:* 25 minutes    *Cook:* 30 to 35 minutes
*Makes* 8 accompaniment servings

| | |
|---|---|
| 3 tablespoons olive oil | ¾ teaspoon salt |
| 1 large onion, cut into ¾-inch pieces | 1 package (9 ounces) fresh mozzarella cheese balls, drained and each cut in half (optional) |
| 2 medium eggplants (about 1½ pounds each), cut into 2-inch pieces | 1 large tomato (about 8 ounces), cut into ¾-inch pieces |
| ½ cup pimiento-stuffed olives | ¼ cup loosely packed basil leaves, coarsely chopped |
| 2 tablespoons dark brown sugar | |
| 1 tablespoon balsamic vinegar | |

◆ In nonstick 12-inch skillet (2 inches deep) or nonstick 5-quart saucepot, heat 1 tablespoon oil over medium heat. Add onion; cook, stirring often, 10 minutes, or until golden.

◆ Increase heat to medium-high. Add remaining 2 tablespoons oil and eggplant to onion in skillet; cook, stirring often, about 10 minutes, until eggplant is browned. Stir in olives, next 3 ingredients, and *½ cup water*; heat to boiling over high heat. Reduce heat to low; cover and simmer 10 to 15 minutes longer, until eggplant is tender. Remove from heat; stir in mozzarella, if using, tomato, and basil.

**Each serving: About 125 calories, 2g protein, 18g carbohydrate, 6g total fat (1g saturated), 0mg cholesterol, 290mg sodium**

### EGGPLANTS

Eggplants come in different shapes, sizes, and colors, ranging from tiny green Thai pea eggplants and baby white to the large, purple Western variety, which can be oval or egg-shaped.

Eggplants can be peeled or not, depending on the type of dish you are preparing and whether the skin is tough or tender. For example, dips are best made with peeled eggplant. Always cook eggplants until completely tender and creamy.

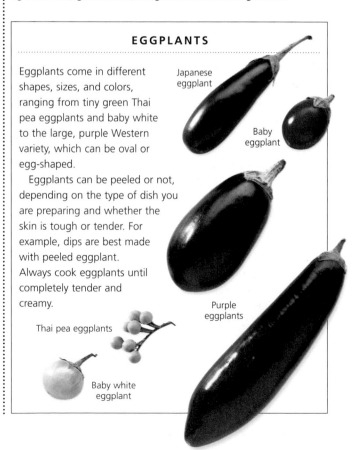

Japanese eggplant

Baby eggplant

Purple eggplants

Thai pea eggplants

Baby white eggplant

# Peppers

Bright bell peppers can be green, red, yellow, orange, or even purple. Unlike hot peppers, or chiles, bell peppers lack a fiery bite since they contain no capsaicin, the chemical substance responsible for the heat. Roasting and broiling intensifies the subtle sweetness of bell peppers and makes them easy to peel. They are also natural candidates for stuffing and baking whole.

## PEPPER AND EGGPLANT SALAD

◆◆◆◆◆◆◆◆◆◆◆◆◆◆

*Prep:* 30 minutes
*Broil:* 35 minutes
*Makes* 8 accompaniment servings

1 medium eggplant (about 1½ pounds)
1 medium onion
Salt
2 medium yellow peppers
2 medium red peppers
1 cup loosely packed basil leaves, cut into thin strips
2 tablespoons olive or vegetable oil
1 tablespoon fresh lemon juice
1 teaspoon sugar
½ teaspoon coarsely ground black pepper
Basil sprigs for garnish

**1** Preheat broiler. Cut eggplant crosswise into ½-inch-thick slices; cut slices into ½-inch-wide strips. Cut onion in half through root end; cut each half into thin wedges, discarding tough root end.

**2** In large bowl, toss eggplant and onion with ½ teaspoon salt. Spread on rack in large broiling pan. Broil at closest position to heat source, stirring occasionally, 20 minutes, or until eggplant is browned on all sides.

**3** Meanwhile, cut yellow and red peppers into ½-inch-wide strips. In medium bowl, toss pepper strips with ½ teaspoon salt. When eggplant mixture is done, return mixture to large bowl.

**4** Spoon pepper strips onto rack in broiling pan. Broil at closest position to heat source, stirring occasionally, 15 minutes, or until browned on all sides. Add to bowl with eggplant.

**5** To vegetable mixture in bowl, add basil strips, next 4 ingredients, and *1 tablespoon water*; toss to mix. Spoon onto platter. Serve warm or cover and refrigerate to serve cold later. Garnish with basil.

**EACH SERVING: ABOUT 80 CALORIES, 2g PROTEIN, 12g CARBOHYDRATE, 4g TOTAL FAT (0g SATURATED), 0mg CHOLESTEROL, 270mg SODIUM**

## BARLEY-STUFFED PEPPERS

*Prep: 1 hour 15 minutes    Bake: 1 hour*
*Makes 6 main-dish servings*

1 cup pearl barley
2⅔ cups vegetable or chicken
  broth
2 tablespoons olive or
  vegetable oil
1 large onion, chopped
3 medium carrots, shredded
½ teaspoon salt
1 cup frozen peas
2 tablespoons chopped fresh
  parsley

6 ounces sharp Cheddar
  cheese, shredded (1½ cups)
2 cans (14½ to 16 ounces
  each) Italian-style stewed
  tomatoes
2 medium red peppers
2 medium green peppers
2 medium yellow peppers

◆ In 3-quart saucepan, heat barley and broth to boiling over high heat. Reduce heat to low; cover and simmer 1 hour, or until barley is tender and liquid is absorbed.

◆ Meanwhile, in 10-inch skillet, heat oil over medium-high heat; add onion and cook, stirring often, until almost tender. Stir in carrots and salt; cook 5 minutes, or until vegetables are tender and lightly browned.

◆ When barley is done, stir in carrot mixture, peas, parsley, and 1 cup cheese. In food processor with knife blade attached or in blender at medium speed, blend tomatoes until almost smooth; pour into shallow 2½-quart casserole.

◆ Preheat oven to 350°F. Cut off top from each pepper; reserve tops for garnish. Remove seeds. Cut thin slice from bottom of each pepper, if necessary, so it will stand level. Fill peppers with barley mixture. Stand peppers in tomato sauce in casserole; sprinkle with remaining ½ cup cheese.

◆ Bake peppers 1 hour, or until tender when pierced with a knife. Loosely cover peppers with foil during last 30 minutes of baking to prevent overbrowning. To serve, arrange reserved pepper tops on stuffed peppers.

**Each serving: About 405 calories, 15g protein, 55g carbohydrate, 15g total fat (7g saturated), 30mg cholesterol, 695mg sodium**

## RED AND YELLOW PEPPER SAUTÉ

*Prep: 15 minutes    Cook: 15 minutes*
*Makes 6 accompaniment servings*

2 tablespoons olive or
  vegetable oil
2 large red peppers, cut into
  1-inch-wide slices

2 large yellow peppers, cut
  into 1-inch-wide slices
½ teaspoon dried oregano
¼ teaspoon salt

In 12-inch skillet, heat oil over medium-high heat; add pepper slices, oregano, and salt, and cook, stirring frequently, until peppers are golden and tender-crisp.

**Each serving: About 70 calories, 1g protein, 7g carbohydrate, 5g total fat (1g saturated), 0mg cholesterol, 90mg sodium**

## ROASTED PEPPER AND WALNUT DIP

*Prep: 20 minutes plus standing    Broil: 10 minutes*
*Makes 1⅔ cups*

½ cup walnuts (about 2 ounces)
½ teaspoon ground cumin
4 medium red peppers,
  roasted and peeled (see
  below)
2 slices firm white bread, torn

1 tablespoon olive oil
2 tablespoons raspberry
  vinegar
⅛ teaspoon ground red
  pepper (cayenne)
½ teaspoon salt

◆ Preheat oven to 350°F. Spread walnuts in pie plate; bake 8 to 10 minutes, until toasted. In 1-quart saucepan, toast cumin over low heat 1 to 2 minutes, until very fragrant.

◆ In food processor with knife blade attached, blend walnuts until ground. Add peppers, cumin, and remaining ingredients; blend until smooth. Transfer to bowl. Cover and refrigerate if not serving right away (remove from refrigerator 1 hour before serving).

**Each tablespoon: About 25 calories, 1g protein, 2g carbohydrate, 2g total fat (0g saturated), 0mg cholesterol, 50mg sodium**

### ROASTING PEPPERS

Preheat broiler; line broiling pan with foil. Cut peppers lengthwise in half; discard stems and seeds. Place peppers, skin-side up, on pan. Broil at closest position to heat source 10 minutes, or until charred all over. Wrap in foil; let stand 15 minutes. Remove foil; peel off skin.

# TOMATOES

It's worth waiting all year for garden-ripe juicy tomatoes. Here we celebrate them in a tomato and goat-cheese tart and broiled tomatoes topped with Parmesan. We even turn green tomatoes into a tempting treat, fried for a BLT. For maximum flavor, store tomatoes at room temperature rather than in the refrigerator, unless they are overripe.

## SAVORY TOMATO TART

◆◆◆◆◆◆◆◆◆◆◆◆◆

*Prep:* 30 minutes
*Bake:* 35 minutes
*Makes* 6 main-dish servings

**Pastry for 11-inch Tart**
**1 tablespoon olive or vegetable oil**
**3 medium onions (about 1 pound), thinly sliced**
**Salt**
**1 package (3½ ounces) goat cheese, crumbled**
**3 large tomatoes (about 1½ pounds), cut into ¼-inch-thick slices**
**½ teaspoon coarsely ground black pepper**
**¼ cup Kalamata olives, pitted and chopped**
**Sliced fresh basil leaves for garnish**

1 Prepare Pastry for 11-inch Tart and use it to line a tart pan. Preheat oven to 425°F. Line tart shell with foil; fill with pie weights, dry beans, or uncooked rice. Bake 20 minutes; remove foil with weights. Bake tart shell 10 minutes longer, or until golden. (If crust puffs up during baking, gently press it down with back of spoon.)

3 Turn oven control to broil. Spoon cooked onions in even layer over bottom of tart shell; sprinkle with half of goat cheese.

2 Meanwhile, in nonstick 12-inch skillet, heat oil over medium heat; add onions and ¼ teaspoon salt and cook, stirring frequently, about 15 minutes, until onions are tender and browned.

4 Arrange tomato slices in concentric circles over onion layer. Sprinkle black pepper and ¼ teaspoon salt over tomatoes. Sprinkle remaining goat cheese over top of tart. Place pan in broiler about 5 to 7 inches from heat source. Broil tart about 5 minutes, until cheese just melts. Sprinkle with chopped Kalamata olives and sliced basil leaves. To serve, cut tart into wedges.

EACH SERVING: ABOUT 415 CALORIES, 8g PROTEIN, 33g CARBOHYDRATE, 28g TOTAL FAT (7g SATURATED), 15mg CHOLESTEROL, 650mg SODIUM

## CHERRY TOMATO GRATIN

*Prep:* 10 minutes
*Bake:* 20 minutes
*Makes:* 6 accompaniment servings

¼ cup plain dried bread
  crumbs
¼ cup freshly grated
  Parmesan cheese
1 garlic clove, minced
¼ teaspoon coarsely ground
  black pepper

1 tablespoon olive oil
2 pints cherry tomatoes
2 tablespoons chopped fresh
  parsley

◆ Preheat oven to 425°F. In small bowl, combine bread crumbs, Parmesan cheese, garlic, pepper, and olive oil.

◆ In 9-inch deep-dish pie plate, place cherry tomatoes. Sprinkle bread-crumb mixture on top of tomatoes. Sprinkle with parsley. Bake 20 minutes, or until crumbs are golden.

**Each serving: About 85 calories, 3g protein, 9g carbohydrate, 4g total fat (1g saturated), 3mg cholesterol, 130mg sodium**

## BROILED PARMESAN TOMATOES

*Prep:* 10 minutes    *Broil:* 3 to 4 minutes
*Makes:* 4 accompaniment servings

1 tablespoon margarine or
  butter
1 small garlic clove, minced
¼ cup freshly grated
  Parmesan cheese

4 plum tomatoes (12 ounces),
  each cut lengthwise in half

◆ Preheat broiler. In 1-quart saucepan, melt margarine over low heat. Add garlic and cook just until golden; remove from heat.

◆ Spread Parmesan cheese on waxed paper. Dip cut side of each tomato half in melted margarine mixture, then in Parmesan; place on rack in broiling pan. Spoon any remaining cheese on top of tomatoes and drizzle with any remaining margarine mixture.

◆ Place pan in broiler at position closest to heat source; broil tomatoes 3 to 4 minutes, until cheese is golden brown.

**Each serving: About 70 calories, 3g protein, 4g carbohydrate, 5g total fat (2g saturated), 5mg cholesterol, 155mg sodium**

## FRIED GREEN TOMATO SANDWICHES

*Prep:* 10 minutes    *Cook:* 20 minutes
*Makes:* 4 sandwiches

1 large egg white
¼ teaspoon salt
½ cup yellow cornmeal
Coarsely ground black pepper
3 medium green tomatoes,
  cut into ½-inch-thick slices
½ pound bacon

¼ cup low-fat mayonnaise
  dressing
¼ cup low-fat plain yogurt
2 tablespoons chopped fresh
  chives
8 slices white bread, toasted
4 green-leaf lettuce leaves

◆ In pie plate, beat egg white and salt. In another pie plate or on waxed paper, combine cornmeal with ¼ teaspoon pepper. Dip tomato slices in egg mixture to coat both sides, then dip into cornmeal mixture to coat both sides thoroughly. Place coated slices on waxed paper.

◆ In 12-inch skillet, cook bacon over medium-low heat until browned. Transfer bacon to paper towels to drain.

◆ Increase heat to medium-high. In drippings in skillet, cook tomato slices, a few at a time, until golden brown on both sides. Drain on paper towels.

◆ In small bowl, combine mayonnaise, yogurt, chives, and ¼ teaspoon pepper. Spread mayonnaise mixture on toast slices. Arrange lettuce, tomato slices, then bacon on 4 toast slices; top with remaining toast slices to make 4 sandwiches.

**Each sandwich: About 350 calories, 12g protein, 45g carbohydrate, 13g total fat (3g saturated), 17mg cholesterol, 645mg sodium**

### TOMATOES

Tomatoes come in many shapes and sizes, especially at farmers' markets. Large red beefsteak tomatoes are juiciest, while cherry tomatoes are sweet all year round. Yellow tomatoes are less acidic than red ones, and can be mixed with the red for a pretty effect. For sauces, nothing can beat plum tomatoes, which have the meatiest flesh.

Yellow pear

Cherry

Vine-ripened

Beefsteak

Plum

# SALADS

# SALADS KNOW-HOW

Gone are the days when a salad meant skimpy diet fare. Today's creations are inspired mixtures of bold flavors, colors, and varied textures. Crisp green salads are the classic starter, but there are also more elaborate "chopped," composed, and warm salads that make substantial meals.

## PREPARING SALAD INGREDIENTS

The most basic steps of salad preparation, such as washing and storing lettuce, are crucial. That's because fresh, uncooked ingredients hide few flaws – and nothing spoils a salad faster than biting down on a bit of grit. Tear lettuce into smaller pieces by hand; a knife may bruise the leaves. Most vegetables can be presliced a day in advance; sturdy ones (e.g., cabbage, carrots, or cooked beets) will keep longer. To retain moisture, store prepared vegetables wrapped in damp paper towels in food-storage bags in the crisper drawer. Don't chop fresh herbs in advance – they'll blacken.

## PEELING TOMATOES

1 Cut a shallow X in the bottom end of each tomato; drop into pan of boiling water for 15 seconds.

2 With slotted spoon, transfer tomatoes to bowl of ice water. Use a knife to peel off the skin.

## STORING AND PREPARING LETTUCE

Wash and dry lettuce leaves right after you bring them home from the store; you'll be able to assemble a beautiful salad in a flash. Remove and discard any bruised or spotted leaves, which will deteriorate quickly. A salad spinner makes short work of drying lettuce; the kind with a pull cord is especially fast. Be careful not to overload the spinner, or the lettuce will get crushed and bruised. To keep lettuce crisp, place clean, dry leaves in a zip-tight food storage bag, along with a few damp paper towels. Delicate varieties such as

butterhead will keep 2 to 3 days; iceberg and other sturdy heads will keep up to a week. Fresh herbs such as parsley, basil, chervil, or dill make delightful additions to salads, but don't chop the leaves in advance, or they'll blacken.

To avoid a soggy salad or diluted dressing, dry rinsed lettuce well before using. Place leaves on a clean kitchen towel; pat dry with another towel. (Or, simply pat leaves dry with paper towels or spin dry.)

## CORING FIRM HEAD LETTUCE

With small, sharp knife, cut all the way around core in a cone shape. Holding lettuce head firmly with one hand, twist out the loosened core.

## PREPARING LOOSE HEAD LETTUCE

1 Gently break off leaves at stem end. Discard any bruised or wilted leaves.

2 Swish leaves briefly in cold water. Lift out of bowl; grit will sink to bottom.

### CHOOSING THE RIGHT LETTUCE

Lettuces fall into four basic types: Crisphead (iceberg) varieties are crisp but bland; butterhead (Bibb, Boston) are soft and delicate; loose-leaf (such as red oak leaf) are tender and sweet; and long-leaf lettuces (romaine) have a crisp, mild flavor. Mesclun encompasses many flavors – it's any mix of young, tiny salad greens.

## ASSEMBLING SALADS

Whether you're tossing leafy greens or making a main-dish salad, aim for a balance of texture, color, and flavor. Cut or tear ingredients into manageable pieces, but don't make them too small. It's also important to pick the right serving dish. A jumble of curly leaves is most manageable in a bowl, while neatly arranged sliced ingredients can be shown off on a plate. Chilled plates help keep ingredients cool. To avoid a watered-down dressing, leafy greens – and all other vegetables – must be thoroughly dried. When making a salad of rice, beans, or potatoes, toss the cooked ingredients with the dressing while they're still warm so they'll soak it up.

### SALAD MATH

| LETTUCE | APPROXIMATE YIELD |
| --- | --- |
| 1 medium crisphead lettuce | 10 cups prepared leaves |
| 1 medium butterhead lettuce | 4 cups prepared leaves |
| 1 medium loose-leaf lettuce | 8 cups prepared leaves |
| 1 medium romaine lettuce | 8 cups prepared leaves |

## SALAD LEAVES

**Arugula** An Italian favorite, this highly perishable green has a hot peppery taste that is stronger in older leaves. The leaves tend to be gritty and need thorough rinsing.

**Spinach** Sweet and earthy-tasting, spinach is delicious raw or cooked. Whether flat or crinkly, leaves should be crisp and dark with a fresh smell; spinach harbors grit, so rinse well.

**Iceberg** Juicy but bland-tasting leaves give this crisphead lettuce more crunch than flavor; great with creamy dressings.

**Bibb lettuce** A small butterhead with a sweet, succulent flavor, ranging in color from yellow-green to dark green.

**Romaine** The classic pick for Caesar salads, romaine has a crunchy texture and slightly nutty flavor. Its elongated leaves lighten at the pale, crunchy center.

**Red endive** A variety of Belgian endive with crimson-tipped leaves and a slightly bitter taste.

**Mâche** Also called lamb's lettuce or corn salad, this tender green has a nutty taste.

**Belgian endive** The shoots of a chicory root, with tightly packed leaves and a strong, slightly bitter taste.

**Watercress** This lively green has a peppery bite and can stand on its own or pair with other lettuces; also delicious used in sandwiches, soups, and omelets.

**Radicchio** Burgundy-colored leaves and a slightly bitter flavor make this Italian chicory a memorable addition to the salad bowl. In the Italian tradition, pair it with arugula and endive for a colorful and flavorful mix.

**Frisée** A member of the chicory family, frisée has slender, curly leaves that range in color from yellow-white to pale green; it has a delicately bitter flavor.

**Red oak leaf** This variety of loose-leaf lettuce has crisp, ruffled leaves with a fuller flavor than butterhead varieties.

Arugula

Spinach

Iceberg

Bibb

Romaine

Red endive

Mâche

Red oak leaf

Belgian endive

Watercress

Radicchio

Frisée

## THE BEST-DRESSED SALAD

Dressings should enhance but not overpower the taste and texture of salad greens. Sturdy lettuces such as romaine and iceberg stand up to thick creamy dressings such as blue cheese or Thousand Island. By contrast, delicate greens, such as leaf or butterhead varieties, pair best with simple vinaigrettes. For the crispest results, toss salads just before serving. To create a new taste, you can vary the oils and vinegars used in dressings. Extra-virgin olive oil is classic, or substitute walnut or hazelnut oil for half the olive oil, or add just a drop of Asian sesame oil. Vinegars range from dark, mellow balsamic to the more subtle varieties made from wine, champagne, cider, or sherry. Other delicious options include vinegars infused with fruit (e.g., raspberry or blueberry) or a fresh herb like tarragon.

The best way to emulsify a vinaigrette dressing is to first whisk together the mustard, vinegar or lemon juice, and seasonings. Than add the oil, while whisking constantly, in a slow, steady stream.

## QUICK SALAD FIXINGS

Choose a basic ingredient, then pile on the flavor with pantry staples or quick-to-prepare add-ins:

**Tossed greens** Enliven with herb leaves or sprigs, warm garlic croutons, and Parmesan shavings; add substance with grilled meat or chicken strips or cubes of smoked ham.

**Steamed new potatoes** Dress with vinaigrette and add gutsy flavor with crumbled bacon, anchovies, capers, olives, or crumbled tangy cheese such as feta, blue, or goat cheese.

**Rice or couscous** Add sunshine with grapes, sliced apple or pear, orange chunks, or dried apricots or raisins. Toasted nuts or sunflower seeds give crunch.

---

### SLIM SALADS

You can make low-fat salad dressings by substituting buttermilk or plain yogurt for mayonnaise or sour cream. A zesty salsa or Asian-style vinaigrette of seasoned rice vinegar, soy sauce, and citrus juice will boost flavor without any fat at all. When it comes to toppings, pile on crunchy veggies, but steer clear of fat sources like avocados, nuts, bacon, and cheese. For a main-dish salad, use skinless chicken, water-packed tuna, shrimp, or beans.

---

## GLORIOUS GARNISHES

Edible flowers lend a unique flavor and dazzling color to salads. The fragile blossoms are typically left whole (tiny herb flowers should be plucked from the stem) and sprinkled on just before serving so they aren't discolored by the dressing. Always use the flowers sparingly, as some have a strong flavor. Small herb flowers, such as mint, thyme, oregano, or lavender blossoms, can be particularly pungent, so taste before using. You will need flowers that have not been treated with pesticides or other chemical sprays; flowers from the florist have usually been sprayed. Some supermarkets carry edible flowers, or check your own garden for unsprayed blossoms. However, not all flowers are edible, and some can be dangerous to eat. If you are not certain that a flower is edible, contact a local poison control center. Nontoxic flowers include carnations, pansies, borage, geraniums, nasturtiums, pinks,

roses, marigolds, cornflowers, baby's breath, and most herb flowers. Salad bowls aren't the only thing that benefit from these colorful blooms. Add them to iced punch, herbal teas, or desserts, or use to garnish soup, roasted fish, or meats. Flowers such as roses, pansies, or violets are often crystallized and used to garnish cakes.

Oregano flowers

Nasturtiums

Chive flowers

Pinks

Marjoram flowers

Mint flowers

Thyme flowers

# VEGETABLE SALADS

Whether your supply of fresh produce is reaped from your own garden, a roadside farmstand, or the local supermarket, a warm or cold salad of tasty, vibrantly colored vegetables is sure to make an irresistible side dish. For the best texture, cook vegetables just until they are tender.

## SUMMER BEET AND ASIAN PEAR SALAD

◆◆◆◆◆◆◆◆◆◆◆◆◆◆◆◆◆◆◆◆◆◆◆◆◆◆◆◆

*Prep: 20 minutes    Cook: 40 minutes*
*Makes 6 accompaniment servings*

| | |
|---|---|
| 8 medium beets (about 4 pounds with tops) | ½ teaspoon salt |
| 1 tablespoon light brown sugar | 1 large Asian pear or Red Delicious apple, peeled, cored, and cut into thin wedges |
| 1 tablespoon red wine vinegar | |
| 1 tablespoon olive or vegetable oil | 1 tablespoon chopped fresh parsley |
| 2 teaspoons Dijon mustard | Lettuce leaves |

**1** Trim stems and leaves from beets. With vegetable brush, scrub beets. In 4-quart saucepan, heat beets and enough *water* to cover to boiling over high heat. Reduce heat to low. Cover; simmer 30 minutes, or just until tender.

**2** Drain cooked beets and cool thoroughly with cold running water. When beets are cool, with paring knife, peel beets; cut each beet in half or into quarters, if large.

**3** Prepare vinaigrette: In large bowl, with wire whisk or fork, mix brown sugar, red wine vinegar, oil, Dijon mustard, and salt. Add beets, Asian pear, and chopped parsley to bowl with vinaigrette.

**4** Toss beet mixture to coat with vinaigrette. Serve at room temperature or cover and refrigerate to serve cold later. To serve, line platter with lettuce leaves; spoon beet mixture on top.

---

### ASIAN PEAR

This delicious fruit was first planted in the United States by Chinese prospectors during the Gold Rush, as they traveled through the Sierra Nevada. Asian pears can be smooth-skinned or speckled with a matte russeting. Unlike regular pears, they are low in acid and aroma, and quite hard even when ripe. This firm texture means that thin slices will hold up to tossing – making them perfect in salads. Asian pears can be stored in the refrigerator for at least 2 weeks. Crunchy and juicy at the same time, delicate in flavor, they make a light, refreshing dessert and remain crisp even when cooked.

---

**EACH SERVING: ABOUT 130 CALORIES, 3g PROTEIN, 24g CARBOHYDRATE, 3g TOTAL FAT (0g SATURATED), 0mg CHOLESTEROL, 350mg SODIUM**

## CHUNKY VEGETABLE SALAD

*Prep: 20 minutes    Makes 4 accompaniment servings*

2 tablespoons olive or vegetable oil

2 tablespoons red wine vinegar

¾ teaspoon salt

½ teaspoon sugar

¼ teaspoon coarsely ground black pepper

2 large tomatoes, cut into thin wedges

1 large yellow pepper, cut into bite-size chunks

1 medium cucumber, unpeeled, cut into bite-size chunks

½ small red onion, finely chopped

1 tablespoon chopped fresh chervil, cilantro, or parsley

Prepare dressing: In medium bowl, with wire whisk or fork, mix first 5 ingredients until blended. Add remaining ingredients; toss to coat.

**Each serving: About 110 calories, 2g protein, 12g carbohydrate, 7g total fat (1g saturated), 0mg cholesterol, 410mg sodium**

## WARM PEAS AND CARROTS SALAD

*Prep: 15 minutes    Cook: 10 minutes*
*Makes 4 accompaniment servings*

1 cup frozen peas

1 tablespoon vegetable oil

3 medium carrots, thinly sliced

1 small onion, thinly sliced

½ teaspoon salt

1 tablespoon fresh lemon juice

1 small head romaine lettuce, washed and well dried

◆ In small bowl, place frozen peas; cover with *boiling water* and let stand 5 minutes.

◆ Meanwhile, in nonstick 10-inch skillet, heat oil over medium-high heat; add carrots, onion, and salt and cook, stirring often, until vegetables are tender and lightly browned.

◆ Drain peas; stir into carrot-onion mixture in skillet. Stir in lemon juice; remove skillet from heat.

◆ Cut lettuce leaves crosswise into ¼-inch-wide strips (you should have about 4 cups loosely packed). In large bowl, toss lettuce with carrot mixture to mix well.

**Each serving: About 115 calories, 5g protein, 17g carbohydrate, 4g total fat (1g saturated), 0mg cholesterol, 330mg sodium**

## GREEN BEANS WITH TOASTED SESAME SEEDS

*Prep: 25 minutes    Cook: 20 minutes*
*Makes 8 accompaniment servings*

3 tablespoons olive oil

2 tablespoons fresh lemon juice

2 teaspoons Dijon mustard

½ teaspoon salt

2 pounds green beans, ends trimmed

1 tablespoon sesame seeds, toasted

◆ Prepare dressing: In large bowl, with wire whisk or fork, mix olive oil, lemon juice, mustard, and salt until blended. Set aside.

◆ In 8-quart Dutch oven, in *1 inch boiling water*, heat green beans to boiling over high heat.

◆ Reduce heat to low and simmer, uncovered, 5 to 10 minutes, until beans are tender. Transfer beans to colander to drain well.

◆ Add warm beans to dressing in bowl; toss to mix well. Cover and refrigerate if not serving right away. Just before serving, toss beans with sesame seeds.

**Each serving: About 80 calories, 2g protein, 7g carbohydrate, 6g total fat (1g saturated), 0mg cholesterol, 180mg sodium**

◆◆◆◆◆◆◆◆◆◆◆◆◆◆◆◆◆◆◆◆◆◆◆◆◆

**TOASTING SESAME SEEDS**

Sesame seeds are the tiny, oval seeds of a tropical herb. They have a mild, nutty flavor that is best brought out by toasting: In a small skillet, toast sesame seeds over medium-low heat 1 to 2 minutes, stirring and shaking the pan often to prevent burning, until the seeds are lightly browned.

◆◆◆◆◆◆◆◆◆◆◆◆◆◆◆◆◆◆◆◆◆◆◆◆◆

## BEET, ORANGE, AND WATERCRESS SALAD

*Prep:* 45 minutes   *Cook:* 40 minutes
*Makes* 10 accompaniment servings

10 medium beets (about 5 pounds with tops), trimmed
4 large navel oranges
¼ cup olive oil
¼ cup red wine vinegar
1 tablespoon Dijon mustard
1 teaspoon sugar
¾ teaspoon salt
¼ teaspoon coarsely ground black pepper
3 bunches watercress (about 12 ounces), tough stems removed
1 medium red onion, thinly sliced

◆ In 4-quart saucepan, heat beets and enough *water* to cover to boiling over high heat. Reduce heat to low; cover and simmer 30 minutes, or until beets are tender.

◆ Meanwhile, grate 1 teaspoon peel from 1 orange; set aside. With knife, cut peel and white pith from all oranges; discard. Holding oranges over large bowl to catch juice, cut sections from oranges between membranes. Place orange sections on plate; reserve juice.

◆ Prepare dressing: Into orange juice in bowl, with wire whisk or fork, mix olive oil, vinegar, mustard, sugar, salt, pepper, and grated orange peel.

◆ Drain beets and cool with cold running water. Peel and cut each beet lengthwise in half, then cut each half crosswise into ¼-inch-thick slices.

◆ To dressing in bowl, add beets, orange sections, watercress, and red-onion slices; toss beet mixture to coat with dressing.

**Each serving: About 150 calories, 4g protein, 23g carbohydrate, 6g total fat (1g saturated), 0mg cholesterol, 310mg sodium**

## FENNEL, PEAR, AND ENDIVE SALAD

*Prep:* 35 minutes
*Makes* 8 accompaniment servings

¼ cup extra-virgin olive oil
¼ cup tarragon vinegar
1 tablespoon Dijon mustard
¾ teaspoon salt
¼ teaspoon coarsely ground black pepper
5 medium Bartlett pears (about 2 pounds), unpeeled, each cored and sliced into 12 wedges
2 large fennel bulbs (about 1 pound each)
4 medium heads Belgian endive (2 red, if available)
¾ cup walnuts, toasted and coarsely chopped

◆ Prepare dressing: In small bowl, with wire whisk or fork, mix olive oil, tarragon vinegar, Dijon mustard, salt, and pepper until blended; set aside.

◆ In large bowl, place pear wedges. Trim top and bottom from each fennel bulb. Slice each bulb lengthwise in half; remove and discard core. Slice fennel-bulb halves crosswise into paper-thin slices; place in bowl with pear wedges.

◆ Cut 2 heads of endive (1 yellow and 1 red, if using both colors) crosswise into ⅛-inch-thick slices; toss with fennel mixture. Separate leaves from remaining heads of endive.

◆ Add dressing to fennel mixture; toss well to coat with dressing.

◆ Arrange endive leaves around edge of large shallow bowl or platter; top with fennel salad. Sprinkle with toasted walnuts.

**Each serving: About 245 calories, 4g protein, 30g carbohydrate, 15g total fat (2g saturated), 0mg cholesterol, 320mg sodium**

## SPINACH AND TANGERINE SALAD

*Prep:* 30 minutes
*Makes* 8 accompaniment servings

4 medium tangerines or navel oranges
1 bunch (10 to 12 ounces) spinach, trimmed, washed, and well dried
2 small heads Bibb lettuce (about 4 ounces each)
3 tablespoons extra-virgin olive oil
3 tablespoons cider vinegar
1 teaspoon sugar
1 teaspoon Dijon mustard
⅛ teaspoon salt
⅛ teaspoon coarsely ground black pepper

◆ Coarsely grate peel from 1 tangerine. Cut remaining peel and white pith from all tangerines; discard. Cut each tangerine in half (from top to bottom), then cut each half crosswise into ¼-inch-thick slices. Tear spinach and lettuce into bite-size pieces.

◆ Prepare vinaigrette: In large bowl, with wire whisk or fork, mix olive oil, vinegar, sugar, mustard, salt, pepper, and grated tangerine peel.

◆ Add spinach, lettuce, and tangerine slices to vinaigrette in bowl; toss well.

**Each serving: About 75 calories, 2g protein, 8g carbohydrate, 5g total fat (1g saturated), 0mg cholesterol, 80mg sodium**

## BABY-GREENS SALAD WITH GRAPEFRUIT VINAIGRETTE

*Prep: 25 minutes*  *Makes 8 accompaniment servings*

2 medium grapefruits
2 medium heads Belgian
  endive
1 tablespoon balsamic vinegar
1 tablespoon Dijon mustard
2 teaspoons capers, drained
½ teaspoon sugar
½ teaspoon salt
¼ cup olive or vegetable oil
1 pound mixed baby salad
  greens or mixed salad
  greens (about 12 cups
  loosely packed)

◆ With knife, cut peel and white pith from grapefruits; discard. Holding grapefruits over small bowl to catch juice, cut sections from grapefruits between membranes. Place grapefruit sections on plate; reserve juice in bowl. Cut each endive lengthwise into matchstick-thin strips.

◆ Prepare vinaigrette: In large bowl, combine balsamic vinegar, mustard, capers, sugar, salt, and 2 tablespoons grapefruit juice (reserve remaining juice for use another day). With wire whisk or fork, slowly beat in oil.

◆ Add greens, grapefruit sections, and endive to vinaigrette in bowl; toss to coat.

**Each serving: About 105 calories, 2g protein, 10g carbohydrate, 7g total fat (1g saturated), 0mg cholesterol, 230mg sodium**

## GRILLED VEGETABLES VINAIGRETTE

*Prep: 15 minutes*  *Grill: 15 to 20 minutes*
*Makes 4 accompaniment servings*

6 tablespoons olive or
  vegetable oil
6 tablespoons white wine
  vinegar
2 tablespoons chopped fresh
  tarragon
1 teaspoon salt
1 teaspoon coarsely ground
  black pepper
1 teaspoon sugar
1 medium portobello
  mushroom (4 ounces) or
  4 jumbo white mushrooms,
  stems trimmed
1 medium red pepper, cut
  lengthwise into quarters
1 medium yellow pepper, cut
  lengthwise into quarters
2 small zucchini (6 ounces
  each), each cut lengthwise
  in half
2 baby eggplants (4 ounces
  each), each cut lengthwise
  in half
Tarragon sprigs for garnish

◆ Prepare outdoor grill. Prepare vinaigrette: In large bowl, with wire whisk or fork, mix oil and next 5 ingredients.

◆ Wipe mushroom clean with damp paper towel. Add mushroom, both peppers, zucchini, and eggplants to vinaigrette in bowl; toss to coat.

◆ Place vegetables on grill over medium heat. Grill, turning occasionally and brushing with some of vinaigrette remaining in bowl, until vegetables are browned and tender when pierced with a fork.

◆ To serve, slice mushroom; toss with vegetables and remaining vinaigrette. Garnish with tarragon sprigs.

**Each serving: About 235 calories, 3g protein, 14g carbohydrate, 21g total fat (3g saturated), 0mg cholesterol, 540mg sodium**

## BABY GREENS WITH RASPBERRY VINAIGRETTE

*Prep: 20 minutes*  *Makes 4 accompaniment servings*

1 tablespoon sugar
3 tablespoons white wine
  vinegar
1 tablespoon Dijon mustard
½ pint raspberries (1 cup)
¼ cup extra-virgin olive oil
8 ounces mixed baby salad
  greens or mixed salad greens
  (6 cups loosely packed)
4 ounces ricotta salata or
  feta cheese, crumbled
  (about 1 cup)
8 quail eggs or 4 small eggs,
  hard-cooked and each cut
  lengthwise in half

◆ Prepare vinaigrette: In large bowl, combine sugar, vinegar, and mustard. Add ½ cup raspberries to vinegar mixture; with wire whisk or fork, crush berries slightly. Slowly beat in olive oil.

◆ Add salad greens to vinaigrette in bowl; toss to coat. To serve, place greens on 4 plates. Sprinkle with cheese and remaining raspberries; tuck eggs into greens.

**Each serving: About 295 calories, 10g protein, 12g carbohydrate, 24g total fat (7g saturated), 185mg cholesterol, 470mg sodium**

# TOMATO SALADS

No flavor captures the essence of summer like vine-ripened tomatoes. Whether simply drizzled with vinaigrette or paired with hearty cubes of toasted bread and pancetta, they create an immensely satisyfying dish. We've even included an easy method for making home-dried tomatoes to perk up countless dishes all year round. Once cut, fresh tomatoes release juices that dilute dressings, so serve immediately.

## DRIED TOMATO, GOAT CHEESE, AND ARUGULA

◆◆◆◆◆◆◆◆◆◆◆◆◆

*Prep: 15 minutes plus preparing Home-Dried Tomatoes (optional)*
*Makes 6 accompaniment servings*

**Home-Dried Tomatoes (see right) or 24 oil-packed dried tomato halves**
**Coarsely ground black pepper**
**3 logs (3½ ounces each) goat cheese**
**2 tablespoons red wine vinegar**
**1 tablespoon extra-virgin olive oil**
**½ teaspoon dried basil**
**¼ teaspoon sugar**
**2 bunches arugula or watercress (about 3 cups loosely packed)**

**1** Prepare Home-Dried Tomatoes, if using. Sprinkle 2 tablespoons coarsely ground black pepper on waxed paper. Roll cheese logs in pepper; slice each log into 6 pieces.

**2** Prepare vinaigrette: In small bowl, with wire whisk or fork, mix vinegar, olive oil, basil, sugar, and ¼ teaspoon coarsely ground black pepper until well combined.

**3** Arrange arugula on 6 plates with goat cheese pieces. If using dried tomato halves in oil, drain well. Arrange tomatoes over arugula and goat cheese; drizzle with vinaigrette.

## HOME-DRIED TOMATOES

◆◆◆◆◆◆◆◆◆◆◆◆◆

Store in a zip-tight plastic bag in the refrigerator up to 2 months or in the freezer up to 6 months. Makes 24 tomato halves.

**12 plum tomatoes (3 pounds)**
**2 tablespoons extra-virgin olive oil**
**½ teaspoon dried basil**
**½ teaspoon dried thyme**
**½ teaspoon salt**
**¼ teaspoon coarsely ground black pepper**

**1** Preheat oven to 250°F. Peel tomatoes (see page 314). Cut each lengthwise in half; remove seeds. In large bowl, toss tomatoes with remaining ingredients.

**2** Arrange tomatoes, cut-side down, on wire rack on cookie sheet. Bake 5½ hours, or until tomatoes are shriveled and partially dried. Cool completely.

EACH SERVING: ABOUT 220 CALORIES, 8g PROTEIN, 14g CARBOHYDRATE, 16g TOTAL FAT (1g SATURATED), 44mg CHOLESTEROL, 365mg SODIUM

## PANZANELLA SALAD WITH TOMATO VINAIGRETTE

*Prep: 30 minutes    Cook: 15 minutes*
*Makes 6 main-dish servings*

¼ pound pancetta or bacon, cut into ¼-inch pieces
3 tablespoons olive oil
6 ounces sourdough bread, cut into ½-inch cubes (6 cups)
2 tablespoons freshly grated Parmesan cheese
Ground black pepper
1 small tomato (about 6 ounces), peeled (see page 72) and coarsely chopped
1 small shallot, chopped
1 tablespoon red wine vinegar

1 tablespoon balsamic vinegar
1 teaspoon sugar
1 teaspoon chopped fresh oregano
2 teaspoons Dijon mustard with seeds
¼ teaspoon salt
1 pound arugula (4 bunches)
1 pound red cherry and/or yellow pear-shaped tomatoes, each cut in half, or 1 pound medium tomatoes, cut into ½-inch chunks

◆ In nonstick 12-inch skillet, cook pancetta over medium heat until lightly browned. With slotted spoon, transfer pancetta to large bowl.

◆ Pour off all but 2 tablespoons drippings from skillet and add 1 tablespoon olive oil; add bread cubes and cook about 10 minutes, until lightly browned. Add toasted bread cubes to bowl with pancetta; toss with grated Parmesan and ¼ teaspoon pepper. Set aside.

◆ Prepare tomato vinaigrette: In blender at medium speed, blend peeled tomato, shallot, red wine vinegar, balsamic vinegar, sugar, oregano, mustard, salt, ¼ teaspoon pepper, and remaining 2 tablespoons olive oil until blended and smooth.

◆ Toss bread-cube mixture with tomato vinaigrette, arugula, and cherry tomatoes.

Each serving: About 225 calories, 10g protein, 25g carbohydrate, 11g total fat (2g saturated), 11mg cholesterol, 615mg sodium

## TWO-TOMATO SALAD

*Prep: 30 minutes    Cook: 10 seconds*
*Makes 8 accompaniment servings*

¼ cup chopped fresh basil
2 tablespoons olive or vegetable oil
2 tablespoons white wine vinegar
1 teaspoon Dijon mustard

¾ teaspoon salt
½ teaspoon sugar
2 pints cherry tomatoes
2 medium tomatoes, sliced
Basil sprigs for garnish

◆ Prepare vinaigrette: In large bowl, with wire whisk or fork, mix chopped basil, oil, vinegar, Dijon mustard, salt, and sugar until blended. Set vinaigrette aside.

◆ In 5-quart saucepan, heat *3 quarts water* to boiling over high heat. Fill a large bowl with *ice water*. Meanwhile, cut small "x" in stem end of each cherry tomato.

◆ Add half of cherry tomatoes to boiling water; blanch 5 seconds. With slotted spoon, transfer tomatoes to ice water to cool. Repeat with remaining cherry tomatoes, heating water in saucepan to boiling before adding.

◆ Drain cherry tomatoes. With fingers, slip tomatoes from their skins, one at a time, and add to vinaigrette; toss to coat.

◆ To serve, arrange tomato slices on platter. Spoon cherry tomatoes and vinaigrette over tomato slices; garnish with basil sprigs.

Each serving: About 55 calories, 1g protein, 6g carbohydrate, 4g total fat (1g saturated), 0mg cholesterol, 225mg sodium

## CHERRY TOMATO-LEMON SALAD

*Prep: 20 minutes    Makes 8 accompaniment servings*

2 medium lemons
2 pints red cherry tomatoes, each cut in half
1 pint yellow cherry tomatoes, each cut in half
1 tablespoon sugar
2 tablespoons chopped fresh chives

2 tablespoons extra-virgin olive oil
¾ teaspoon salt
½ teaspoon coarsely ground black pepper

◆ With knife, cut peel and white pith from lemons; discard. Cut each lemon crosswise into slightly less than ¼-inch-thick slices.

◆ In medium bowl, toss lemon slices, tomatoes, and remaining ingredients.

Each serving: About 65 calories, 1g protein, 9g carbohydrate, 4g total fat (1g saturated), 0mg cholesterol, 210mg sodium

# POTATO SALADS

Dress up your basic burger or steak with a novel approach to potato salad: Toss potato chunks with roasted green beans and blue cheese; with fresh herbs and cool, crunchy celery; or with ripe olives, balsamic vinegar, and feta cheese. Red potatoes add color and, since you don't need to peel them, save time. As is true of most potato salads, these recipes are just as delicious when they are prepared several hours in advance. For the best flavor, remove the salad from the refrigerator about 30 minutes before serving to bring it to room temperature.

1 Preheat oven to 425°F. Peel shallots (if using onions, peel and cut each lengthwise in half). Cut potatoes into 1½-inch chunks.

2 In large roasting pan (about 17" by 11½"), combine shallots, potatoes, salt, and 1 tablespoon oil. Roast 30 minutes.

## ROASTED POTATO SALAD

◆◆◆◆◆◆◆◆◆◆◆◆◆◆◆◆◆◆◆◆◆◆◆◆◆◆◆◆◆◆

*Prep: 25 minutes    Roast: 45 minutes*
*Makes 6 accompaniment servings*

16 shallots or 8 small white onions

2 pounds medium red potatoes (about 8)

1 teaspoon salt

3 tablespoons olive or vegetable oil

8 ounces French green beans (haricots verts) or green beans, ends trimmed

1 tablespoon fresh lemon juice

1 teaspoon Dijon mustard

1 ounce blue cheese, crumbled (about ¼ cup)

3 After vegetables have roasted 30 minutes, stir in green beans and 1 more tablespoon oil. Roast 15 minutes longer, or until vegetables are tender.

4 Meanwhile, prepare vinaigrette: In large bowl, with wire whisk or fork, mix lemon juice, Dijon mustard, and remaining 1 tablespoon oil. Add roasted vegetables to bowl, tossing to coat with vinaigrette. Serve salad warm or cover and refrigerate to serve later. To serve, place potato salad in serving dish or on platter; sprinkle with crumbled blue cheese.

### GREEK ROASTED POTATO SALAD

Prepare salad as directed, but add ½ cup pitted Kalamata olives when tossing vegetables with vinaigrette, and 2 to 4 tablespoons chopped fresh oregano, mint, or parsley, if desired. Omit blue cheese; sprinkle salad with 2 ounces feta cheese, crumbled (about ½ cup).

Each serving: About 280 calories, 5g protein, 39g carbohydrate, 12g total fat (3g saturated), 8mg cholesterol, 700mg sodium

**EACH SERVING: ABOUT 235 CALORIES, 5g PROTEIN, 37g CARBOHYDRATE, 8g TOTAL FAT (2g SATURATED), 3mg CHOLESTEROL, 455mg SODIUM**

## CLASSIC POTATO SALAD

*Prep: 25 minutes plus cooling*
*Cook: 45 to 50 minutes*
*Makes 8 accompaniment servings*

3 pounds medium all-purpose potatoes (about 9), unpeeled
Salt
2 large celery stalks, thinly sliced
1 cup mayonnaise
½ cup milk
2 tablespoons white vinegar
1 tablespoon grated onion
1 teaspoon sugar
¼ teaspoon coarsely ground black pepper

◆ In 4-quart saucepan, heat potatoes, 1 teaspoon salt, and enough *water* to cover to boiling over high heat. Reduce heat to low; cover and simmer 25 to 30 minutes, until potatoes are fork-tender. Drain potatoes; cool slightly. Peel and cut potatoes into ¾-inch cubes.

◆ In large bowl, gently toss potatoes with celery, mayonnaise, milk, vinegar, onion, sugar, pepper, and 2 teaspoons salt to coat well. If not serving right away, cover and refrigerate.

**Each serving: About 360 calories, 4g protein, 37g carbohydrate, 23g total fat (4g saturated), 18mg cholesterol, 740mg sodium**

## MEDITERRANEAN POTATO SALAD

*Prep: 15 minutes plus cooling*
*Cook: 40 to 45 minutes*
*Makes 6 accompaniment servings*

2 pounds medium red potatoes (about 8)
Salt
½ cup pitted ripe olives, minced
3 tablespoons olive oil
2 tablespoons balsamic vinegar
½ (8-ounce) package feta cheese with dried tomatoes and basil, crumbled, or your favorite feta (1 cup)
Basil sprigs for garnish

◆ In 4-quart saucepan, heat potatoes, 1 teaspoon salt, and enough *water* to cover to boiling over high heat. Reduce heat to low; cover and simmer 20 to 25 minutes, until potatoes are fork-tender. Drain; cool slightly. Cut potatoes into ½-inch pieces.

◆ In large bowl, with fork, mix olives, olive oil, balsamic vinegar, ½ teaspoon salt, and half of feta cheese. Add potatoes; gently toss to coat. Sprinkle remaining feta cheese on top. If not serving right away, cover and refrigerate. Garnish with basil sprigs.

**Each serving: About 320 calories, 9g protein, 34g carbohydrate, 17g total fat (7g saturated), 38mg cholesterol, 790mg sodium**

## LEMON-CHIVE POTATO SALAD

*Prep: 25 minutes plus cooling*
*Cook: 30 to 35 minutes*
*Makes 12 accompaniment servings*

5 pounds red potatoes, cut into 1½-inch chunks
Salt
2 medium lemons
3 tablespoons olive oil
1 teaspoon sugar
¾ cup mayonnaise
½ cup milk
⅓ cup sour cream
5 large celery stalks, thinly sliced
½ cup chopped fresh chives or green-onion tops

◆ In 8-quart Dutch oven or saucepot, heat potatoes, 2 teaspoons salt, and enough *water* to cover to boiling. Reduce heat to low; cover and simmer 10 to 12 minutes, until potatoes are fork-tender.

◆ Meanwhile, prepare lemon dressing: Grate 1½ teaspoons peel and squeeze ¼ cup juice from lemons. In large bowl, with wire whisk or fork, mix lemon peel and juice, oil, sugar, and 1½ teaspoons salt until blended.

◆ Drain potatoes. Add hot potatoes to lemon dressing in large bowl. With rubber spatula, stir gently to coat thoroughly with dressing. Let potatoes cool at room temperature 30 minutes, stirring occasionally.

◆ In small bowl, stir mayonnaise, milk, sour cream, and ½ teaspoon salt until mixture is smooth. Add mayonnaise mixture, celery, and chopped chives to potatoes; stir gently to coat well. If not serving right away, cover and refrigerate.

**Each serving: About 320 calories, 5g protein, 41g carbohydrate, 16g total fat (3g saturated), 12mg cholesterol, 505mg sodium**

---

### PERFECT POTATO SALADS

• All-purpose and red potatoes are ideal for salads because they retain their firm texture when cut. Avoid using baking potatoes, which can fall apart in salads.

• Choose potatoes of about the same size so they cook evenly.

• It's important that potatoes are neither under- nor overcooked. They are ready if just tender when tested with the tip of a knife. If overcooked, they will absorb too much dressing and fall apart.

• When adding the dressing, don't overdo it. Potatoes taste best when they are lightly coated rather than swimming in dressing.

• Always make potato salad with warm, freshly cooked potatoes. Cold leftover potatoes will not absorb the dressing as well.

• If your finished salad still needs a flavor fillip, try adding some crumbled cooked bacon, capers, anchovy fillets, dried tomatoes, or diced pickles.

# VEGETABLE SLAWS

As good as basic coleslaw can be, slaw-style salads are not limited to cabbage and mayonnaise alone. Celery root and broccoli add their crunch and flavor, while cilantro and sesame oil lend Asian nuances to special slaws. There's even a cabbage-less slaw here: a crunchy carrot, apple, and date blend that's especially good with grilled meats.

## THREE-C SLAW

◆◆◆◆◆◆◆◆◆◆◆◆◆

*Prep: 1 hour plus chilling*
**Makes** *10 accompaniment servings*

½ cup light mayonnaise
¼ cup Dijon mustard with seeds
¼ cup fresh lemon juice
1 tablespoon sugar
1 tablespoon rice vinegar
¼ teaspoon salt
¼ teaspoon coarsely ground black pepper
2 small bulbs celery root (celeriac), about 8 ounces each (if you can't find celery root, use another 3 medium carrots and ¼ teaspoon celery seeds)
3 medium carrots
1 small head green cabbage (about 1¼ pounds)

**1** Prepare dressing: In small bowl, with wire whisk or fork, mix mayonnaise, mustard, lemon juice, sugar, vinegar, salt, and pepper.

**2** Peel and finely shred celery root and carrots. With chef's knife, cut cabbage into quarters; cut out core. Thinly slice cabbage; discard tough ribs.

**3** Place vegetables in large bowl. Add dressing and toss to coat well. Cover bowl with plastic wrap; refrigerate at least 1½ hours to allow flavors to blend.

◆◆◆◆◆◆◆◆◆◆◆◆◆◆◆◆◆◆◆◆◆◆◆◆◆◆◆◆◆◆◆◆◆◆◆◆◆◆◆

### SMART SHREDDING

• Use a stainless steel knife for slicing cabbage; carbon steel may react with the juices in the cabbage, causing the cut edges to discolor (this will turn green cabbage black, and red cabbage blue).

• Slicing or shredding vegetables in advance causes a loss of vitamin C. If you must do this, seal the shredded vegetables tightly in a plastic bag and refrigerate.

• For shredding, use the coarse side of a grater, the shredding disk in a food processor, or an adjustable-blade slicer (right), which makes short work of shredding and gives attractive long, fine, uniform shreds.

◆◆◆◆◆◆◆◆◆◆◆◆◆◆◆◆◆◆◆◆◆◆◆◆◆◆◆◆◆◆◆◆◆◆◆◆◆◆◆◆◆◆◆◆◆◆◆◆◆

EACH SERVING: ABOUT 80 CALORIES, 2g PROTEIN, 10g CARBOHYDRATE, 4g TOTAL FAT (0g SATURATED), 4mg CHOLESTEROL, 250mg SODIUM

## ASIAN COLESLAW

*Prep: 40 minutes*   *Makes 12 accompaniment servings*

⅓ cup seasoned rice vinegar
2 tablespoons vegetable oil
2 teaspoons Asian sesame oil
¾ teaspoon salt
1 bag (16 ounces) carrots, shredded

1 large head savoy cabbage (about 2½ pounds), thinly sliced and tough ribs removed
4 green onions, thinly sliced
½ cup chopped fresh cilantro

◆ Prepare vinaigrette: In large bowl, with wire whisk or fork, mix seasoned rice vinegar, vegetable oil, sesame oil, and salt until blended.

◆ Add carrots, cabbage, green onions, and cilantro to vinaigrette in bowl; toss to mix well.

**Each serving: About 80 calories, 2g protein, 12g carbohydrate, 3g total fat (1g saturated), 0mg cholesterol, 280mg sodium**

## CABBAGE AND BEET-GREEN SLAW

*Prep: 35 minutes plus chilling*   *Makes 12 accompaniment servings*

1 medium head green cabbage (2 pounds)
1 medium head red cabbage (2 pounds)
1 medium red onion
¾ cup mayonnaise
¼ cup cider vinegar

2 tablespoons sugar
2 tablespoons Dijon mustard
1 teaspoon salt
½ teaspoon coarsely ground black pepper
3 cups loosely packed beet greens or spinach leaves

◆ Quarter, core, and thinly slice both cabbages; discard tough ribs. Place cabbage in large bowl. Cut red onion lengthwise in half, then cut each half crosswise into paper-thin slices. Add onion to cabbage in bowl.

◆ Prepare dressing: In small bowl, with wire whisk or fork, mix mayonnaise, cider vinegar, sugar, Dijon mustard, salt, and coarsely ground black pepper. Add dressing to cabbage mixture and toss to coat well. Cover bowl with plastic wrap and refrigerate at least 3 hours before serving to allow flavors to blend.

◆ Meanwhile, rinse beet greens with cold running water and pat dry with paper towels. Cut beet greens into julienne strips; wrap with plastic wrap and refrigerate until ready to serve slaw.

◆ To serve, add julienned beet greens to cabbage mixture; toss to mix well.

**Each serving: About 160 calories, 3g protein, 14g carbohydrate, 12g total fat (2g saturated), 8mg cholesterol, 400mg sodium**

## CARROT AND APPLE SLAW WITH DATES

*Prep: 20 minutes*   *Makes 6 accompaniment servings*

1 tablespoon fresh lemon juice
1 teaspoon honey
¼ teaspoon dried mint
¼ teaspoon salt
1 bag (16 ounces) carrots, shredded

2 Granny Smith apples, peeled, cored, and shredded
⅓ cup chopped pitted dates
2 tablespoons chopped fresh parsley

◆ Prepare dressing: In large bowl, stir lemon juice, honey, mint, and salt until combined.

◆ Add carrots, apples, dates, and parsley to dressing in bowl; toss to mix well.

**Each serving: About 90 calories, 1g protein, 23g carbohydrate, 0g total fat (0g saturated), 0mg cholesterol, 25mg sodium**

## SWEET BROCCOLI SLAW

*Prep: 10 minutes*   *Makes 4 accompaniment servings*

⅓ cup mayonnaise
¼ cup cider vinegar
4 teaspoons sugar
2 teaspoons celery seeds
1 bunch watercress

1 package (15 to 16 ounces) broccoli coleslaw or shredded cabbage mix for coleslaw

◆ Prepare dressing: In large bowl, with wire whisk or fork, mix mayonnaise, cider vinegar, sugar, and celery seeds.

◆ Remove tough stems from watercress. Add watercress and broccoli slaw to dressing in bowl; toss to mix well.

**Each serving: About 185 calories, 2g protein, 14g carbohydrate, 15g total fat (2g saturated), 11mg cholesterol, 140mg sodium**

---

### HISTORIC FAVORITE

◆◆◆◆◆◆◆◆◆◆◆◆◆◆◆◆◆◆◆◆◆◆◆◆◆◆◆◆◆

Coleslaw was brought to the American colonies around 1627 by Dutch immigrants. Cabbage was an important staple of the pioneer cooks, who made good use of the sturdy vegetable that kept well through long winters in the root cellar. They called their creation of shredded cabbage, seasonings, and a boiled dressing *koolsla*, from the Dutch *kool*, for cabbage, and *sla*, for salad. By 1792, coleslaw had become a standard in kitchens all over America, and there are now many variations that include other vegetables besides cabbage. The cool, crisp, refreshing flavor of coleslaw makes it ideal with fried and barbecued foods.

# PASTA SALADS

Pasta salads are terrific room-temperature dishes: They pack up nicely in a picnic basket, and are the ideal addition to any barbecue. They are best eaten the same day they're made because pasta continues to absorb dressing as it stands. For pasta salads, rinse the hot pasta under cold running water – this stops the cooking and ensures a firm texture.

## SZECHUAN PEANUT-NOODLE SALAD

◆◆◆◆◆◆◆◆◆◆◆◆◆◆

*Prep: 25 minutes*
*Cook: 12 minutes*
*Makes 5 main-dish or*
*8 accompaniment servings*

**1 package (16 ounces) linguine or spaghetti**
**4 ounces snow peas, strings removed**
**¾ cup creamy peanut butter**
**3 tablespoons soy sauce**
**2 tablespoons vegetable oil**
**1 tablespoon hot Asian sesame oil**
**1 tablespoon cider vinegar**
**2 teaspoons grated, peeled fresh ginger**
**1 medium red pepper, thinly sliced**
**Dry-roasted peanuts and chopped green onion (optional)**

**1** Prepare linguine as label directs. Drain, reserving 1 cup pasta cooking water. Rinse linguine with cold running water; drain well.

**2** In 3-quart saucepan, in *1 inch boiling water*, heat snow peas to boiling over high heat. Reduce heat to low; simmer 1 minute, or until tender-crisp.

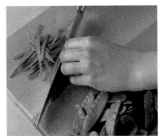

**3** Rinse snow peas with cold running water to stop cooking; drain. Cut snow peas into matchstick-thin strips.

### SESAME OIL

◆◆◆◆◆◆◆◆◆◆◆

Pressed from toasted sesame seeds, dark-amber Asian sesame oil has an intense, nutty aroma; use in preference to pale sesame oil, which is neutral in flavor. "Hot" Asian sesame oil is flavored with chiles. Refrigerate after opening to prolong freshness.

**4** Prepare peanut-butter dressing: In large bowl, with wire whisk or spoon, mix peanut butter, soy sauce, vegetable oil, hot Asian sesame oil, cider vinegar, grated ginger, and reserved pasta cooking water until mixture is thoroughly blended and smooth.

**5** Add linguine, snow-pea strips, and sliced red pepper to peanut-butter dressing in bowl; toss to coat well. Sprinkle with dry-roasted peanuts and chopped green onion, if you like. Serve noodle salad immediately or cover and refrigerate to serve later. If noodles become too sticky upon standing, toss with a little hot water until dressing is of desired consistency.

EACH MAIN-DISH SERVING: ABOUT 595 CALORIES, 21g PROTEIN, 62g CARBOHYDRATE, 32g TOTAL FAT (6g SATURATED), 101mg CHOLESTEROL, 835mg SODIUM

## TORTELLINI SALAD

*Prep: 25 minutes    Cook: 10 to 15 minutes*
*Makes 6 main-dish servings*

2 packages (9 ounces each) refrigerated or 1 package (16 ounces) frozen cheese tortellini
¼ cup white wine vinegar
3 tablespoons extra-virgin olive oil
1 teaspoon sugar
½ teaspoon salt
¼ teaspoon coarsely ground black pepper
1 medium red pepper, cut into thin strips
1 medium yellow pepper, cut into thin strips
1 medium tomato, seeded and diced
1 jar (6 ounces) marinated artichoke hearts, drained and each cut in half
2 bunches arugula or watercress (about 3 cups lightly packed)

◆ Prepare tortellini as label directs. Drain and rinse with cold running water; drain well.

◆ Prepare dressing: In large bowl, with wire whisk or fork, mix white wine vinegar, olive oil, sugar, salt, and coarsely ground black pepper. Add red and yellow peppers, tomato, artichokes, and tortellini; toss to coat. Cover and refrigerate if not serving right away.

◆ To serve, set aside a few whole arugula leaves for garnish. Tear remaining arugula into bite-size pieces; toss with tortellini mixture. Garnish with arugula leaves.

Each serving: About 350 calories, 14g protein, 46g carbohydrate, 13g total fat (3g saturated), 40mg cholesterol, 540mg sodium

## ORZO SALAD WITH FETA CHEESE

*Prep: 20 minutes    Cook: 10 minutes*
*Makes 6 accompaniment servings*

1½ cups orzo (rice-shaped pasta)
2 tablespoons fresh lemon juice
2 tablespoons olive oil
¾ teaspoon salt
½ teaspoon ground black pepper
¼ cup pitted, chopped Kalamata olives
¼ cup chopped fresh parsley
1 large ripe tomato, diced (1½ cups)
3 ounces feta cheese, crumbled (¾ cup)

◆ Cook orzo as label directs. Drain and rinse with cold running water; drain well.

◆ Prepare vinaigrette: In large bowl, with wire whisk or fork, mix lemon juice, olive oil, salt, and pepper.

◆ Add orzo to vinaigrette in bowl and toss to coat. Stir in chopped olives and parsley. Add diced tomato and feta cheese and toss gently, just until combined.

Each serving: About 260 calories, 9g protein, 33g carbohydrate, 10g total fat (3g saturated), 12mg cholesterol, 530mg sodium

## MACARONI SALAD

*Prep: 15 minutes    Cook: 20 minutes*
*Makes 6 accompaniment servings*

1½ cups tubetti or ditalini pasta
3 medium carrots, diced (1 cup)
⅓ cup mayonnaise
¼ cup chopped fresh dill
1 tablespoon fresh lemon juice
½ teaspoon salt
½ teaspoon ground black pepper
3 medium celery stalks, diced (1 cup)
1 cup frozen peas, thawed

◆ In 5-quart Dutch oven, prepare tubetti as label directs, but cook only 8 minutes.

◆ Add carrots to tubetti and cook 3 minutes longer. Drain and rinse with cold running water. Drain well.

◆ Prepare dressing: In large bowl, mix mayonnaise, dill, lemon juice, salt, and pepper until blended.

◆ Add tubetti and carrots to dressing in bowl; toss to coat. Add celery and peas and toss to combine.

Each serving: About 225 calories, 5g protein, 28g carbohydrate, 10g total fat (2g saturated), 7mg cholesterol, 300mg sodium

# Rice salads

Whether you're celebrating summer with a picnic or rounding out a holiday buffet, a rice salad is a side dish to consider. Vegetables or chunks of fresh or dried fruit make welcome additions. Tossing the hot rice with the dressing allows it to absorb maximum flavor as it cools. Rice salads are best eaten within two hours of preparation (rice hardens when it's refrigerated).

## MINTED RICE SALAD WITH CORN

◆◆◆◆◆◆◆◆◆◆◆◆◆

*Prep: 20 minutes plus cooling*
*Cook: 20 minutes*
*Makes 8 accompaniment servings*

**1 cup regular long-grain rice**
**Salt**
**2 tablespoons fresh lemon juice**
**2 tablespoons olive oil**
**¼ teaspoon ground black pepper**
**3 medium ears corn, husks and silk removed**
**¾ cup finely diced radishes**
**¾ cup frozen peas, thawed**
**¼ cup chopped fresh mint leaves**

**1** Prepare rice as label directs, using ½ teaspoon salt. Meanwhile, prepare vinaigrette: In large bowl, with wire whisk or fork, mix lemon juice, oil, pepper, and ¾ teaspoon salt.

**2** Add cooked rice to vinaigrette in bowl and toss gently but thoroughly to coat. Let cool 30 minutes, tossing mixture occasionally with fork.

**3** Meanwhile, in 5-quart Dutch oven, heat *3 quarts water* to boiling. Add corn; cook 5 minutes. Drain and cool.

### ALMOST-INSTANT RICE SALADS

◆◆◆◆◆◆◆◆◆◆◆◆◆◆◆◆◆◆◆◆◆◆

Make a rice salad with any vinaigrette plus a few choice leftover meats or vegetables, or try the following:

• Canned tuna, diced tomatoes, capers, chopped flat-leaf parsley, and a lemon juice and olive oil vinaigrette.

• Diced cooked chicken, celery, apple, chopped walnuts, and a mayonnaise and lemon juice dressing.

• Rinsed and drained canned black beans, crumbled feta cheese, some diced avocado, and a dressing of fresh lime juice, olive oil, garlic, and cumin.

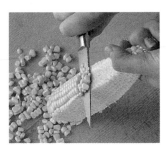

**4** Cut corn kernels from cobs and add to rice mixture with diced radishes, peas, and chopped fresh mint; toss to combine.

EACH SERVING: ABOUT 160 CALORIES, 3g PROTEIN, 28g CARBOHYDRATE, 4g TOTAL FAT (1g SATURATED), 0mg CHOLESTEROL, 325mg SODIUM

## WHITE AND WILD RICE SALAD

*Prep: 20 minutes plus cooling    Cook: 50 to 60 minutes*
*Makes 8 accompaniment servings*

½ cup wild rice
Salt
¾ cup regular long-grain rice
⅓ cup dried cranberries or
   currants
2 tablespoons red wine
   vinegar
2 tablespoons olive oil
½ teaspoon grated orange
   peel
¼ teaspoon ground black
   pepper

2 cups seedless red grapes,
   each cut in half
2 medium celery stalks, thinly
   sliced (1 cup)
2 tablespoons chopped fresh
   parsley
Lettuce leaves (optional)
½ cup pecans, toasted and
   coarsely chopped

◆ Prepare wild rice as label directs, using ½ teaspoon salt.
Meanwhile, cook long-grain rice as label directs, using
¼ teaspoon salt.

◆ In small bowl, combine dried cranberries with *boiling
water* just to cover; let stand 5 minutes. Drain.

◆ Prepare dressing: In large bowl, with wire whisk or fork,
mix vinegar, olive oil, orange peel, pepper,
and ¾ teaspoon salt.

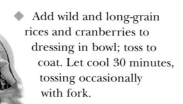

◆ Add wild and long-grain
rices and cranberries to
dressing in bowl; toss to
coat. Let cool 30 minutes,
tossing occasionally
with fork.

◆ Add grapes, celery,
and parsley to rice mixture
in bowl; toss until evenly
combined. To serve, line
salad bowl or platter with
lettuce leaves, if you like.
Spoon in rice salad; sprinkle
with pecans.

**Each serving: About 205 calories, 4g protein, 32g carbohydrate,
8g total fat (1g saturated), 0mg cholesterol, 410mg sodium**

## JAPANESE RICE SALAD

*Prep: 20 minutes plus cooling    Cook: 20 minutes*
*Makes 8 accompaniment servings*

1½ cups regular long-grain
   rice
Salt
3 tablespoons seasoned rice
   vinegar
2 tablespoons vegetable oil
1 teaspoon grated, peeled
   fresh ginger

¼ teaspoon ground black
   pepper
4 ounces green beans, ends
   trimmed, cut into ¼-inch
   pieces (1 cup)
2 medium carrots, shredded
3 green onions, thinly sliced
Watercress (optional)

◆ Prepare rice as label directs, using ½ teaspoon salt.

◆ Prepare dressing: In large bowl, with wire whisk or
fork, mix seasoned rice vinegar, oil, ginger, pepper, and
½ teaspoon salt.

◆ Add rice and toss to coat. Let cool 30 minutes, tossing
occasionally with fork.

◆ Meanwhile, in 2-quart saucepan, heat *2 cups water* to
boiling with 1 teaspoon salt; add green beans and cook
5 minutes. Drain and rinse with cold running water.

◆ Add green beans to rice with carrots and green onions;
toss to combine. To serve, arrange watercress, if using,
around edge of platter; spoon rice salad into center.

**Each serving: About 175 calories, 3g protein, 32g carbohydrate,
4g total fat (1g saturated), 0mg cholesterol, 395mg sodium**

## BROWN RICE AND MANGO SALAD

*Prep: 25 minutes    Cook: 1 hour*
*Makes 8 accompaniment servings*

1 cup long-grain brown rice
Salt
1 large lime
2 tablespoons olive oil
¼ teaspoon ground black
   pepper

1 ripe mango, peeled and cut
   into ½-inch cubes
¼ cup chopped fresh cilantro
2 green onions, thinly sliced

◆ Prepare brown rice as label directs, using ½ teaspoon salt.
Rinse with cold running water; drain well. Meanwhile, grate
½ teaspoon peel and squeeze 2 tablespoons juice from lime.

◆ Prepare dressing: In large bowl, with wire whisk or fork,
mix lime peel, lime juice, olive oil, pepper, and ½ teaspoon
salt. Add rice and toss to coat. Add mango, cilantro, and
green onions; toss until evenly combined.

**Each serving: About 135 calories, 2g protein, 24g carbohydrate,
4g total fat (1g saturated), 0mg cholesterol, 205mg sodium**

# GRAIN SALADS

Barley and wheat, both whole (wheat berries) and cracked (bulgur), make appearances in some wonderfully satisfying salads. Cooked (or soaked, for bulgur) until just tender but still slightly firm, they lend excellent texture and a delicately nutty flavor to these nutritious and irresistible combinations. If the grains in these recipes aren't available at the supermarket, look for them in health-food stores.

## BARLEY SALAD WITH NECTARINES

◆◆◆◆◆◆◆◆◆◆◆◆◆◆◆◆◆◆◆◆◆◆◆◆◆◆◆◆◆

*Prep: 30 minutes    Cook: 40 to 50 minutes*
*Makes 12 accompaniment servings*

| | |
|---|---|
| 1 package (16 ounces) pearl barley | 1½ pounds nectarines (about 4 medium), pitted and cut into ½-inch pieces |
| Salt | |
| 3 to 4 medium limes | 1 pound tomatoes (about 2 large), seeded and cut into ½-inch pieces |
| ⅛ cup olive oil | |
| 1 tablespoon sugar | 4 green onions, thinly sliced |
| ¾ teaspoon coarsely ground black pepper | ½ cup chopped fresh mint |

**1** In 4-quart saucepan, heat *6 cups water* to boiling over high heat. Add barley and 1½ teaspoons salt; heat to boiling. Reduce heat to low; cover and simmer 35 to 45 minutes, until barley is tender and most of liquid is absorbed. Drain and rinse with cold running water. Drain well.

**2** Meanwhile, prepare lime dressing: Grate 1 tablespoon peel and squeeze ½ cup juice from limes. Place grated lime peel and lime juice in large bowl. Add olive oil, sugar, pepper, and 1¼ teaspoons salt. With wire whisk or fork, mix until blended.

**3** Add barley, nectarines, tomatoes, green onions, and mint to lime dressing; with rubber spatula, stir gently to coat. If not serving right away, cover and refrigerate.

---

### BARLEY

This hearty, ancient grain is often identified with beer, breads, cereals, and soups, but it also makes delicious, healthy salads. When cooked until tender, the whole grain has a nutty taste and chewy texture, making it the perfect partner for bold vinaigrettes, herbs, crunchy vegetables, and even fruit. Instead of rice, try barley (or quick-cooking barley) as an easy side dish. Pearl barley is scoured six times to remove the bran and husk for quicker cooking.

---

EACH SERVING: ABOUT 230 CALORIES, 5g PROTEIN, 40g CARBOHYDRATE, 7g TOTAL FAT (1g SATURATED), 0mg CHOLESTEROL, 405mg SODIUM

## WHEAT-BERRY SALAD WITH SPINACH

*Prep:* 15 minutes plus soaking   *Cook:* 1 hour 15 minutes
*Makes* 4 main-dish servings

1½ cups wheat berries
  (whole-grain wheat)
1 bunch (10 to 12 ounces)
  spinach, tough stems
  removed
1 medium tomato
10 dried tomato halves
  (about 1 ounce)
3 tablespoons olive oil

2 tablespoons red wine
  vinegar
1 teaspoon salt
½ teaspoon sugar
½ teaspoon Dijon mustard
¼ teaspoon coarsely ground
  black pepper
1 cup golden raisins

◆ In large bowl, soak wheat berries overnight in enough *water* to cover by 2 inches.

◆ Drain wheat berries. In 4-quart saucepan, heat *7 cups water* to boiling over high heat. Add soaked wheat berries; heat to boiling. Reduce heat to low; cover and simmer 1 hour, or until wheat berries are tender. Drain.

◆ Meanwhile, coarsely chop spinach. Dice tomato. Place dried tomato halves in small bowl; pour over *1 cup boiling water*. Let stand 5 minutes to soften; drain well. Coarsely chop dried tomatoes.

◆ Prepare dressing: In medium bowl, with wire whisk or fork, mix olive oil, red wine vinegar, salt, sugar, mustard, and coarsely ground black pepper. Add raisins, diced tomato, chopped dried tomatoes, spinach, and wheat berries; toss until blended.

**Each serving: About 455 calories, 12g protein, 82g carbohydrate, 12g total fat (1g saturated), 0mg cholesterol, 625mg sodium**

## BARLEY SUCCOTASH SALAD

*Prep:* 15 minutes plus cooling   *Cook:* 40 to 50 minutes
*Makes* 6 accompaniment servings

¾ cup pearl barley
Salt
1 cup frozen baby lima beans
3 ears corn, husks and silk
  removed

2 tablespoons cider vinegar
1 tablespoon olive oil
¼ teaspoon ground black
  pepper
¼ cup chopped fresh parsley

◆ In 2-quart saucepan, heat *2½ cups water* to boiling over high heat. Add barley and ½ teaspoon salt; heat to boiling. Reduce heat to low; cover and simmer 35 to 45 minutes, until tender. Drain and rinse with cold running water. Drain well.

◆ Meanwhile, cook baby lima beans as label directs. Drain and rinse with cold running water; drain well. In 5-quart Dutch oven, heat *4 quarts water* to boiling over high heat. Add corn; cook 5 minutes. Drain corn and cool. Cut kernels from cobs.

◆ Prepare dressing: In large bowl, with wire whisk or fork, mix vinegar, olive oil, pepper, and ¾ teaspoon salt. Add barley, lima beans, corn kernels, and chopped parsley; toss until blended.

**Each serving: About 180 calories, 6g protein, 35g carbohydrate, 3g total fat (0g saturated), 0mg cholesterol, 320mg sodium**

## TOMATO AND MINT TABBOULEH

*Prep:* 20 minutes plus standing and chilling
*Makes* 8 accompaniment servings

1½ cups bulgur (cracked
  wheat)
¼ cup fresh lemon juice
3 medium-size ripe tomatoes
  (about 1 pound), cut into
  ½-inch pieces
1 medium cucumber (about
  8 ounces), peeled and cut
  into ½-inch pieces

3 green onions, chopped
¾ cup loosely packed fresh
  parsley leaves, chopped
½ cup loosely packed fresh
  mint leaves, chopped
1 tablespoon olive oil
¾ teaspoon salt
¼ teaspoon coarsely ground
  black pepper

◆ In medium bowl, combine bulgur, lemon juice, and *1½ cups boiling water*, stirring to mix. Let mixture stand about 30 minutes, until liquid is absorbed.

◆ When bulgur mixture is cool, stir in tomatoes and remaining ingredients. Cover and refrigerate bulgur mixture at least 1 hour to blend flavors.

**Each serving: About 125 calories, 4g protein, 24g carbohydrate, 2g total fat (0g saturated), 0mg cholesterol, 215mg sodium**

# Bean salads

With their soft, creamy texture and mild taste, beans absorb the flavors of any dressing and make a wonderful foundation for a salad. If you cannot find one variety, simply substitute another. For the freshest taste and consistency – and to cut some of their sodium – always rinse canned beans before using. Keep your pantry stocked with a good assortment of canned beans and you'll always be able to prepare delicious salads at a moment's notice.

**1** Trim ends from green beans; cut into 1½-inch pieces. In 3-quart saucepan, in *1 inch boiling water*, heat green beans to boiling over high heat. Reduce heat to low; cover and simmer 5 to 10 minutes, until tender-crisp. Drain. Prepare lima beans as label directs; drain. Meanwhile, chop onion.

## Fiesta bean salad

❖❖❖❖❖❖❖❖❖❖❖❖❖❖❖❖❖❖❖❖❖❖❖❖❖

*Prep: 20 minutes plus chilling  Cook: 20 minutes*
*Makes 12 accompaniment servings*

1 pound green beans
1 package (10 ounces) frozen lima beans
1 small onion
¼ cup olive or vegetable oil
1 tablespoon chili powder
⅓ cup distilled white vinegar
1½ teaspoons sugar
1½ teaspoons salt
1 can (15 to 19 ounces) red kidney beans, rinsed and drained

1 can (15 to 19 ounces) white kidney beans (cannellini), rinsed and drained
1 can (15 to 19 ounces) black beans, rinsed and drained
1 can (16 to 17 ounces) whole-kernel corn, drained
¼ cup chopped fresh cilantro or parsley

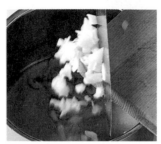

**2** In 2-quart saucepan, heat oil over medium-high heat; add chopped onion and cook, stirring, 10 minutes, or until tender.

**3** Stir chili powder into onion; cook, stirring, 1 minute. Remove from heat; stir in vinegar, sugar, and salt.

**4** Place red and white kidney beans and black beans in large bowl. Add corn, chopped cilantro, green beans, lima beans, and onion mixture; toss to coat. Cover with plastic wrap and refrigerate at least 1 hour to blend flavors.

❖❖❖❖❖❖❖❖❖❖❖❖

**LEFTOVER CILANTRO**

Left with half a bunch? Add cilantro to omelets, tuna salad, or mixed greens, or use it instead of basil in your favorite pesto recipe. To avoid discoloration, don't chop cilantro in advance.

❖❖❖❖❖❖❖❖❖❖❖❖

**EACH SERVING: ABOUT 190 CALORIES, 9g PROTEIN, 32g CARBOHYDRATE, 5g TOTAL FAT (1g SATURATED), 0mg CHOLESTEROL, 790mg SODIUM**

## AVOCADO AND BLACK BEAN SALAD

*Prep: 20 minutes*

*Makes 4 accompaniment servings*

2 small avocados (8 ounces each)

2 medium plum tomatoes

2 medium navel oranges

1 can (15 to 19 ounces) black beans, rinsed and drained

1 tablespoon chopped fresh cilantro or parsley

1 teaspoon salt

Cut each avocado in half; discard seeds. Peel avocados. Cut avocados and tomatoes into bite-size chunks. Cut peel and white pith from oranges; discard. Cut each orange crosswise into ¼-inch-thick slices. In large bowl, with rubber spatula, toss avocados, tomatoes, orange slices, and remaining ingredients to mix well.

Each serving: About 325 calories, 10g protein, 35g carbohydrate, 20g total fat (3g saturated), 0mg cholesterol, 955mg sodium

## GARBANZO SALAD

*Prep: 20 minutes*

*Makes 4 accompaniment servings*

2 tablespoons red wine vinegar

2 tablespoons olive oil

1 teaspoon Dijon mustard

¼ teaspoon salt

3 small tomatoes (about 12 ounces), each cut into 8 wedges

½ cup Kalamata olives, pitted and coarsely chopped

1 green onion, thinly sliced

1 can (15 to 19 ounces) garbanzo beans, rinsed and drained

2 tablespoons chopped fresh oregano, basil, or parsley

Prepare vinaigrette: In medium bowl, with wire whisk or fork, mix red wine vinegar, olive oil, mustard, and salt. To vinaigrette in bowl, add tomato wedges, olives, green onion, garbanzo beans, and oregano; toss to mix well.

Each serving: About 235 calories, 6g protein, 24g carbohydrate, 14g total fat (2g saturated), 0mg cholesterol, 900mg sodium

## BLACK-EYED PEA SALAD

*Prep: 10 minutes plus chilling   Cook: 20 minutes*

*Makes 8 accompaniment servings*

2 packages (10 ounces each) frozen black-eyed peas

1 large red pepper, diced

½ cup chopped red onion

1 package (10 ounces) frozen peas, thawed

3 tablespoons cider vinegar

2 tablespoons olive oil

1 teaspoon sugar

1 teaspoon chopped fresh thyme or ¼ teaspoon dried thyme

¾ teaspoon salt

¼ teaspoon coarsely ground black pepper

1 large tomato

◆ Cook black-eyed peas as label directs; drain. Rinse with cold running water. In large bowl, toss black-eyed peas with remaining ingredients except tomato. Cover and refrigerate at least 3 hours to blend flavors.

◆ To serve, cut tomato into ¼-inch-thick slices. Arrange tomato slices and black-eyed pea salad on large platter.

Each serving: About 165 calories, 8g protein, 25g carbohydrate, 4g total fat (1g saturated), 0mg cholesterol, 235mg sodium

## TWO-BEAN AND TOMATO SALAD

*Prep: 20 minutes   Cook: 10 minutes*

*Makes 6 accompaniment servings*

12 ounces French green beans (haricots verts) or green beans, ends trimmed

2 tablespoons extra-virgin olive oil

1 tablespoon fresh lemon juice

½ large shallot, finely chopped

½ teaspoon Dijon mustard

¼ teaspoon salt

¼ teaspoon coarsely ground black pepper

2 medium tomatoes, each cut into 12 wedges

1 can (15 to 19 ounces) Great Northern beans, rinsed and drained

◆ In 10-inch skillet, heat ¾ *inch water* to boiling over high heat. Add green beans; heat to boiling. Reduce heat to medium; cook, uncovered, 3 to 5 minutes, until beans are tender-crisp. Drain. Rinse beans with cold running water, then drain and pat dry with paper towels.

◆ Prepare dressing: In large bowl, with wire whisk or fork, mix olive oil, lemon juice, chopped shallot, mustard, salt, and pepper until blended.

◆ To dressing in bowl, add green beans, tomato wedges, and Great Northern beans; with rubber spatula, gently toss to mix well.

Each serving: About 145 calories, 6g protein, 21g carbohydrate, 5g total fat (1g saturated), 0mg cholesterol, 115mg sodium

# SALAD DRESSINGS

Fast, fresh, and delicious, these salad dressings provide some intriguing possibilities. From a creamy buttermilk and chive dressing to a classic vinaigrette flavored with Dijon mustard and shallots, there's something here to suit every salad. Each of these dressings can be prepared a day or two in advance and refrigerated in a jar with a tight-fitting lid. If made ahead, bring the dressing to room temperature for fullest flavor, and shake the jar well before tossing the dressing with salad greens.

## MUSTARD-SHALLOT VINAIGRETTE

*Prep:* 10 minutes   *Makes* about ¾ cup

| | |
|---|---|
| 6 tablespoons olive oil | ½ teaspoon salt |
| ⅓ cup red wine vinegar | ½ teaspoon coarsely ground |
| 4 teaspoons Dijon mustard | black pepper |
| 1 tablespoon minced shallot | ½ teaspoon sugar |

In small bowl, with wire whisk or fork, mix all ingredients.

**Each tablespoon: About 65 calories, 0g protein, 1g carbohydrate, 7g total fat (1g saturated), 0mg cholesterol, 125mg sodium**

## JAPANESE MISO VINAIGRETTE

*Prep:* 10 minutes   *Makes* about 1 cup

| | |
|---|---|
| 2 tablespoons miso | 1 tablespoon minced, peeled |
| (fermented soybean paste) | fresh ginger |
| ½ cup rice vinegar | 1 tablespoon sugar |
| ¼ cup olive oil | |

In small bowl, stir miso into vinegar until smooth. Add to blender with remaining ingredients; blend until smooth.

**Each tablespoon: About 35 calories, 0g protein, 1g carbohydrate, 4g total fat (0g saturated), 0mg cholesterol, 80mg sodium**

### VINAIGRETTE VARIATIONS

**Blue-cheese vinaigrette** Prepare Mustard-Shallot Vinaigrette, adding 2 ounces blue cheese, crumbled (½ cup), to ingredients. Makes about 1 cup.

Each tablespoon: About 60 calories, 1g protein, 1g carbohydrate, 6g total fat (1g saturated), 3mg cholesterol, 140mg sodium

**Balsamic vinaigrette** Prepare Mustard-Shallot Vinaigrette, using balsamic vinegar instead of red-wine vinegar. Makes about ¾ cup.

Each tablespoon: About 70 calories, 0g protein, 2g carbohydrate, 7g total fat (1g saturated), 0mg cholesterol, 125mg sodium

### HERB VINEGARS

Wash several 3- to 4-cup capacity bottles with corks (or jars with clamp-top lids) in hot soapy water. To sterilize, put bottles in large pot (and corks in small pan) with water to cover; heat to boiling over high heat. Boil 15 minutes; drain.

Place 3 or 4 sprigs of desired herbs (washed and dried) and other ingredients (see below) in each bottle; you may need a skewer to push them in. For each bottle, in nonreactive saucepan, heat vinegar (3 to 4 cups, depending on bottle size) to boiling. Pour through funnel into bottle. Cork; let stand in cool, dark place about 2 weeks (it is not necessary to refrigerate). Strain through fine sieve into measuring cup or pitcher. Discard herbs and fruits, return vinegar to bottle, and add sprigs of fresh herbs, if you like. Store at room temperature up to 3 months. If the cork pops, discard the vinegar.

**Chive-garlic** Rice vinegar, 2 to 3 peeled garlic cloves, chives

**Dill-peppercorn** Cider vinegar, 1 tablespoon whole black peppercorns, dill sprigs

**Sage-rosemary** Red wine vinegar, sage and rosemary sprigs

**Basil-orange** White wine vinegar, strips of peel of 1 orange, basil sprigs

**Raspberry-mint** (below left) White wine vinegar, 1½ cups fresh raspberries, mint sprigs

**Chile-cilantro** (below center) Distilled white vinegar, 1 to 4 fresh chiles, cilantro sprigs

**Lemon-thyme** (far right) White wine vinegar, strips of peel of 1 lemon, thyme sprigs

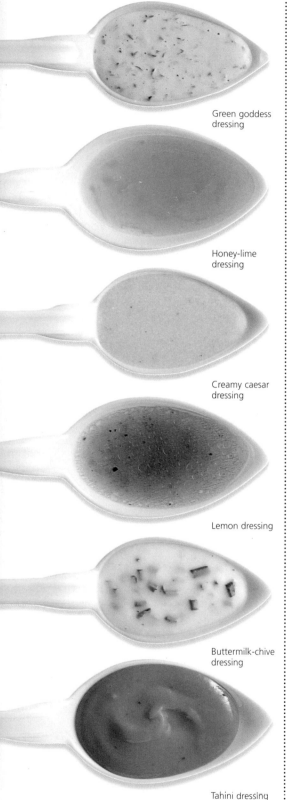

Green goddess dressing

Honey-lime dressing

Creamy caesar dressing

Lemon dressing

Buttermilk-chive dressing

Tahini dressing

## GREEN GODDESS DRESSING

*Prep: 10 minutes*   *Makes about ¾ cup*

½ cup mayonnaise
½ cup loosely packed fresh parsley leaves
¼ cup sour cream
1 tablespoon red wine vinegar
1 teaspoon anchovy paste
¼ teaspoon ground black pepper

In blender, blend all ingredients until smooth, scraping sides as necessary.

**Each tablespoon: About 80 calories, 1g protein, 1g carbohydrate, 9g total fat (2g saturated), 8mg cholesterol, 125mg sodium**

## HONEY-LIME DRESSING

*Prep: 5 minutes*   *Makes about ½ cup*

⅓ cup fresh lime juice
4 teaspoons honey
1 tablespoon rice vinegar
⅛ teaspoon salt

In small bowl, with wire whisk or fork, mix all ingredients.

**Each tablespoon: About 15 calories, 0g protein, 4g carbohydrate, 0g total fat, 0mg cholesterol, 35mg sodium**

## BUTTERMILK-CHIVE DRESSING

*Prep: 5 minutes*   *Makes about ¾ cup*

½ cup buttermilk
2 tablespoons distilled white vinegar
2 tablespoons chopped fresh chives
1 tablespoon low-fat mayonnaise dressing
¼ teaspoon salt
¼ teaspoon coarsely ground black pepper

In small bowl, with wire whisk or fork, mix all ingredients.

**Each tablespoon: About 10 calories, 0g protein, 1g carbohydrate, 0g total fat, 1mg cholesterol, 55mg sodium**

## LEMON DRESSING

*Prep: 5 minutes*   *Makes about ¾ cup*

¼ cup fresh lemon juice
½ teaspoon salt
¼ teaspoon ground black pepper
½ cup olive oil

In bowl, with wire whisk or fork, mix lemon juice, salt, and pepper. In thin, steady stream, gradually whisk in oil.

**Each tablespoon: About 80 calories, 0g protein, 1g carbohydrate, 9g total fat (1g saturated), 0mg cholesterol, 90mg sodium**

## CREAMY CAESAR DRESSING

*Prep: 10 minutes*   *Makes about 1¼ cups*

⅓ cup olive oil
⅓ cup freshly grated Parmesan cheese
¼ cup fresh lemon juice
¼ cup mayonnaise
1 teaspoon anchovy paste
½ teaspoon coarsely ground pepper
1 small garlic clove, minced

In small bowl, with wire whisk or fork, mix all ingredients until smooth.

**Each tablespoon: About 60 calories, 1g protein, 0g carbohydrate, 6g total fat (1g saturated), 3mg cholesterol, 90mg sodium**

## TAHINI DRESSING

*Prep: 10 minutes*   *Makes about ¾ cup*

⅓ cup tahini (sesame seed paste)
2 tablespoons fresh lemon juice
4 teaspoons soy sauce
1 tablespoon honey (optional)
½ teaspoon ground black pepper
½ small garlic clove, minced

In small bowl, with wire whisk or fork, mix all ingredients until smooth.

**Each tablespoon: About 40 calories, 1g protein, 2g carbohydrate, 3g total fat (0g saturated), 0mg cholesterol, 115mg sodium**

# PASTA

Delicious, healthy, and easy to prepare, pasta is the perfect food for the way we eat today – and there have never been more enticing noodles to choose from. So whether you're cooking fresh fettuccine, dried penne, or lasagna, here's how to get great results every time.

## BUYING AND STORING

For the best taste and texture, buy dried pasta made from durum wheat or semolina flour (semolina is more coarsely ground durum wheat). Good-quality pasta will have a clear yellow color and feel hard and smooth. Stored in a cool, dry, dark place, dried pasta will keep up to 1 year (whole-wheat pasta up to 6 months). Store commercially made fresh pasta in the refrigerator according to package directions – or up to 1 week – or freeze up to 1 month.

## HOMEMADE PASTA

It's easy to make your own fresh pasta. Although the dough can be rolled out with a rolling pin, a pasta machine makes it easy. A machine thins the dough gradually – through a series of thickness settings controlled by a knob – which results in an even, chewy texture. Support longer strips of dough as they come through the machine so they won't fold and stick together. Cut unwieldy lengths into more manageable pieces. You can refrigerate homemade pasta, tightly covered, up to 3 days, or freeze up to 1 month. Do not thaw before cooking.

1 With machine on widest setting, pass through portion of dough. Fold dough into thirds and roll again. Repeat folding and rolling 8 to 10 times, until dough is smooth and elastic.

2 Continue rolling dough (unfolded), reducing thickness setting by 1 notch each time, until it reaches the desired thickness; pass dough through cutting blades. Cut pasta into lengths.

## THE SECRETS OF PERFECT PASTA

**Start with plenty of water** Use at least 4 quarts of water for every pound of pasta. Add the pasta – and salt – after the water comes to a rapid boil. (If the water stops boiling when you add the pasta, cover pot just until boil returns.)

**Stir frequently** This ensures even cooking and prevents strands from clumping or sticking to the bottom of the pot.

**Check early (and often) for doneness** Cooking times on packages are guides, not rules; start checking doneness early.

**Test the texture** Perfectly cooked pasta should feel firm to the bite. This texture is described in Italian as *al dente*, or "to the tooth." At this stage, the pasta will have no raw flour taste, but will reveal a tiny chalky-white center. (Residual heat will continue to cook pasta as it's drained and tossed, so gauge cooking time accordingly.)

**Avoid a soggy sauce** Drain cooked pasta thoroughly by shaking excess moisture through the colander. Unless it's indicated in a recipe, never rinse pasta. (Except for lasagna, pasta is rinsed only when it is to be used in a cold salad.)

**Serve it hot** Remember that pasta will wait for no one! The noodles tend to absorb liquid (creamy sauces can practically disappear), and the pasta will cool down quickly. So for best results, call everyone to the table while you're tossing, and serve the pasta in prewarmed bowls.

## TO SALT OR NOT TO SALT

Almost all pasta recipes suggest adding salt to the pasta's cooking water – and purists wouldn't have it any other way. However, some people shy away from this step because they're worried about sodium. But in truth, the salt (we recommend 2 teaspoons per pound of pasta) added to the water isn't all absorbed by the noodles – it merely seasons them. When you drain the noodles, you're draining much of the sodium as well (only about 10 percent is absorbed by the pasta). The sodium analyses for all our pasta recipes are based on pasta cooked in salted water. Most important, salting the water results in noodles with a much fuller flavor.

### FRESH VS. DRIED

There's no doubt that fresh, tender pasta is a delight to eat. But fresh pasta isn't superior to dried – it's simply different. Fresh noodles (typical of the cooking of northern Italy), are finer-textured and richer because they're made with eggs, and pair best with delicate sauces. By contrast, dried pasta (favored by southern Italian cooks), which is made from flour and water, is more economical, lower in fat, and the best choice for robust, highly flavored sauces.

## A MORE NUTRITIOUS NOODLE

Storing pasta in a clear glass or plastic container on an open shelf or counter exposes it to light, which destroys riboflavin, a B vitamin and key nutrient in pasta. Instead, store pasta in an opaque container or in the cupboard. Buy pasta sold in cardboard cartons, which keep out the light.

## COOKING LONG PASTA

1 Add pasta all at once to boiling water, pushing ends down as they soften until all strands are immersed. Cover pot until water returns to a boil.

2 To prevent noodles from sticking to the bottom of the pot, stir often. A spaghetti fork grips and separates strands, allowing for easier draining and neater serving.

## COMMON PASTA DILEMMAS – SOLVED

**How much do I make?** Most packages list a 2-ounce serving size, but a more generous main-dish measure is 4 ounces dry pasta (3 ounces fresh) per person. For rich dishes you're apt to use less. The cooked yield depends on the shape: 4 ounces of dried *penne, ziti, corkscrews* = 2½ cups cooked; of *spaghetti, fettuccine, linguine* = 2 cups cooked; of *egg noodles* = 3 cups cooked.

**How should I store leftover noodles?** Toss them with a small amount of oil and store in a zip-tight plastic bag.

**What's the best way to reheat noodles?** Microwave them in a microwave-safe container or glass bowl on high for about 2 minutes, or simply place in a colander under hot running water just until warm; toss with hot sauce.

**What can I do with leftover noodles?** Layer them with sautéed vegetables and tomato sauce in a gratin dish, top with grated Parmesan cheese, and bake; use as an omelet or frittata filling; toss with salad dressing and a variety of crisp, colorful vegetables for a quick lunch.

**How can I keep cooked lasagna noodles from sticking together?** Rinse cooked noodles under cold running water, then return to saucepot with enough cold water to cover. Drain on a clean kitchen towel before using.

## KNOW YOUR PASTA

These days pasta can be purchased in a dizzying array of shapes and sizes; each one has a special texture and its own cooking time. Many shapes have whimsical Italian names that reflect their shape: Ditalini means "thimbles"; penne, "quills"; orecchiette, "little ears"; manicotti, "sleeves"; and linguine, "little tongues." One shape may go by different names in different regions, and one name may refer to several different shapes.

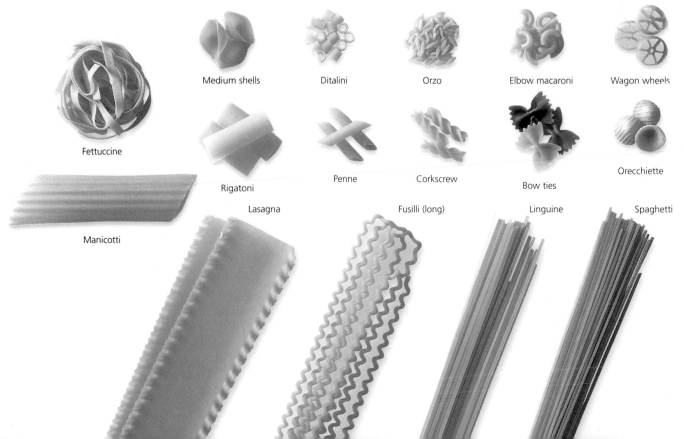

Fettuccine

Medium shells

Ditalini

Orzo

Elbow macaroni

Wagon wheels

Manicotti

Rigatoni

Penne

Corkscrew

Bow ties

Orecchiette

Lasagna

Fusilli (long)

Linguine

Spaghetti

## PASTA PARTNERS

**Tiny shapes and skinny strands** Alphabets, acini di pepe, stars, ditalini, orzo, and vermicelli are excellent in soups, particularly well-seasoned homemade broths.

**Long, thin strands** Spaghetti or linguine goes well with smooth tomato or seafood sauces. You should use just enough sauce to keep the strands wet and slippery.

**Sturdy, hollow, medium-sized shapes** Rigatoni, ziti, and similar shapes are good for baked dishes, since their thick walls will hold up to prolonged cooking. Their sturdiness also makes them the perfect match for robust meat sauces and grilled vegetables.

**Wide, flat noodles** Pastas such as pappardelle, mafalde, and fettuccine are best with simple, rich sauces made with cream, butter, or a selection of cheeses.

**Ridged, curved shapes** Penne, farfalle, gemelli, fusilli, orecchiette, or small shells are designed to catch chunky sauces that contain chopped vegetables, olives, or chunks of cheese. These also make terrific pasta salads, because they cradle other ingredients and can stand up to lively vinaigrettes or creamy dressings.

**Large shapes** Manicotti and jumbo shells are strictly for stuffing with vegetables, meat, and/or cheese mixtures.

## ALMOST-INSTANT PASTA DISHES

• Mix diced ham, frozen peas (add to the pasta cooking water just before draining pasta to thaw), some chopped fresh rosemary, Parmesan cheese, and olive oil with penne.

• Toss slivered jarred roasted red peppers, quartered oil-packed artichoke hearts, chunks of smoked mozzarella, and a generous amount of chopped flat-leaf parsley with rigatoni; moisten with chicken broth.

• Sauté shrimp or scallops in hot olive oil with some fresh bread crumbs and crushed red pepper; toss with spaghetti.

• Mix corkscrew pasta with chunks of deli-roasted turkey, a handful each of toasted pine nuts and golden raisins, some crushed red pepper, and a little olive oil.

• Toss bow ties with ricotta cheese, chopped toasted pecans, a spoonful of milk, and some grated Parmesan.

• Cook cheese-filled tortellini in chicken broth to cover until almost tender; stir in sliced spinach leaves until wilted. Serve in soup bowls with freshly grated Parmesan cheese.

• Heat garbanzo beans and diced salami in chicken broth; toss with wagon-wheel pasta. Then toss again with olive oil, freshly grated Parmesan cheese, and cracked black pepper.

## KNOW YOUR ASIAN PASTA

Unlike most Western pastas, which are made from wheat flour, Asian noodles are made from a variety of flours, including rice and bean or vegetable starches such as yam, soybean, or potato. The versatility of these delicious noodles is limited only by your imagination. They can be served alongside meat and fish dishes, made into salads with tasty Asian-style vinaigrettes and other favorite ingredients (crisp vegetables, fresh herbs, seafood), or added to steaming broth to make a nourishing soup. Thinner noodles can be softened in hot water; others are boiled like spaghetti.

**Soba** These thin, brownish-gray noodles are made from buckwheat flour and served cold with a dipping sauce or steaming-hot in broth.

**Flat rice noodles** Made from rice flour, these noodles are typically boiled or stir-fried for salads or soups.

**Rice stick noodles** These thread-thin sticks can be softened in hot water for soups and salads, or deep-fried, which causes them to puff dramatically into crunchy strands used in salads.

**Cellophane noodles** When softened, these thin, translucent strands (made from mung bean flour) have a slippery texture and glassy look; they're used in stir-fries, soups, and salads.

**Chinese-style egg noodles** Made from wheat flour, these tender strands are similiar in texture and flavor to Western egg noodles. Available fresh or dried in a variety of widths, they're excellent added to soups, topped with meat, or eaten cold with sesame dressing.

**Udon noodles** These long, thick, chewy Japanese noodles made from wheat flour can be flat or round; they're usually eaten in soup.

Soba

Udon noodles

Chinese-style egg noodles

Rice stick noodles

Flat rice noodles

Cellophane noodles

# TOMATO PASTA SAUCES

With a few choice ingredients or a clever cooking technique, a simple tomato sauce becomes the base for a sensational meal. We've roasted plum tomatoes and garlic, for example, to create a sauce of incredible depth and sweetness. There's also a fresh tomato sauce with chunks of mozzarella; a rich tomato-cream sauce; and a marinara with a host of tasty variations.

## ROASTED TOMATO SAUCE

◆◆◆◆◆◆◆◆◆◆◆◆◆◆◆◆◆◆◆◆◆◆◆◆◆◆◆◆◆

*Prep: 20 minutes plus cooling    Roast: 50 to 60 minutes*
*Makes 4 main-dish servings*

| | |
|---|---|
| 3 pounds medium-size ripe plum tomatoes | ¼ teaspoon coarsely ground black pepper |
| 6 medium garlic cloves, unpeeled | 1 package (16 ounces) penne or corkscrew pasta, cooked |
| 2 tablespoons olive oil | Grated Romano cheese |
| ¾ teaspoon salt | (optional) |

**1** Preheat oven to 450°F. Cut each plum tomato lengthwise in half. In 15½" by 10½" jelly-roll pan, toss plum tomatoes and garlic cloves with 1 tablespoon olive oil. Roast tomatoes and garlic 50 to 60 minutes, until tomatoes are well browned and garlic cloves are soft.

**2** Let tomatoes and garlic cool 20 minutes in pan. When tomatoes and garlic are cool, over medium bowl, carefully peel tomatoes. Squeeze garlic cloves from skins into bowl.

**3** With spoon, break up peeled tomatoes and garlic. Stir in salt, pepper, and remaining 1 tablespoon olive oil until blended. To serve, toss cooked pasta with sauce. Sprinkle with grated Romano cheese, if you like.

### GARLIC

• Choose plump, rock-hard heads of garlic with dry, papery skins (avoid soft or moist heads, as well as those that are refrigerated at the grocery store).

• Store garlic in an open container in a cool, dry place up to 2 months. If any clove begins to sprout, cut it in half and simply cut out the bitter-tasting green core.

• For easy peeling, crush the clove with the flat side of a chef's knife to loosen the skin.

• When sautéing garlic, stir it often to prevent it from overbrowning and taking on a bitter taste.

• Raw, garlic is pungent (and its flavor in a dish builds if it sits); roasting or blanching sweetens and mellows it.

EACH SERVING: ABOUT 560 CALORIES, 18g PROTEIN, 102g CARBOHYDRATE, 10g TOTAL FAT (1g SATURATED), 0mg CHOLESTEROL, 545mg SODIUM

## SUMMER TOMATO SAUCE WITH MOZZARELLA

*Prep: 15 minutes plus standing    Makes 4 main-dish servings*

2¼ pounds ripe tomatoes, cut into ½-inch pieces
8 ounces fresh mozzarella cheese, cut into ½-inch pieces
1 cup packed fresh basil leaves
1 tablespoon olive oil
1 tablespoon red wine vinegar
1 teaspoon salt
¼ teaspoon coarsely ground black pepper
1 package (16 ounces) penne or ziti, cooked

In medium bowl, combine tomatoes with their juice and remaining ingredients except pasta, stirring gently to mix well. Allow sauce to stand 15 minutes to develop flavor. To serve, toss cooked pasta with sauce.

**Each serving: 665 calories, 28g protein, 99g carbohydrate, 18g total fat (8g saturated), 44mg cholesterol, 885mg sodium**

## MARINARA SAUCE

*Prep: 10 minutes    Cook: 35 minutes*
*Makes 4 cups sauce or 4 main-dish servings*

2 tablespoons olive oil
1 small onion, chopped
1 garlic clove, minced
1 can (29 to 35 ounces) plum tomatoes in juice
1 can (6 ounces) tomato paste
2 tablespoons chopped fresh basil or parsley (optional)
1 package (16 ounces) spaghetti or rigatoni, cooked

In 3-quart saucepan, heat oil over medium heat; add onion and garlic and cook until tender. Stir in tomatoes with their juice, tomato paste, and basil, if using; heat to boiling over high heat, breaking up tomatoes with back of spoon. Reduce heat to low. Partially cover pan; simmer, stirring occasionally, 20 minutes. To serve, toss cooked pasta with sauce, or use in your favorite recipe.

**Each serving: About 570 calories, 18g protein, 104g carbohydrate, 9g total fat (1g saturated), 0mg cholesterol, 1130mg sodium**

### MARINARA PLUS

Our Marinara Sauce is so versatile, it's worth doubling the recipe (use a 5-quart Dutch oven, and simmer 30 instead of 20 minutes) to freeze half. Try the following add-ins:

• 8 ounces mushrooms, sliced and sautéed

• 8 ounces Italian-sausage links (casings removed), crumbled, and cooked

• 2 green or red peppers, sliced and sautéed

## CREAMY TOMATO SAUCE WITH PEAS

*Prep: 10 minutes    Cook: 10 minutes*
*Makes 4 main-dish servings*

1 tablespoon olive oil
1 medium onion, chopped
2 cans (14½ ounces each) diced tomatoes
1 package (10 ounces) frozen peas, thawed
¼ cup packed fresh basil leaves, chopped
½ cup heavy or whipping cream
½ teaspoon salt
¼ teaspoon crushed red pepper
1 package (16 ounces) medium shell or corkscrew pasta, cooked

◆ In 12-inch nonstick skillet, heat oil over medium heat; add onion and cook until tender.

◆ Add tomatoes with their juice and remaining ingredients except pasta; heat through, stirring constantly. To serve, toss cooked pasta with sauce.

**Each serving: 665 calories, 21g protein, 108g carbohydrate, 17g total fat (8g saturated), 41mg cholesterol, 790mg sodium**

## TOMATO-SAGE SAUCE

*Prep: 15 minutes    Cook: 1 hour*
*Makes 6 main-dish servings*

2 tablespoons olive oil
1 small onion, finely chopped
3 pounds medium-size ripe plum tomatoes, peeled (see page 72) and chopped
½ cup chicken broth
⅓ cup dry white wine
2 tablespoons butter
1 tablespoon chopped fresh sage
1 teaspoon salt
1½ pounds spaghetti or cavatelli, cooked

◆ In 10-inch skillet, heat olive oil over medium-low heat. Add onion and cook 15 to 20 minutes, until very tender and slightly golden.

◆ Stir in tomatoes with their juice, chicken broth, and white wine; heat to boiling over high heat.

◆ Reduce heat to low; cover and simmer 30 minutes, stirring occasionally, and pressing on tomatoes with back of slotted spoon to crush.

◆ Uncover skillet and simmer, stirring occasionally, 25 minutes longer, or until sauce has reduced and thickened slightly. Add butter, chopped fresh sage, and salt and stir until butter melts. To serve, toss cooked pasta with tomato sauce.

**Each serving: 420 calories, 12g protein, 69g carbohydrate, 11g total fat (3g saturated), 12mg cholesterol, 580mg sodium**

# OLIVE OIL PASTA SAUCES

A bottle of good olive oil comes in handy for creating a variety of easy pasta sauces. By adding a few flavorful ingredients such as broccoli rabe, anchovies, dried tomatoes, or Kalamata olives, you can whip up a splendid sauce in next to no time. Or, try our classic Italian pesto, a no-cook sauce that's packed with fresh basil taste. Because these sauces are simple, it's best to use good-quality ingredients so the pure flavors shine through.

## LINGUINE WITH BROCCOLI RABE AND ANCHOVIES

◆◆◆◆◆◆◆◆◆◆◆◆◆

*Prep: 5 minutes*
*Cook: 15 minutes*
*Makes 4 main-dish servings*

1 package (16 ounces) linguine or spaghetti
2 bunches broccoli rabe (about 1 pound each)
2 teaspoons salt
3 tablespoons olive oil
3 garlic cloves, crushed with side of knife
1 can (2 ounces) anchovy fillets, undrained
¼ teaspoon crushed red pepper
½ cup golden raisins

1 Prepare linguine as label directs. Drain, reserving ¼ cup pasta cooking water. Return linguine to saucepot; keep warm. Meanwhile, trim ends of stems from broccoli rabe. In 5-quart Dutch oven, heat *4 quarts water* to boiling over high heat. Add broccoli rabe and salt; heat to boiling. Boil 2 minutes; drain. Wipe Dutch oven dry.

2 In same Dutch oven, heat oil over medium heat. Add garlic; cook until golden. Add anchovies with their oil and red pepper; cook, stirring, just until anchovies begin to dissolve.

3 Add broccoli rabe and raisins to anchovy mixture in Dutch oven; cook, stirring, until broccoli rabe is heated through and well coated with oil.

### OLIVE OIL

The fragrant oil pressed from tree-ripened olives is prized around the world for cooking and salads. Olive oil is classified in categories that indicate color and taste. Extra-virgin, with a greenish hue, fruity aroma and taste, and the lowest acidity, is the finest. It is cold-pressed, a process that relies only on pressure and yields the most flavor. Virgin olive oil is slightly more acidic, and regular olive oil contains blends of refined and virgin oils. Light olive oil isn't low-fat, but instead has been filtered for a neutral aroma and taste. Stored in a cool, dark place, olive oil will last up to 6 months.

4 Add linguine and reserved pasta cooking water to broccoli rabe mixture in Dutch oven; toss well to combine.

EACH SERVING: ABOUT 660 CALORIES, 27g PROTEIN, 111g CARBOHYDRATE, 14g TOTAL FAT (2g SATURATED), 12mg CHOLESTEROL, 1075mg SODIUM

# PESTO

*Prep:* 10 minutes   *Makes* 4 main-dish servings

2 cups loosely packed fresh
  basil leaves
¼ cup olive oil
¼ cup freshly grated
  Parmesan cheese
2 tablespoons pine nuts
  (pignoli) or chopped walnuts

½ teaspoon salt
1 package (16 ounces) long
  fusilli or linguine, cooked
Fresh basil leaves for garnish

In food processor with knife blade attached or in blender at medium speed, process basil, olive oil, Parmesan cheese, pine nuts, and salt with ¼ *cup water* until smooth. To serve, toss cooked pasta with pesto; garnish.

**Each serving: About 590 calories, 18g protein, 86g carbohydrate, 19g total fat (4g saturated), 5mg cholesterol, 500mg sodium**

## OIL AND GARLIC SAUCE

*Prep:* 10 minutes   *Cook:* 10 minutes
*Makes* 4 main-dish servings

¼ cup olive oil
1 large garlic clove, minced
2 tablespoons minced fresh
  parsley
2 tablespoons freshly grated
  Parmesan cheese
¼ teaspoon salt

¼ teaspoon ground black
  pepper
1 package (16 ounces)
  spaghetti or linguine,
  cooked
2 tablespoons pine nuts
  (pignoli), toasted (optional)

In 1-quart saucepan, heat olive oil over medium heat; add garlic and cook just until golden. Remove saucepan from heat; stir in parsley, Parmesan cheese, salt, and pepper. To serve, toss cooked pasta with sauce. Sprinkle pine nuts over pasta, if you like.

**Each serving: About 555 calories, 16g protein, 85g carbohydrate, 16g total fat (3g saturated), 2mg cholesterol, 310mg sodium**

# SPINACH, GARBANZO, AND RAISIN SAUCE

*Prep:* 15 minutes   *Cook:* 10 minutes
*Makes* 4 main-dish servings

3 tablespoons olive oil
4 garlic cloves, minced
1 bunch (10 to 12 ounces)
  spinach, tough stems
  removed
1 can (15 to 19 ounces)
  garbanzo beans, rinsed and
  drained

½ cup golden raisins
¼ teaspoon salt
¼ teaspoon crushed red
  pepper
½ cup reduced-sodium
  chicken broth
1 package (16 ounces) penne
  or corkscrew pasta, cooked

In nonstick 12-inch skillet, heat oil over medium heat; add garlic and cook until golden. Increase heat to medium-high; stir in spinach, garbanzo beans, raisins, salt, and red pepper and cook until spinach wilts. Stir in chicken broth and heat through. To serve, toss cooked pasta with sauce.

**Each serving: 700 calories, 23g protein, 122g carbohydrate, 14g total fat (2g saturated), 0mg cholesterol, 740mg sodium**

# DRIED TOMATO AND OLIVE SAUCE

*Prep:* 15 minutes   *Cook:* 15 minutes
*Makes* 4 main-dish servings

2 tablespoons olive oil
3 garlic cloves, minced
⅓ cup chopped dried
  tomatoes (1 ounce)
1 can (13¾ to 14½ ounces)
  chicken broth
½ cup Kalamata olives, pitted
  and chopped

¼ cup packed fresh parsley
  leaves, chopped
1 package (16 ounces)
  spaghetti or corkscrew
  pasta, cooked
2 ounces goat cheese,
  crumbled (½ cup)

In nonstick 12-inch skillet, heat oil over medium heat; add garlic and cook 30 seconds. Add dried tomatoes and chicken broth; heat to boiling over medium-high heat. Reduce heat to low and simmer 10 minutes. Stir in olives and parsley. To serve, toss cooked pasta with sauce; sprinkle with crumbled goat cheese.

**Each serving: 580 calories, 19g protein, 92g carbohydrate, 15g total fat (4g saturated), 14mg cholesterol, 745mg sodium**

# Baked and stuffed pasta

Ever popular as a comforting family meal and for fuss-free entertaining, baked pastas are loved by all for their fragrant, zesty sauces and gooey strings of melted cheese. When cooking the pasta for these recipes, it's essential to undercook it slightly, so it doesn't become soft and mushy during baking.

## Zucchini and cheese manicotti

◆◆◆◆◆◆◆◆◆◆◆◆◆◆◆◆◆◆◆◆◆◆◆◆◆◆

*Prep: 40 minutes    Bake: 40 minutes*
*Makes 7 main-dish servings*

1 package (8 ounces)
   manicotti shells (14 shells)
2 small zucchini (about
   6 ounces each)
1 small onion
2 tablespoons olive oil
1 container (15 ounces)
   ricotta cheese
4 ounces mozzarella cheese,
   shredded (1 cup)
4 ounces Provolone cheese,
   shredded (1 cup)

2 large eggs
4 cups Marinara Sauce (see
   page 100) or 1 jar
   (30 ounces) chunky garden-
   style spaghetti sauce mixed
   with 1 cup water
1 tablespoon chopped fresh
   basil or parsley
Basil sprigs for garnish
Italian bread (optional)

**1** Prepare manicotti shells as label directs but do not add salt to water. Drain. Meanwhile, shred zucchini and mince onion.

**2** In 10-inch skillet, heat oil over high heat; add zucchini and onion and cook, stirring often, until lightly browned and all liquid evaporates. Remove from heat.

**3** Prepare filling: In large bowl, combine ricotta cheese, shredded mozzarella, shredded Provolone, and eggs; stir until well mixed. Stir in zucchini mixture. Set aside.

**4** Preheat oven to 375°F. Measure and reserve ½ cup marinara sauce. Spoon remaining sauce into bottom of 13" by 9" glass baking dish or shallow 3½- to 4-quart casserole; spread in even layer.

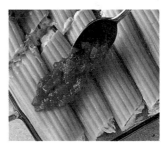

**5** Spoon filling into cooked shells. Or, spoon filling into zip-tight plastic bag, snip off one corner of bag, and squeeze filling into shells. Arrange shells in sauce in casserole in single layer, making sure that shells do not touch sides of casserole.

**6** Spoon reserved marinara sauce over top of filled manicotti shells. Cover casserole with foil and bake 40 minutes, or until pasta is heated through and sauce is bubbly. To serve, sprinkle with chopped basil. Garnish with basil sprigs. Serve manicotti with Italian bread, if you like.

EACH SERVING: ABOUT 485 CALORIES, 23g PROTEIN, 41g CARBOHYDRATE, 26g TOTAL FAT (12g SATURATED), 115mg CHOLESTEROL, 1010mg SODIUM

## BAKED RIGATONI AND PEAS

*Prep: 35 minutes    Bake: 30 to 35 minutes*
*Makes 8 main-dish servings*

1 package (16 ounces)
  rigatoni or ziti
Salt
7 tablespoons margarine or
  butter
¼ cup all-purpose flour
3½ cups milk
1 cup freshly grated Parmesan
  cheese

1 package (10 ounces) frozen
  peas, thawed
1 can (14½ ounces) diced
  tomatoes
½ cup loosely packed fresh
  basil leaves, cut into strips
¼ cup plain dried bread
  crumbs

◆ Prepare rigatoni as label directs, using 2 teaspoons salt in water; drain. Return rigatoni to saucepot; keep warm. Preheat oven to 350°F. Meanwhile, in 2-quart saucepan, melt 5 tablespoons margarine over low heat. Stir in flour; cook, stirring constantly, 2 minutes. With wire whisk, gradually blend in milk. Increase heat to medium; cook, stirring frequently, about 15 minutes, until mixture thickens slightly and boils. Stir in 1 teaspoon salt and ¾ cup Parmesan.

◆ Pour sauce over rigatoni in saucepot, stirring to combine. Stir in peas, tomatoes with their juice, and basil. Spoon mixture into shallow 3½- to 4-quart casserole or 13" by 9" glass baking dish. In small saucepan, melt remaining 2 tablespoons margarine over low heat. Remove from heat; stir in bread crumbs and remaining ¼ cup Parmesan. Sprinkle topping on rigatoni. Bake 30 to 35 minutes, until top is golden brown.

**Each serving: About 485 calories, 19g protein, 60g carbohydrate, 19g total fat (7g saturated), 24mg cholesterol, 870mg sodium**

## REDUCED-FAT MACARONI AND CHEESE

*Prep: 30 minutes    Bake: 20 minutes*
*Makes 6 main-dish servings*

12 ounces (about 3 cups)
  elbow macaroni twists
Nonstick cooking spray
1 container (16 ounces) low-
  fat cottage cheese (1%)
2 tablespoons all-purpose flour
2 cups skim milk
4 ounces sharp Cheddar
  cheese, shredded (1 cup)

1 teaspoon salt
¼ teaspoon ground black
  pepper
¼ teaspoon ground nutmeg
¼ cup freshly grated
  Parmesan cheese

◆ Prepare macaroni as label directs but do not add salt to water; drain. Preheat oven to 375°F. Spray shallow, broiler-safe 2½-quart casserole with nonstick cooking spray. In food processor with knife blade attached, blend cottage cheese until smooth. (Or, in blender at high speed, blend cottage cheese with ¼ cup of the milk called for in recipe.)

◆ In 2-quart saucepan, whisk flour with ¼ cup milk until smooth. Gradually stir in remaining milk until blended. Cook over medium heat, stirring frequently, until mixture thickens slightly and just boils. Remove saucepan from heat; stir in cottage cheese, Cheddar, salt, pepper, and nutmeg.

◆ Place macaroni in casserole; pour cheese sauce over. Bake, uncovered, 20 minutes. Remove casserole from oven; turn oven control to broil. Sprinkle Parmesan on top of macaroni. Place casserole in broiler at closest position to heat source; broil 2 to 3 minutes, until top is golden brown.

**Each serving: About 400 calories, 26g protein, 51g carbohydrate, 9g total fat (6g saturated), 28mg cholesterol, 900mg sodium**

## SOUTHWESTERN-STYLE PASTA

*Prep: 35 minutes    Bake: 15 minutes*
*Makes 4 main-dish servings*

½ (16-ounce) package wagon
  wheel or corkscrew pasta
½ pound fully cooked chorizo
  sausage, thinly sliced
1 large green pepper, diced
1 large onion, diced
2 cans (14½ to 16 ounces
  each) stewed tomatoes
1 small zucchini (about
  6 ounces), diced

1 can (16 to 17¼ ounces)
  whole-kernel corn, drained
1 can (4 to 4½ ounces) diced
  mild green chiles
2 ounces Monterey Jack
  cheese, coarsely shredded
  (½ cup)

◆ Prepare pasta as label directs but do not add salt to water; drain. Meanwhile, preheat oven to 400°F. In 12-inch skillet, cook sausage, green pepper, and onion over medium-high heat, stirring frequently, until vegetables are tender. Spoon off and discard any fat in skillet.

◆ Stir in tomatoes, zucchini, corn, and chiles with their liquid; heat to boiling. Reduce heat to low; cook 5 minutes. Stir in pasta. Spoon mixture into shallow 2-quart casserole or 11" by 7" glass baking dish. Sprinkle with shredded cheese and bake 15 minutes, or until top is golden brown.

**Each serving: About 445 calories, 31g protein, 86g carbohydrate, 29g total fat (11g saturated), 13mg cholesterol, 1305mg sodium**

# LASAGNA

A pan of hot, bubbly lasagna has timeless appeal. Here are recipes for every appetite, from a robust beef and sausage version to tempting cheese-filled lasagna rolls. Because lasagna freezes beautifully, it's a perfect make-ahead meal.

## THREE-CHEESE LASAGNA ROLLS

◆◆◆◆◆◆◆◆◆◆◆◆◆

*Prep:* 35 minutes
*Bake:* 35 to 40 minutes
*Makes* 6 main-dish servings

½ (16-ounce) package curly lasagna noodles (9 noodles)
2 cans (14½ ounces each) stewed tomatoes
1 can (8 ounces) tomato sauce
1 container (15 ounces) part-skim ricotta cheese
6 ounces part-skim mozzarella cheese, shredded (1½ cups)
3 tablespoons freshly grated Parmesan cheese
½ teaspoon coarsely ground black pepper
4 tablespoons chopped fresh basil
2 teaspoons olive oil
1 small onion, chopped
1 small zucchini (4 ounces), diced
1 small tomato, diced
1 tablespoon capers, drained and chopped

**1** Prepare lasagna noodles as label directs. Drain and rinse with cold running water. Return noodles to saucepot with *cold water* to cover. Meanwhile, in 3-quart ceramic or glass baking dish, combine stewed tomatoes and tomato sauce; break up tomatoes with back of spoon. Prepare filling: In large bowl, mix all cheeses, pepper, and 3 tablespoons chopped basil.

**2** Preheat oven to 375°F. Drain lasagna noodles on clean kitchen towels. Spread rounded ¼ cup filling on each lasagna noodle and roll up jelly-roll fashion. Slice each rolled noodle crosswise in half.

**3** Arrange lasagna rolls, cut-side down, in sauce in baking dish; cover loosely with foil. Bake 35 to 40 minutes, until hot.

**4** Meanwhile, prepare topping: In nonstick 10-inch skillet, heat oil over medium heat. Add onion; cook until tender and browned. Stir in zucchini; cook until tender.

**5** Stir in diced tomato, capers, and remaining 1 tablespoon basil; heat through. To serve, place sauce and lasagna rolls on 6 plates; spoon topping over lasagna rolls.

EACH SERVING: ABOUT 385 CALORIES, 24g PROTEIN, 43g CARBOHYDRATE, 14g TOTAL FAT (7g SATURATED), 40mg CHOLESTEROL, 910mg SODIUM

## BEEF AND SAUSAGE LASAGNA

*Prep: 1 hour plus standing    Bake: 45 minutes*
*Makes 10 main-dish servings*

⅔ (16-ounce) package lasagna noodles (about 12 noodles)
½ pound hot Italian-sausage links, casings removed
½ pound ground beef
1 medium onion, diced
1 can (28 ounces) Italian plum tomatoes
2 tablespoons tomato paste
1 teaspoon salt
1 teaspoon sugar
¾ teaspoon dried Italian seasoning
1 container (15 ounces) part-skim ricotta cheese
1 large egg
¼ cup chopped fresh parsley
8 ounces part-skim mozzarella cheese, shredded (2 cups)

◆ Prepare lasagna noodles as label directs but do not add salt to water; drain and rinse with cold running water. Return to saucepot with *cold water* to cover. Set aside.

◆ Meanwhile, prepare meat sauce: In 4-quart saucepan, cook sausage, ground beef, and onion over high heat, stirring often to break up sausage, until meat is well browned. Spoon off and discard fat. Add tomatoes with their juice and next 4 ingredients. Heat to boiling, breaking up tomatoes with back of spoon. Reduce heat to low; cover and simmer, stirring occasionally, 30 minutes. Set aside.

◆ Preheat oven to 375°F. In medium bowl, mix ricotta, egg, and parsley. Drain noodles on clean kitchen towels.

◆ In 13" by 9" glass baking dish, arrange half of lasagna noodles, overlapping slightly; top with ricotta mixture. Sprinkle with half of mozzarella; top with half of meat sauce. Layer with remaining noodles and meat sauce; top with remaining mozzarella. Cover with foil; bake 30 minutes.

◆ Uncover and bake 15 minutes longer, or until sauce is bubbly and top is lightly browned. Let stand 15 minutes for easier serving.

**Each serving: About 385 calories, 23g protein, 28g carbohydrate, 20g total fat (8g saturated), 82mg cholesterol, 800mg sodium**

## MUSHROOM LASAGNA

*Prep: 1 hour plus standing    Bake: 50 minutes*
*Makes 12 main-dish servings*

½ ounce dried porcini mushrooms
¾ (16-ounce) package lasagna noodles (about 16 noodles)
5 cups milk
5 tablespoons margarine or butter
⅓ cup all-purpose flour
Pinch ground nutmeg
Salt and ground black pepper
½ cup finely chopped shallots
1½ pounds white mushrooms, sliced
2 tablespoons chopped fresh parsley
1 container (15 ounces) ricotta cheese
1 package (10 ounces) frozen chopped spinach, thawed and squeezed dry
1 cup freshly grated Parmesan cheese

◆ In bowl, combine porcini and *¾ cup hot water*; let stand 30 minutes. With slotted spoon, remove porcini; rinse to remove any grit. Chop and set aside. Strain soaking liquid through sieve lined with paper towel; set aside. Meanwhile, prepare lasagna noodles as label directs, but do not add salt to water; drain and rinse with cold running water. Return noodles to saucepot with *cold water* to cover. Set aside.

◆ Prepare béchamel sauce: In 3-quart saucepan, heat milk to boiling over medium-high heat. Meanwhile, in 4-quart saucepan, melt 3 tablespoons margarine over medium heat. Stir in flour; cook, stirring, 1 minute. Gradually whisk in milk, nutmeg, ½ teaspoon salt, and ⅛ teaspoon pepper. Heat to boiling. Reduce heat to low; simmer 5 minutes, stirring. Remove from heat.

◆ In 12-inch skillet, melt remaining 2 tablespoons margarine over medium-high heat. Add shallots; cook 1 minute. Stir in white mushrooms, ½ teaspoon salt, and ⅛ teaspoon pepper and cook 10 minutes, or until liquid has evaporated. Stir in porcini and soaking liquid; cook until liquid has evaporated. Remove from heat; stir in parsley.

◆ Preheat oven to 375°F. In large bowl, mix ricotta, spinach, ¼ cup Parmesan, ½ teaspoon salt, ¼ teaspoon pepper, and ½ cup béchamel. Drain noodles on clean kitchen towels.

◆ In 13" by 9" glass baking dish, spread ½ cup béchamel. Arrange 4 lasagna noodles over sauce, overlapping slightly. Top with half of mushroom mixture, 1 cup béchamel, ¼ cup Parmesan, and 4 more noodles. Add all of ricotta mixture, 4 more noodles, remaining mushrooms, 1 more cup béchamel, and ¼ cup Parmesan. Top with remaining noodles, béchamel, and Parmesan. Cover with foil; bake 30 minutes.

◆ Uncover and bake 20 minutes longer, or until sauce is bubbly and top is lightly browned. Let stand 15 minutes.

**Each serving: About 355 calories, 18g protein, 36g carbohydrate, 16g total fat (8g saturated), 38mg cholesterol, 580mg sodium**

# GRAINS & BEANS

 Long a staple and source of protein in the cuisines of cultures around the globe, grains and beans have finally taken a prominent place on the American table – and it's easy to see why. Grains and beans are inexpensive, low in fat, rich in nutrients, and, if served together, form a complete protein. When it comes to meal planning, few foods are as versatile, creating satisfying side dishes and salads or hearty entrées in bold, robust flavors.

## BUYING AND STORING

Dry beans and grains will keep for a year or longer, but they become less flavorful and drier with time. For best results, buy them in small quantities and use within 6 months. Avoid packages with any hint of dust or mold. Store grains and beans in airtight containers in a cool, dry place. The bran left in brown rice and other whole grains makes them more perishable, so refrigerate or freeze them for a longer shelf life.

Cooked beans can be refrigerated, tightly covered, for 4 or 5 days or frozen for 6 months (thaw them at room temperature for about 1 hour). Cooked grains can be refrigerated for up to 5 days. Since they keep so well, it's a good idea to cook extra beans and grains to use for fast salads, soups, pilafs, and stir-fries. Cooked rice becomes hard if refrigerated, but reheats beautifully in the microwave.

## SOAKING BEANS

There are two reasons to soak dry beans in water before they're cooked. The first is that this process softens and returns moisture to the beans, which will reduce cooking time. The second is that soaking allows some of the gas-causing oligosaccharides (complex sugars that the human body cannot digest) to dissolve in the water, which makes digestion easier. Always discard the soaking liquid and cook the beans in fresh water.

To soak, combine beans with enough cold water to cover by 2 inches. (Remember that beans will rehydrate to triple their dry size, so start with a large enough bowl or pot.) The standard soaking time is overnight, or about 8 hours. It's not true that longer is better, though; if left to soak too long, beans may start to ferment, so follow the recipe or package directions. When time is of the essence, you can use the quick-soak method instead. To do this, simply boil the water and beans for 3 minutes; remove from heat. Cover and set aside for 1 hour; discard the soaking liquid.

## REASONS TO RINSE

There's no need to rinse most domestic packaged rice before cooking. That's because the rice has already been cleaned during milling – and you'll rinse away the starchy coating on enriched rice that contains nutrients such as thiamin, niacin, and iron. You should, however, rinse wild rice and imported varieties such as basmati or jasmine, which may be dirty or dusty.

By contrast, dry beans and lentils should be picked over to remove any shriveled beans, stones, or twigs, then rinsed with cold running water to remove dust before cooking. Canned beans of all kinds should also be rinsed, for best appearance and texture in the finished dish.

## COOKING SUCCESS

• For the lightest texture, be sure to allow cooked rice a 5-minute "standing time" before fluffing and serving.
• For enhanced flavor, cook rice in broth.
• Don't lift the lid when cooking rice. This allows steam and heat to escape from the pan and results in a mushy texture.
• Never add anything acidic (e.g., tomatoes, vinegar, wine, or citrus juices) or salt to beans at the start of cooking. These can toughen the skins and result in a longer cooking time, so add toward the end of cooking.
• Test rice and beans for doneness by tasting: Freshness and variety can influence their cooking times. Rice should be soft and fluffy; beans should be creamy, not mushy, in texture.
• Cool cooked beans in their cooking liquid to prevent them from drying out.

### RICE COOKING METHODS

There are two basic methods of cooking rice, immersion and absorption. For the immersion method, rice is boiled like pasta, in a large amount of salted water until tender, then drained; the disadvantage is that nutrients are poured away with the cooking water. Good Housekeeping prefers the absorption method, where rice is cooked in a measured quantity of liquid, all of which is absorbed, thus conserving nutrients. (Rice cookers use the absorption method and have a built-in timer; some also double up as steamers for other foods.) The cooking time and amount of liquid will vary depending on the variety of rice (see chart on page 109). For long-grain white rice, combine 1 cup rice with 2 cups cooking liquid, 1 teaspoon salt (optional), and 1 tablespoon margarine or butter (optional) in a 2- to 3-quart saucepan. Heat to boiling. Reduce heat; cover and simmer 18 to 20 minutes. Remove from heat; let stand, covered, 5 minutes.

## KNOW YOUR RICE

**Regular long-grain** Slender, polished white elongated grains; it cooks into dry grains that separate easily.

**Parboiled (also called converted)** Rice that has been steamed and pressure-treated; the grains remain firm and separate after cooking.

**Instant** Rice that has been partially or fully cooked, then dehydrated. It cooks in minutes but remains dry and chewy.

**Arborio** The traditional rice for Italian risotto; this fat, almost round grain has a high starch content and yields a moist, creamy texture. Vialone Nano and Carnaroli rice varieties have a similar starch content.

**Brown** The least processed form of rice; it has the outer hull removed but retains the nutritious, high-fiber bran layers that give it a light tan color, nutty flavor, and chewy texture.

**Basmati** A long-grain rice native to India; valued for its fragrant perfume, delicate taste, and fluffy texture. When cooked, the slender grains swell only lengthwise, resulting in thin, dry grains perfect for pilafs.

**Wild rice** Not truly a rice but the seed of an aquatic grass. The long, dark-brown grains have a chewy texture and nutty, earthy flavor; rinse well before cooking.

Regular long-grain Instant Arborio

Brown Basmati Wild

### WHAT IS STICKY RICE?

Sticky, or glutinous, rice is a short-grain Asian rice with a slightly sweet taste and soft, sticky texture resulting from a high starch content. Typically used in dim sum, sushi, and desserts, it can be purchased in Asian or Caribbean markets.

### RICE SENSE

| RICE VARIETY (1 CUP) | AMOUNT OF LIQUID | COOKING TIME | COOKED YIELD |
|---|---|---|---|
| Regular long-grain | 1¾–2 cups | 18–20 mins | 3 cups |
| Medium- or short-grain | 1½–1¾ cups | 18–20 mins | 3 cups |
| Brown | 2–2½ cups | 45–50 mins | 3–4 cups |
| Wild | 2–2½ cups | 45–60 mins | 2⅔ cups |

## KNOW YOUR GRAINS

**Couscous (Moroccan pasta)** Grains of precooked semolina; in North African cooking, it is steamed and served with spiced meats and vegetables to make a dish of the same name.

**Bulgur** Wheat kernels that have been steamed, dried, and crushed. A staple in Middle Eastern cuisine and the grain for tabbouleh, bulgur has a tender, chewy texture.

**Barley** An ancient grain used to make cereal, bread, salads, and soups. Pearl barley has been polished to remove the outer hull; quick-cooking pearl barley has been pre-steamed.

**Wheat berries** Unprocessed whole wheat kernels with a chewy texture; used for salads, pilafs, breakfast porridge, or baking.

**Quinoa** A staple grain of the ancient Incas, quinoa is rich in protein and vital nutrients. The tiny seeds cook quickly; they have a slightly earthy taste and springy texture.

**Cornmeal** Dried corn kernels (yellow, white, or blue) ground to a fine, medium, or coarse texture. Much used in baking, it is also cooked to make polenta, a staple dish in Northern Italy. Stone-ground cornmeal has not been degerminated and has the best flavor; store in the freezer or refrigerator.

Couscous Bulgur Barley

Wheat berries Quinoa Cornmeal

**Buckwheat** A grain with an earthy flavor. The kernels, whole (groats) or ground (grits), may be cooked like rice. Kasha is roasted buckwheat kernels. Buckwheat flour is used in blinis.

# KNOW YOUR BEANS

**Black beans** Also called turtle beans, these are a staple bean in Latin America and the Caribbean. With a slightly sweet taste, they're prized as the base for black bean soup, as a partner with rice, or as a robust filling for burritos.

**Navy** A small white bean, also called the pea or Yankee bean, these have long been a staple of the U.S. Navy. They're used for canned pork and beans, soups, and Boston baked beans.

**Yellow or green split peas** Dried peas that have been peeled and split in half, these have a slightly sweet flavor that pairs well with ham, and they can be cooked to a soft puree that makes excellent soup.

**Cranberry** These plump, beautiful beans are cream-colored with red streaks, but become uniform in color during cooking. Also called shell beans, they have a nutty flavor.

**Pink** A smooth, reddish-brown dry bean popular in the Southwest, where it's used to make refried beans and chili; interchangeable with pinto beans.

**Great Northern** These large white beans have a delicate flavor. Popular in soup and baked-bean dishes; they can be substituted for other white beans in most recipes.

**Black-eyed peas** Oval, beige-colored beans with a black circular "eye," also called cowpeas. Used to make Hoppin' John, a Southern specialty, as well as soups and salads; they have a mealy texture and earthy taste.

**Garbanzo beans** Also called chick-peas, they're perhaps best known as the base for hummus, a creamy Middle Eastern dip; they're also a favorite in Italian and Indian cooking. Their cooking time can vary greatly, so always taste for doneness.

**Red kidney** The choice for chili, this medium-size bean has a firm, burgundy-colored skin, pale flesh, and a sweet, meaty flavor.

**White kidney** Also called cannellini beans, they have a creamy texture and milder taste than the red variety. White kidney beans are common in Italian cooking, where they're used for soup or pasta dishes, or with tuna to make a salad.

**Pinto** Named for the Spanish word for "speckled," these pale pink beans are splotched with reddish-brown streaks. Grown in the Southwest and prized in most Spanish-speaking countries, they are used to make refried beans or in soup or stew. Pinto beans are interchangeable with pink beans.

**Fava** Also called broad beans, these flat, light brown beans resemble large limas. They have a tough skin that should be removed by blanching before cooking. Fava beans are popular in Mediterranean countries, where they are commonly used to make salads and soups.

**Lima** Also called butter beans, these large oval, cream-colored beans hold their shape well when cooked; often served alone as a hot vegetable or in salads.

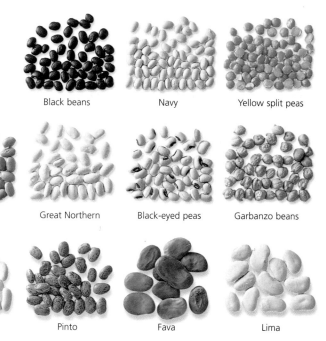

Black beans    Navy    Yellow split peas

Cranberry    Pink    Great Northern    Black-eyed peas    Garbanzo beans

Red kidney    White kidney    Pinto    Fava    Lima

# KNOW YOUR LENTILS

Protein-packed lentils, one of our oldest cultivated crops, cook into countless savory, satisfying dishes including Indian dals and hearty stews and salads. They don't need to be presoaked and they cook faster than other dry beans.

**Small green French lentils (Puy)** These tiny, plump lentils are grown in central France. Considered to have the best flavor, they cook quickly, hold their shape, and have a nutty taste.

**Red** A smaller, round variety, these lighten to yellow and become very soft when cooked. They are often used in Indian dals.

**Green lentils** Popular in European cooking; they have a firm texture and a nutty, earthy taste.

**Brown lentils** The most common variety; they have a firm texture and a mild nutty flavor.

Puy    Red    Green    Brown

# RICE

Perhaps the word's most versatile staple, rice is the basis of flavorful dishes from paella to jambalaya. In a hurry? A dash of herbs or spice transforms plain white rice into an exciting side dish.

## VEGETABLE PAELLA

◆◆◆◆◆◆◆◆◆◆◆◆◆◆◆◆◆◆◆◆◆◆◆◆◆◆◆◆◆◆

*Prep: 40 minutes plus standing    Bake: 50 minutes*
*Makes 8 main-dish servings*

1 small eggplant (1 pound), cut lengthwise in half, then crosswise into ½-inch-thick slices

2 tablespoons plus ¼ cup olive or vegetable oil

1 medium onion, diced

8 ounces mushrooms, each cut in half or quarters

2 small zucchini (about 6 ounces each), cut into 1-inch pieces

2 medium tomatoes, cut into ¾-inch pieces

3 cans (13¾ to 14½ ounces each) reduced-sodium vegetable broth

1 package (16 ounces) parboiled rice

1 package (10 ounces) frozen artichoke hearts, thawed

¼ teaspoon salt

½ teaspoon crushed saffron threads

¼ teaspoon ground black pepper

1 can (15 to 19 ounces) garbanzo beans, rinsed and drained

1 package (10 ounces) frozen peas

¼ cup pimiento-stuffed olives, rinsed and drained

½ teaspoon chopped fresh thyme

**1** Preheat oven to 450°F. Brush eggplant slices on both sides with 2 tablespoons oil. Spread eggplant in jelly-roll pan. Bake 15 minutes, turning slices once. Set aside. Turn oven control to 350°F.

**2** Meanwhile, in 12-inch skillet, heat remaining ¼ cup oil over medium-high heat; add onion and cook, stirring occasionally, until tender.

**3** Add mushrooms to onion in skillet; cook, stirring occasionally, until tender and brown. Stir in zucchini and cook 1 minute.

**4** Stir in tomatoes, vegetable broth, rice, artichoke hearts, salt, saffron, pepper, and eggplant; heat to boiling over high heat. Transfer rice mixture to shallow 4-quart casserole. Bake, uncovered, about 50 minutes, until rice is tender and liquid is absorbed.

**5** Remove casserole from oven; stir in garbanzo beans, peas, olives, and thyme. Let paella stand 10 minutes to allow ingredients to heat through.

## SAFFRON

◆◆◆◆◆◆◆◆◆◆◆

The most expensive spice you can buy, saffron is the yellow-orange stigmas of the crocus flower, which are hand-picked and dried. Available as threads or powder, saffron should be used sparingly – too much produces a medicinal flavor. Use the threads in preference to powder, which loses its pungency in storage. The golden color and distinct flavor of saffron are traditional in paella, bouillabaisse, and risotto Milanese.

**EACH SERVING: ABOUT 475 CALORIES, 12g PROTEIN, 78g CARBOHYDRATE, 13g TOTAL FAT (2g SATURATED), 0mg CHOLESTEROL, 660mg SODIUM**

## CUMIN RICE WITH BLACK BEANS

*Prep: 10 minutes plus standing    Cook: 30 minutes*
*Makes 6 accompaniment servings*

| | |
|---|---|
| 1 tablespoon vegetable oil | ¼ teaspoon salt |
| 1 medium onion, finely chopped | 1 can (15 to 19 ounces) black beans, rinsed and drained |
| 1 garlic clove, minced | 2 tablespoons chopped fresh cilantro |
| 2 teaspoons cumin seeds | Lime wedges |
| 1½ cups regular long-grain rice | |
| 1 can (13¾ to 14½ ounces) chicken or vegetable broth | |

◆ In 3-quart saucepan, heat oil over medium heat. Add onion and cook 5 minutes, or until tender. Stir in garlic and cumin seeds; cook until fragrant. Add rice and cook, stirring, 1 minute.

◆ Stir in chicken broth plus enough *water* to equal 3 cups and salt; heat to boiling over high heat. Reduce heat to low; cover and simmer 15 minutes.

◆ Stir black beans into rice. Cover and simmer 5 minutes longer. Remove from heat and let stand 5 minutes. Spoon rice mixture into serving bowl and sprinkle with chopped cilantro. Serve with lime wedges.

**Each serving: About 270 calories, 9g protein, 53g carbohydrate, 4g total fat (1g saturated), 5mg cholesterol, 650mg sodium**

## INDIAN-SPICED RICE

*Prep: 2 minutes plus standing    Cook: 25 minutes*
*Makes 4 accompaniment servings*

| | |
|---|---|
| 1 tablespoon vegetable oil | 4 whole cloves |
| 1 cinnamon stick (3 inches) | 1 cup regular long-grain rice |
| 10 black peppercorns | ½ teaspoon salt |
| 6 cardamom pods | |

◆ In 2-quart saucepan, heat oil over medium heat. Add cinnamon stick, peppercorns, cardamom, and cloves and cook, stirring often, just until spices begin to darken. Add rice and cook, stirring, 1 minute.

◆ Stir in salt and *2 cups water*; heat to boiling over high heat. Reduce heat to low; cover and simmer 20 minutes.

◆ Remove rice from heat and let stand 5 minutes. Fluff with fork.

**Each serving: About 205 calories, 3g protein, 38g carbohydrate, 4g total fat (1g saturated), 0mg cholesterol, 270mg sodium**

## PERSIAN RICE PILAF

*Prep: 10 minutes plus standing    Cook: 30 minutes*
*Makes 4 accompaniment servings*

| | |
|---|---|
| 1 tablespoon margarine or butter | ⅛ teaspoon ground black pepper |
| 1 small onion, finely chopped | ½ teaspoon grated orange peel |
| 1 cup regular long-grain rice | ¼ cup pine nuts (pignoli), toasted |
| 1 can (13¾ to 14½ ounces) chicken or vegetable broth | ¼ cup chopped fresh parsley |
| ¼ cup dried currants | |
| Pinch ground cinnamon | |

◆ In 2-quart saucepan, melt margarine over medium heat. Add onion and cook, stirring often, 4 minutes, or until tender. Add rice and cook, stirring, 1 minute.

◆ Stir in chicken broth plus enough *water* to equal 2 cups, currants, cinnamon, and ground black pepper; heat to boiling over high heat. Reduce heat to low; cover and simmer 20 minutes.

◆ Remove rice from heat and let stand 5 minutes. Add orange peel; fluff with fork until combined. Gently stir in pine nuts and parsley.

**Each serving: About 285 calories, 7g protein, 49g carbohydrate, 8g total fat (2g saturated), 8mg cholesterol, 475mg sodium**

### WORLD OF RICE

There are over 40,000 varieties of rice, and more than half the world's people eat rice as their main sustenance. Specialties come from all over: In the Near East and India, rice pilaf is prepared by browning rice in hot oil or butter before cooking it in broth, which helps keep the grains separate. Japanese cooks prefer a starchier variety of rice, while in northern Thailand, sticky rice holds together enough to be eaten with the hands. In China, rice is served as a breakfast porridge called congee.

Rijsttafel, Dutch for "rice table," is an adaptation of an Indonesian meal that's popular in Holland: A platter of hot spiced rice is accompanied by various small side dishes including fried seafood and meats, curries, and relishes. In Spain and Mexico, arroz con pollo, or "rice with chicken," may get added flavor from tomatoes, pimientos, onions, peppers, and peas. Paella is a Spanish rice dish that usually contains a combination of chicken, seafood, sausages, pork, and vegetables, with saffron for a bright yellow color. Jambalaya, the New Orleans version of paella, may include ham and shrimp, and replaces the saffron with cayenne pepper. "Dirty" rice was also created in New Orleans; it gets its "dirty" appearance from chicken livers.

# RISOTTO

Rich, creamy risotto, a specialty from Northern Italy, relies on starchy, short-grain Arborio rice – and a little patience. The grains of rice are first sautéed, then hot broth is added gradually, as it is absorbed. Almost constant stirring ensures even cooking. Perfect risotto is just tender, yet still slightly "al dente."

## SPRING RISOTTO

◆◆◆◆◆◆◆◆◆◆◆◆◆

*Prep:* 30 minutes
*Cook:* 55 minutes
*Makes* 4 main-dish servings

1 can (13¾ to 14½ ounces) vegetable or chicken broth
2 tablespoons olive oil
3 medium carrots, diced
¾ pound asparagus, tough ends removed, cut into 2-inch pieces
6 ounces sugar snap peas, strings removed and each cut crosswise in half
¼ teaspoon coarsely ground black pepper
Salt
1 small onion, chopped
2 cups Arborio rice (Italian short-grain rice) or medium-grain rice
½ cup dry white wine
½ cup freshly grated Parmesan cheese
¼ cup chopped fresh basil or parsley

**1** In 2-quart saucepan, heat broth and *3½ cups water* to boiling over high heat. Reduce heat to low to maintain simmer; cover. In 4-quart saucepan, heat 1 tablespoon olive oil over medium heat. Add carrots and cook 10 minutes. Add asparagus, sugar snap peas, pepper, and ¼ teaspoon salt; cover and cook about 5 minutes, until vegetables are tender-crisp. Transfer vegetables to bowl; set aside.

**2** In same saucepan, heat remaining 1 tablespoon oil over medium heat. Add onion; cook 5 minutes, or until tender. Add rice and ¼ teaspoon salt; cook, stirring, until rice is opaque.

**3** Add white wine; cook, stirring constantly, until wine is absorbed. Add about ½ cup simmering broth to rice mixture, stirring until liquid is absorbed.

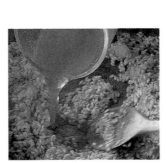

**4** Continue cooking, adding simmering broth, ½ cup at a time, and stirring after each addition, about 25 minutes, until all liquid is absorbed and rice is tender but still firm.

**5** When risotto is done (it should have a creamy consistency), stir in vegetables; heat through. Stir in Parmesan and basil. Spoon risotto into 4 shallow bowls; serve hot.

### RISOTTO TIPS

◆◆◆◆◆◆◆◆◆◆

• Serve risotto at once; it continues to absorb liquid as it stands.

• Use a heavy pan with a thick base that heats evenly; maintain the rice at a steady, gentle simmer.

• Keep the broth at a constant simmer, or the risotto will cook too slowly and become gluey.

EACH SERVING: ABOUT 645 CALORIES, 18g PROTEIN, 107g CARBOHYDRATE, 12g TOTAL FAT (4g SATURATED), 18mg CHOLESTEROL, 965mg SODIUM

## SHRIMP RISOTTO WITH BABY PEAS

*Prep: 35 minutes    Cook: 35 minutes*
*Makes 4 main-dish servings*

1 pound medium shrimp
1 can (13¾ to 14½ ounces) reduced-sodium chicken or vegetable broth
1 tablespoon margarine or butter
⅛ teaspoon ground black pepper
½ teaspoon salt
1 tablespoon olive oil
1 small onion, finely chopped
2 cups Arborio rice (Italian short-grain rice) or medium-grain rice
½ cup dry white wine
1 cup frozen baby peas
¼ cup chopped fresh parsley

◆ Shell and devein shrimp, reserving shells. In 3-quart saucepan, combine broth, *4 cups water*, and reserved shells. Heat to boiling over high heat. Reduce heat to low; simmer 20 minutes. Strain broth through sieve; if necessary, add *water* to equal 5½ cups. Return broth to clean saucepan and heat to boiling over high heat. Reduce heat to low to maintain simmer; cover.

◆ In 4-quart saucepan, melt margarine over medium-high heat. Add shrimp, pepper, and salt; cook, stirring, 2 minutes, or just until shrimp are opaque. Transfer to bowl.

◆ In same saucepan, heat oil over medium heat. Add onion; cook 5 minutes, until tender. Add rice and cook, stirring often, until grains are opaque. Add wine; cook until absorbed. Add ½ cup simmering broth; stir until absorbed. Continue cooking, adding broth, ½ cup at a time, and stirring after each addition, about 25 minutes, until all liquid is absorbed and rice is tender and creamy but still firm. Stir in peas and cooked shrimp and heat through. Stir in parsley.

**Each serving: About 645 calories, 30g protein, 100g carbohydrate, 8g total fat (2g saturated), 183mg cholesterol, 565mg sodium**

## MUSHROOM RISOTTO

*Prep: 20 minutes plus standing*
*Cook: 50 minutes*
*Makes 4 main-dish servings*

½ ounce dried porcini mushrooms
1 can (13¾ to 14½ ounces) reduced-sodium chicken or vegetable broth
2 tablespoons margarine or butter
1 pound white mushrooms, sliced
¼ teaspoon ground black pepper
½ teaspoon salt
Pinch dried thyme
1 tablespoon olive oil
1 small onion, finely chopped
2 cups Arborio rice (Italian short-grain rice) or medium-grain rice
½ cup dry white wine
½ cup freshly grated Parmesan cheese
2 tablespoons chopped fresh parsley

◆ In small bowl, combine porcini with *½ cup boiling water*; let stand 30 minutes. With slotted spoon, remove porcini; rinse and chop. Strain soaking liquid through sieve lined with paper towel. In 2-quart saucepan, heat broth, *3¼ cups water*, and porcini liquid to boiling over high heat. Reduce heat to low to maintain simmer; cover.

◆ In 4-quart saucepan, melt margarine over medium heat. Add white mushrooms, pepper, salt, and thyme; cook, stirring occasionally, 10 minutes. Stir in porcini. Transfer mushroom mixture to bowl.

◆ In same saucepan, heat oil over medium heat. Add onion; cook 5 minutes. Add rice and cook, stirring often, until grains are opaque. Add wine; cook until absorbed. Add ½ cup simmering broth; stir until absorbed. Continue cooking, adding broth, ½ cup at a time, and stirring after each addition, about 25 minutes, until all liquid is absorbed and rice is tender and creamy but still firm. Stir in mushroom mixture and Parmesan; heat through. Stir in parsley.

**Each serving: About 645 calories, 17g protein, 102g carbohydrate, 14g total fat (4g saturated), 18mg cholesterol, 600mg sodium**

## BUTTERNUT SQUASH RISOTTO WITH SAGE

*Prep: 20 minutes    Cook: 50 minutes*
*Makes 4 main-dish servings*

1 medium butternut squash (2 pounds)
1 can (13¾ to 14½ ounces) reduced-sodium chicken or vegetable broth
2 tablespoons margarine or butter
¼ teaspoon ground black pepper
3 tablespoons chopped fresh sage
¼ teaspoon salt
1 tablespoon olive oil
1 small onion, finely chopped
2 cups Arborio rice (Italian short-grain rice) or medium-grain rice
⅓ cup dry white wine
½ cup freshly grated Parmesan cheese

◆ Cut squash into chunks; cut off peel. Cut enough squash into ½-inch pieces to equal 2 cups. Shred enough remaining squash to equal 2 cups. In 2-quart saucepan, heat broth and *3½ cups water* to boiling over high heat. Reduce heat to low to maintain simmer; cover.

◆ In 4-quart saucepan, melt margarine over medium heat. Add squash pieces, pepper, 2 tablespoons sage, and salt. Cook, stirring often, 10 minutes, or until squash is tender (add *2 to 4 tablespoons water* if squash sticks to pan before it is tender). Transfer to small bowl.

◆ Add oil, onion, and shredded squash to same saucepan; cook, stirring frequently, until vegetables are tender. Add rice; cook, stirring often, until grains are opaque. Add wine; cook until absorbed. Add ½ cup simmering broth; stir until absorbed. Continue cooking, adding broth, ½ cup at a time, and stirring after each addition, about 25 minutes, until all liquid is absorbed and rice is tender and creamy but still firm. (Add *½ cup water* if necessary.) Stir in squash pieces, Parmesan, and remaining 1 tablespoon sage; heat through.

**Each serving: About 690 calories, 17g protein, 119g carbohydrate, 14g total fat (4g saturated), 18mg cholesterol, 470mg sodium**

# Couscous

The grain-like semolina pasta called couscous, originally from North Africa, is quickly transformed into a refreshing main-course salad or an exotic side dish for chicken, lamb, or beef. The boxed supermarket version is ready in about five minutes (traditional couscous is soaked, steamed, and dried several times).

## Nutty couscous salad

*Prep: 20 minutes    Cook: 5 minutes*
*Makes 8 accompaniment servings*

1½ cups (10 ounces) couscous (Moroccan pasta)
½ cup pitted dates
1 bunch flat-leaf parsley
1 large orange
2 tablespoons olive or vegetable oil
2 tablespoons cider vinegar
½ teaspoon sugar
¼ teaspoon salt
1 cup dried currants or dark seedless raisins
2 tablespoons coarsely chopped crystallized ginger
1 can (6 ounces) salted cashews

**1** Prepare couscous as label directs. Cut each date crosswise into 3 pieces. Reserve a few sprigs parsley to use for garnish.

**2** With large chef's knife, finely chop enough remaining parsley to equal 3 tablespoons. Set aside.

**3** Prepare orange dressing: Grate peel and squeeze juice from orange. In large bowl, with wire whisk or fork, mix orange peel, orange juice, oil, cider vinegar, sugar, and salt until blended.

**4** To dressing in bowl, add couscous, dates, chopped parsley, currants, ginger, and cashews; toss to mix well. Garnish with parsley sprigs. Cover and refrigerate if not serving right away.

---

### DATES

With at least 50 percent sugar, dates are the sweetest of fruits. They are categorized as soft, semisoft, or dry according to how soft they are when ripe: The Deglet Noor, the most commonly available, is a medium-size semisoft date, while the Medjool, a very large premium date, is the best known of the soft dates.

Dates are available both fresh on the stem and dried; most supermarket dates have beeen dried and partially rehydrated. When buying, avoid very shriveled dates (though a wrinkled skin is normal) and any with mold or sugar crystals on the skin. Dates will last up to a year in an airtight container in the refrigerator and up to five years in the freezer.

Dates are frequently used in baking (you can substitute chopped dates for raisins), and are good in salads, pilafs, poultry stuffings, and lamb stews.

Medjool

Deglet Noor

---

**EACH SERVING: ABOUT 410 CALORIES, 9g PROTEIN, 60g CARBOHYDRATE, 17g TOTAL FAT (4g SATURATED), 8mg CHOLESTEROL, 370mg SODIUM**

**Lime couscous** Prepare 1 cup couscous (Moroccan pasta) as label directs, but add 1 tablespoon fresh lime juice and ½ teaspoon grated lime peel to water before boiling. Makes 4 accompaniment servings.

Each serving: About 210 calories, 6g protein, 36g carbohydrate, 5g total fat (1g saturated), 0mg cholesterol, 245mg sodium

**Moroccan couscous** Prepare 1 cup couscous (Moroccan pasta) as label directs, but add ¼ cup golden raisins, ¼ teaspoon ground cinnamon, ¼ teaspoon ground turmeric, and ¼ teaspoon ground cumin to water before boiling. Makes 4 accompaniment servings.

Each serving: About 245 calories, 6g protein, 44g carbohydrate, 5g total fat (1g saturated), 0mg cholesterol, 255mg sodium

**Green onion and dried tomato couscous** Prepare 1 cup couscous (Moroccan pasta) as label directs, but add 1 medium green onion, sliced, and 5 oil-packed dried tomato halves, chopped, to water before boiling. Makes 4 accompaniment servings.

Each serving: About 225 calories, 6g protein, 37g carbohydrate, 6g total fat (1g saturated), 0mg cholesterol, 270mg sodium

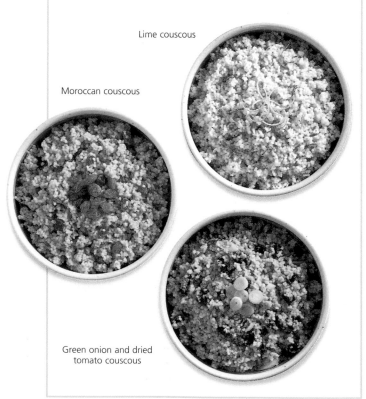

Lime couscous

Moroccan couscous

Green onion and dried tomato couscous

# FRAGRANT VEGETABLE COUSCOUS

*Prep: 10 minutes plus standing    Cook: 15 minutes*
*Makes 4 accompaniment servings*

| | |
|---|---|
| 1 tablespoon olive or vegetable oil | ⅛ teaspoon ground cinnamon |
| 3 green onions, finely chopped | 1 can (13¾ to 14½ ounces) chicken broth |
| 2 medium carrots, diced | 1 cup (7 ounces) couscous (Moroccan pasta) |
| ¼ teaspoon salt | ½ teaspoon grated orange peel (optional) |
| ¼ teaspoon ground black pepper | |

◆ In 3-quart saucepan, heat oil over medium-high heat; add green onions, carrots, salt, and pepper and cook, stirring occasionally, until carrots are tender-crisp. Stir in cinnamon.

◆ Add chicken broth to vegetable mixture; heat to boiling over high heat. Stir in couscous. Cover saucepan; remove from heat and let stand 5 minutes.

◆ With fork, fluff couscous mixture. Stir in grated orange peel, if you like.

Each serving: About 235 calories, 7g protein, 40g carbohydrate, 5g total fat (1g saturated), 8mg cholesterol, 585mg sodium

# COUSCOUS SALAD WITH RADISHES

*Prep: 15 minutes    Cook: 5 minutes*
*Makes 8 accompaniment servings*

| | |
|---|---|
| 1½ cups (10 ounces) couscous (Moroccan pasta) | 1 cup frozen peas, thawed |
| 1 can (14½ ounces) vegetable broth | 1 cup frozen whole-kernel corn, thawed |
| 1 bunch radishes, coarsely chopped | 3 tablespoons olive oil |
| | 1 teaspoon grated lemon peel |
| | ½ teaspoon salt |

◆ Prepare couscous as label directs, but use vegetable broth plus *water* to equal amount of water called for on label, and do not use margarine or butter or salt.

◆ In large bowl, mix radishes, peas, corn, olive oil, grated lemon peel, and salt. Stir in couscous until mixed. Cover and refrigerate if not serving right away.

Each serving: About 220 calories, 6g protein, 36g carbohydrate, 5g total fat (1g saturated), 0mg cholesterol, 180mg sodium

# CORNMEAL

Cornmeal – ground dried corn kernels – is the key ingredient of polenta, the silky cornmeal mush of Northern Italy. It's great served as a side dish, like mashed potatoes; layered with cheese; or cooled and sliced to be grilled, broiled, or fried. Spoonbread, a soufflé-like casserole, is the fancy Southern version of cornmeal mush. Always add cornmeal gradually to a liquid, and stir well to prevent lumps.

## POLENTA WITH MUSHROOMS

◆◆◆◆◆◆◆◆◆◆◆◆◆

*Prep: 15 minutes plus standing*
*Cook: 35 minutes*
*Makes 3 main-dish servings*

1 package (0.35 ounce) dried porcini mushrooms
8 ounces shiitake mushrooms
8 ounces cremini or white mushrooms
2 tablespoons olive oil
1 medium onion, coarsely chopped
2 tablespoons margarine or butter
1 teaspoon minced fresh oregano or ¼ teaspoon dried oregano
¼ teaspoon coarsely ground black pepper
½ teaspoon salt
2 cups milk
1 cup yellow cornmeal
¼ cup freshly grated Parmesan cheese
Oregano sprigs for garnish

**1** In bowl, combine porcini and *1 cup boiling water*; let stand 30 minutes. Meanwhile, cut stems from shiitakes; trim stem ends from cremini. Rinse and thickly slice shiitakes and cremini. In 12-inch skillet, heat 1 tablespoon olive oil over medium heat. Add onion and cook 5 minutes, or until tender; transfer to small bowl. In same skillet, heat margarine and remaining 1 tablespoon oil over medium-high heat.

**2** Add shiitakes, cremini, minced oregano, and pepper to skillet; cook, stirring, 10 minutes. Meanwhile, drain porcini in sieve lined with paper towel; reserve ¾ cup liquid. Rinse porcini; chop.

**3** Return onion to skillet. Stir in chopped porcini and reserved liquid; heat to boiling. Boil 1 minute. Remove from heat; keep warm.

### PERFECT POLENTA

◆◆◆◆◆◆◆◆◆◆◆◆◆

This is our tried-and-tested method for lump-free polenta: In pan you intend to cook it in, place one-third of cold liquid called for in recipe, then gradually whisk in cornmeal. In another pan, heat remaining liquid to boiling. Add hot liquid to cornmeal mixture, whisking constantly.

**4** Prepare polenta: In 3-quart saucepan, place salt and 1⅛ cups milk; gradually whisk in cornmeal until smooth. In 2-quart saucepan, heat remaining ⅞ cup milk and *2 cups water* to boiling over high heat; whisk into cornmeal mixture. Heat to boiling over medium-high heat, whisking. Reduce heat to low.

**5** Cook polenta, stirring constantly, 5 minutes, or until thick. Stir in grated Parmesan until well combined. Serve polenta topped with mushroom mixture. Garnish with oregano sprigs.

EACH SERVING: ABOUT 545 CALORIES, 16g PROTEIN, 65g CARBOHYDRATE, 26g TOTAL FAT (8g SATURATED), 28mg CHOLESTEROL, 690mg SODIUM

# ROSEMARY POLENTA WEDGES

*Prep: 15 minutes plus standing*
*Broil: 5 to 10 minutes*
*Makes 8 accompaniment servings*

1½ teaspoons salt
1½ cups yellow cornmeal
3 cups milk
1 tablespoon margarine or butter

½ teaspoon minced fresh rosemary or ¼ teaspoon dried rosemary, crushed
Rosemary sprigs for garnish

◆ Line two 8-inch round cake pans with foil; grease foil. In 3-quart saucepan, place salt and 1¼ cups water. Gradually whisk in cornmeal.

◆ In 2-quart saucepan, heat milk to boiling over medium-high heat; whisk into cornmeal mixture. Heat to boiling over medium-high heat, whisking. Reduce heat to low and cook, stirring constantly, 3 to 5 minutes, until mixture is thick.

◆ Spoon mixture into prepared pans; let stand 10 minutes, or until firm. If not serving right away, cover and refrigerate.

◆ About 20 minutes before serving, preheat broiler. Grease rack in broiling pan. Remove polenta from pans; discard foil. Cut each polenta round into 8 wedges. Place polenta wedges on rack in broiling pan.

◆ In small saucepan, melt margarine with minced rosemary over medium heat. Brush polenta wedges with margarine mixture; garnish each with small rosemary sprig. Broil polenta about 5 to 7 inches from heat source 5 to 10 minutes, until lightly browned and heated through.

**Each serving: About 165 calories, 5g protein, 24g carbohydrate, 5g total fat (2g saturated), 12mg cholesterol, 460mg sodium**

# SPOONBREAD

*Prep: 15 minutes plus standing     Bake: 40 minutes*
*Makes 8 accompaniment servings*

3 cups milk
½ teaspoon salt
¼ teaspoon ground black pepper

1 cup yellow cornmeal
4 tablespoons margarine or butter, cut up
3 large eggs, separated

◆ Preheat oven to 400°F. Grease shallow 1½-quart glass or ceramic baking dish. In 4-quart saucepan, heat milk, salt, and pepper to boiling over medium-high heat. Remove from heat; gradually whisk in cornmeal. Whisk in margarine until melted. Let stand 5 minutes.

◆ Whisk in egg yolks, one at a time. In medium bowl, with electric mixer at high speed, beat egg whites to soft peaks; fold half of whites into cornmeal mixture, then fold in remaining whites. Pour into baking dish. Bake 40 minutes, or until set. Serve immediately.

**Each serving: About 200 calories, 7g protein, 18g carbohydrate, 11g total fat (4g saturated), 92mg cholesterol, 270mg sodium**

# THREE-CHEESE POLENTA

*Prep: 45 minutes plus standing     Bake: 20 minutes*
*Makes 10 main-dish servings*

Chunky Tomato Sauce (see below)
2 cups half-and-half or light cream
1 teaspoon salt
½ teaspoon ground black pepper
3 cups yellow cornmeal

1 tablespoon margarine or butter
4 ounces mozzarella cheese, shredded (1 cup)
4 ounces Fontina cheese, shredded (1 cup)
1 cup freshly grated Parmesan cheese

◆ Prepare Chunky Tomato Sauce; keep warm. Meanwhile, in 5-quart Dutch oven, place half-and-half, salt, pepper, and *1 cup water*. Gradually whisk in cornmeal until smooth. Whisk in *7 cups boiling water*. Heat to boiling over medium-high heat. Reduce heat to low; cook, stirring constantly, about 5 minutes, until mixture is very thick. Stir in margarine until melted. Remove polenta from heat.

◆ Preheat oven to 425°F. Grease 13" by 9" glass baking dish. In medium bowl, mix all cheeses. Spread one-third of polenta in baking dish. Reserve ½ cup cheese mixture for topping; sprinkle polenta with half of remaining cheese. Top with one-third of polenta, remaining cheese, then remaining polenta. Sprinkle with reserved ½ cup cheese. Bake 20 minutes, or until top is browned. Remove from oven; let stand 10 minutes for easier serving.

◆ Cut polenta lengthwise into 2 strips. Cut each strip crosswise into 5 pieces. Serve with Chunky Tomato Sauce.

**Each serving: About 500 calories, 17g protein, 50g carbohydrate, 26g total fat (11g saturated), 48mg cholesterol, 1355mg sodium**

---

### CHUNKY TOMATO SAUCE

In 4-quart saucepan, melt 2 tablespoons margarine or butter over medium heat; stir in 3 large celery stalks, diced, and 3 large carrots, diced, until coated. Cover and cook 20 minutes, stirring occasionally, until vegetables are very tender. Add 1 jar (48 ounces) marinara sauce; heat to boiling over high heat. Reduce heat to low; cover and simmer 15 minutes.

---

# OTHER GRAINS

Whether you're looking for a flavor-packed side dish or a hearty, healthy lunch, delicious grains like quinoa, bulgur, barley, and wheat berries all offer unique texture and taste, and make a nice change of pace from ordinary rice. These wholesome grains are especially appealing when they're speckled with a variety of flavorful ingredients – from nuts and fresh herbs to crunchy vegetables and dried fruits.

## QUINOA WITH CORN

*Prep: 10 minutes    Cook: 20 minutes*
*Makes 6 accompaniment servings*

| | |
|---|---|
| 1 cup quinoa | 1 tablespoon margarine or |
| Salt | butter |
| 3 medium ears corn, silk and | ¼ teaspoon ground black |
| husks removed | pepper |
| 4 green onions | ½ teaspoon grated lemon peel |

1 In fine-mesh sieve, thoroughly rinse quinoa with cold running water. In 2-quart saucepan, heat quinoa, ½ teaspoon salt, and *1¾ cups water* to boiling over high heat.

2 Reduce heat to low; cover saucepan and simmer 15 minutes, or until water is absorbed. Meanwhile, cut corn kernels from cobs. Thinly slice green onions.

3 In 10-inch skillet, melt margarine over medium-high heat. Add corn, green onions, pepper, and ¼ teaspoon salt. Cook, stirring often, 3 minutes, or until tender-crisp. Add quinoa and lemon peel; cook, stirring, until combined.

---

### THE HIGH-PROTEIN GRAIN

Native to the Andes mountains in South America, quinoa was cultivated by the ancient Incas. Although it is considered a grain, quinoa is botanically an herb. Unlike any other grain or vegetable, however, quinoa is a complete protein (containing all eight essential amino acids). It is also high in iron.

Quinoa cooks quickly and has a light, springy texture. Rinse quinoa before using to remove the saponin, a bitter, soapy-tasting coating that acts as a natural insecticide.

Try lightly browning quinoa in a dry skillet for 5 minutes before cooking to give it a delicious toasted flavor. For a salad, toss cooked quinoa with finely chopped raw vegetables and a vinaigrette. Quinoa can also be served with fruit and a little sugar or honey as a breakfast cereal.

---

**EACH SERVING: ABOUT 165 CALORIES, 5g PROTEIN, 29g CARBOHYDRATE, 4g TOTAL FAT (1g SATURATED), 0mg CHOLESTEROL, 300mg SODIUM**

## BULGUR PILAF

*Prep: 10 minutes plus standing*   *Cook: 30 minutes*
*Makes 6 accompaniment servings*

2 tablespoons margarine or
  butter
1 medium onion, finely
  chopped
1 cup bulgur wheat
1 can (13¾ to 14½ ounces)
  reduced-sodium chicken or
  vegetable broth
1 cinnamon stick (3 inches)

1 can (15 to 19 ounces)
  garbanzo beans, rinsed and
  drained
⅓ cup diced dried apricots
¼ teaspoon salt
⅛ teaspoon ground black
  pepper
¼ cup chopped fresh parsley

◆ In 3-quart saucepan, melt margarine over medium heat. Add onion and cook, stirring often, 5 minutes, or until tender. Add bulgur and cook, stirring, 2 minutes longer.

◆ Stir in broth, cinnamon stick, garbanzo beans, dried apricots, salt, and pepper; heat to boiling over high heat.

◆ Reduce heat to low; cover and simmer 15 minutes. Remove from heat and let stand 5 minutes. Stir in parsley; fluff bulgur mixture with fork.

**Each serving: About 220 calories, 7g protein, 37g carbohydrate, 6g total fat (1g saturated), 5mg cholesterol, 350mg sodium**

## WHEAT BERRIES WITH BROWN BUTTER AND PECANS

*Prep: 10 minutes plus soaking*   *Cook: 1 hour 15 minutes*
*Makes 6 accompaniment servings*

1 cup wheat berries (whole-
  grain wheat)
2 tablespoons margarine or
  butter
1 medium onion, finely
  chopped
½ teaspoon salt

⅛ teaspoon ground black
  pepper
½ cup pecans, coarsely
  chopped (about 2 ounces)
2 tablespoons chopped fresh
  parsley

◆ In medium bowl, soak wheat berries overnight in enough *water* to cover by 2 inches.

◆ Drain wheat berries. In 3-quart saucepan, heat wheat berries and *3 cups water* to boiling over high heat.

◆ Reduce heat to low; cover and simmer 1 hour, or just until tender but still firm. Drain. Wipe saucepan clean.

◆ In same saucepan, melt margarine over medium heat. Add onion and cook, stirring frequently, 5 minutes, or until tender. Stir in salt, pepper, and pecans. Cook, stirring, about 3 minutes, until pecans are lightly toasted and margarine begins to brown.

◆ Add wheat berries and *1 tablespoon water* to pecan mixture; stir until well combined. Heat through, stirring. Remove from heat; stir in parsley.

**Each serving: About 235 calories, 6g protein, 31g carbohydrate, 11g total fat (1g saturated), 0mg cholesterol, 225mg sodium**

## MUSHROOM-BARLEY PILAF

*Prep: 15 minutes*   *Cook: 55 minutes*
*Makes 6 accompaniment servings*

1 cup pearl barley
2 tablespoons margarine or
  butter
1 medium onion, finely
  chopped
2 medium celery stalks, cut
  into ¼-inch-thick slices
12 ounces mushrooms, sliced

1 can (13¾ to 14½ ounces)
  chicken or vegetable broth
½ teaspoon salt
⅛ teaspoon ground black
  pepper
⅛ teaspoon dried thyme
¼ cup chopped fresh parsley

◆ In 3-quart saucepan, toast barley over medium heat, shaking pan occasionally, 4 minutes, or until beginning to brown. Transfer to bowl.

◆ In same saucepan, melt margarine over medium heat. Add onion and celery and cook 5 minutes, or until tender. Stir in mushrooms; cook about 10 minutes, until tender and liquid has evaporated.

◆ Stir in barley, broth plus enough *water* to equal 2½ cups, salt, pepper, and thyme. Heat to boiling over high heat. Reduce heat to low; cover and simmer 30 minutes, or until barley is tender. Remove from heat; stir in parsley.

**Each serving: About 190 calories, 6g protein, 32g carbohydrate, 5g total fat (1g saturated), 5mg cholesterol, 530mg sodium**

# CANNED BEANS

Canned beans are the secret to many an easy meal, whether baked in a Greek-style pie or tucked into a hearty vegetarian burrito. Keep your pantry stocked with a variety. For best texture and appearance in the finished dish, rinse beans before using.

## GREEK GREENS AND SPINACH PIE

◆◆◆◆◆◆◆◆◆◆◆◆◆◆◆◆◆◆◆◆◆◆◆◆◆◆◆◆◆

*Prep: 40 minutes   Bake: 30 minutes*
*Makes 8 main-dish servings*

3 cans (15 to 19 ounces each) white kidney beans (cannellini)

2 tablespoons olive or vegetable oil

1 large bunch kale (about 1⅓ pounds), tough stems trimmed, leaves coarsely chopped

1 large bunch escarole (about 1¼ pounds), chopped

1 bunch (10 to 12 ounces) spinach, tough stems removed, leaves coarsely chopped

½ teaspoon salt

½ teaspoon coarsely ground black pepper

2 tablespoons minced fresh dill or 1 teaspoon dillweed

1 package (8 ounces) feta cheese, crumbled

5 sheets (about 16" by 12" each) fresh or frozen (thawed) phyllo (about 3½ ounces)

2 tablespoons margarine or butter, melted

Dill sprigs and chopped fresh dill for garnish

1 Rinse and drain 2 cans beans. In medium bowl, with potato masher, mash drained beans. Spread evenly in 13" by 9" glass baking dish. Rinse and drain remaining can of beans; set aside. In 8-quart Dutch oven or saucepot, heat oil over high heat; add greens, one-third at a time, and cook, stirring, just until wilted. While greens are cooking, stir in salt and pepper. Remove from heat.

2 To greens in Dutch oven, stir in the 1 can drained beans, minced dill, and feta. Spoon evenly over mashed beans in baking dish. Preheat oven to 375°F.

3 Place 1 sheet of phyllo on top of greens mixture in baking dish; brush phyllo sheet lightly with some of melted margarine.

4 Continue layering with 3 more sheets of phyllo, brushing each sheet lightly with some of melted margarine. Top with dill sprigs arranged in pretty design. Top with remaining sheet of phyllo; press down gently so dill is visible through phyllo. Brush lightly with remaining melted margarine.

5 Tuck ends of phyllo into baking dish. Bake pie about 30 minutes, until filling is heated through and phyllo is lightly golden. Garnish with chopped dill; cut into squares.

EACH SERVING: ABOUT 345 CALORIES, 18g PROTEIN, 39g CARBOHYDRATE, 14g TOTAL FAT (5g SATURATED), 25mg CHOLESTEROL, 1035mg SODIUM

## SKILLET BEANS AND RICE

*Prep: 15 minutes    Cook: 30 minutes*
*Makes 5 main-dish servings*

¾ cup regular long-grain rice
1 tablespoon vegetable oil
1 medium green pepper, cut into ½-inch pieces
1 medium red pepper, cut into ½-inch pieces
1 medium onion, chopped
1 can (15 to 19 ounces) black beans

1 can (15 to 19 ounces) garbanzo beans
1 can (15 to 19 ounces) red kidney beans
1 can (15 to 19 ounces) pink beans
1 can (14½ ounces) stewed tomatoes
½ cup bottled barbecue sauce

◆ Prepare rice as label directs.

◆ Meanwhile, in 12-inch skillet, heat oil over medium heat; add green and red peppers and onion and cook until vegetables are tender.

◆ Rinse and drain all beans. Add beans, stewed tomatoes, barbecue sauce, and *1 cup water* to pepper mixture in skillet; heat to boiling over high heat. Reduce heat to low; cover and simmer 15 minutes.

◆ When rice is done, stir rice into bean mixture.

**Each serving: About 465 calories, 21g protein, 88g carbohydrate, 6g total fat (1g saturated), 0mg cholesterol, 1215mg sodium**

## CORN, BLACK BEAN, AND RICE BURRITOS

*Prep: 25 minutes    Bake: 15 minutes*
*Makes 4 main-dish servings*

1 cup regular long-grain rice
1 can (15 to 19 ounces) black beans, rinsed and drained
1 can (15¼ to 16 ounces) whole-kernel corn, drained
1 can (4 to 4½ ounces) chopped mild green chiles, drained

4 ounces Monterey Jack or Cheddar cheese, shredded (1 cup)
¼ cup chopped fresh cilantro
1 package (10 ounces) flour tortillas (eight 6- to 7-inch tortillas)
1 jar (12½ ounces) mild salsa

◆ Preheat oven to 425°F. Prepare rice as label directs.

◆ Meanwhile, in large bowl, combine black beans, corn, chiles, cheese, and cilantro. When rice is done, stir into bean mixture. Spoon rounded ½ cup rice mixture across center of each tortilla.

◆ Spoon about 1 tablespoon salsa on top of rice mixture on each tortilla. Fold sides of tortilla over rice mixture, overlapping slightly.

◆ Grease 13" by 9" glass or ceramic baking dish. Place burritos, seam-side down, in dish. Spoon any remaining rice mixture down center of burritos; top with remaining salsa. Cover loosely with foil and bake 15 minutes, or until burritos are heated through.

**Each serving: About 685 calories, 25g protein, 117g carbohydrate, 15g total fat (6g saturated), 25mg cholesterol, 1415mg sodium**

## BLACK BEAN AND VEGETABLE HASH

*Prep: 15 minutes    Cook: 30 minutes*
*Makes 4 main-dish servings*

1½ pounds all-purpose potatoes (about 4 medium), peeled and cut into ½-inch cubes
2 tablespoons vegetable oil
4 ounces Canadian bacon, cut into ½-inch pieces

1 large red pepper, cut into ½-inch pieces
1 can (15 to 19 ounces) black beans, rinsed and drained
4 large eggs
Salt and coarsely ground black pepper (optional)

◆ In 3-quart saucepan, heat potatoes and enough *water* to cover to boiling over high heat. Reduce heat to low; cover and simmer 4 minutes, or until potatoes are almost tender. Drain.

◆ In nonstick 12-inch skillet, heat oil over medium-high heat. Add Canadian bacon, red pepper, and potatoes; cook, stirring occasionally, about 15 minutes, until vegetables are tender and browned. Stir in black beans; heat through.

◆ Meanwhile, in 10-inch skillet, heat *1½ inches water* to boiling over high heat. Reduce heat to medium-low. One at a time, break eggs into custard cup, then, holding cup close to water's surface, slip each egg into simmering water. Cook eggs 3 to 5 minutes, until desired doneness. When done, with slotted spoon, carefully remove eggs from water. Drain each egg (still held in spoon) on paper towels. Serve poached eggs on vegetable hash. Sprinkle eggs with salt and pepper, if you like.

**Each serving: About 420 calories, 22g protein, 53g carbohydrate, 15g total fat (4g saturated), 229mg cholesterol, 780mg sodium**

# LENTILS

The small, flat legumes called lentils are delicious, economical, and packed with nutrients. And, as a bonus, they do not require the lengthy soaking and cooking times of dry beans. In less than an hour, lentils are ready to serve as an aromatic Indian side dish, a warm salad, a hearty pasta stew, or an elegant French-style accompaniment.

## INDIAN-STYLE LENTILS

*Prep: 20 minutes    Cook: 35 to 45 minutes*
*Makes 6 accompaniment servings*

1 pound sweet potatoes
1 medium onion
1 tablespoon vegetable oil
1 tablespoon minced, peeled fresh ginger
1 large garlic clove, minced
1½ teaspoons cumin seeds
⅛ teaspoon ground red pepper (cayenne)
1 cup lentils, rinsed and picked through

1 can (13¾ to 14½ ounces) chicken or vegetable broth
¼ teaspoon salt
1 container (8 ounces) plain low fat yogurt
¼ cup chopped fresh mint or cilantro
Mint or cilantro leaves for garnish

**1** Peel sweet potatoes and cut into ¾-inch pieces (you should have about 3 cups); set aside.

**2** Finely chop onion. In 3-quart saucepan, heat oil over medium heat. Add onion and cook, stirring occasionally, 5 minutes, or until tender.

**3** Stir in ginger, garlic, cumin seeds, and ground red pepper; cook, stirring, 30 seconds. Stir in sweet potatoes, lentils, chicken broth, salt, and *1 cup water*; heat to boiling over high heat.

**4** Reduce heat to low; cover and simmer 20 to 30 minutes, stirring occasionally, until lentils are just tender. In small bowl, mix yogurt and chopped mint. Garnish and serve with lentils.

### INDIAN LENTIL SOUP

Follow directions for Indian-Style Lentils, but cut sweet potatoes into ½-inch dice and use 2 cans (13¾ to 14½ ounces each) broth. Simmer 45 minutes or until lentils are very tender. Partly mash with potato masher, if you like. Or, blend in batches in the blender, or in food processor with knife blade attached. Reheat if necessary over low heat. Garnish with lemon slices.

Each serving: About 185 calories, 10g protein, 34g carbohydrate, 5g total fat (1g saturated), 13g cholesterol, 705mg sodium

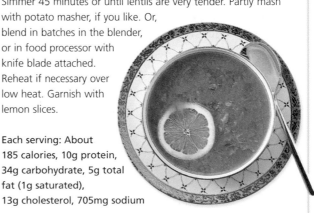

EACH SERVING: ABOUT 175 CALORIES, 9g PROTEIN, 33g CARBOHYDRATE, 4g TOTAL FAT (1g SATURATED), 8mg CHOLESTEROL, 415mg SODIUM

## WARM LENTIL SALAD

*Prep: 10 minutes    Cook: 30 to 40 minutes*
*Makes 4 accompaniment servings*

| | |
|---|---|
| 1 cup lentils | 2 tablespoons fresh lemon |
| 1 bay leaf | juice |
| 1 small carrot, shredded | 2 tablespoons olive oil |
| 1 tablespoon chopped fresh | ¾ teaspoon salt |
| mint or 1 teaspoon dried | ¼ teaspoon ground black |
| mint | pepper |

◆ Rinse lentils with cold running water and discard any stones or shriveled lentils.

◆ In 2-quart saucepan, heat lentils, bay leaf, and enough *water* to cover lentils by 2 inches to boiling over high heat. Reduce heat to medium-low; cover and simmer 20 to 30 minutes, until lentils are just tender.

◆ When lentils are done, drain well; discard bay leaf. In medium bowl, mix lentils, shredded carrot, chopped mint, lemon juice, oil, salt, and pepper until blended.

**Each serving: About 140 calories, 8g protein, 21g carbohydrate, 7g total fat (1g saturated), 0mg cholesterol, 410mg sodium**

## LENTILS AND PASTA

*Prep: 15 minutes    Cook: 50 minutes*
*Makes 4 main-dish servings*

| | |
|---|---|
| 1 cup lentils | ¾ teaspoon salt |
| 1 ounce pancetta or ham, | ¼ teaspoon ground black |
| chopped (¼ cup) | pepper |
| 1 small onion, chopped | 1 cup ditalini or small shell |
| 1 medium carrot, chopped | pasta |
| 1 medium celery stalk, | ¼ cup chopped fresh parsley |
| chopped | Flat-leaf parsley sprig for |
| 1 garlic clove, chopped | garnish |
| 1 tablespoon olive oil | |

◆ Rinse lentils with cold running water and discard any stones or shriveled lentils. On cutting board, chop pancetta, onion, carrot, celery, and garlic together until very fine.

◆ In 3-quart saucepan, heat olive oil over medium heat. Add pancetta-vegetable mixture and cook, stirring often, 10 minutes, or until tender.

◆ Stir in lentils and *3 cups water*; heat to boiling over high heat. Reduce heat to low; cover and simmer 15 minutes. Stir in salt and pepper; cover and cook 15 minutes longer, or until lentils are just tender.

◆ Meanwhile, cook ditalini as label directs; drain. Stir ditalini and chopped parsley into lentils; garnish.

**Each serving: About 235 calories, 14g protein, 44g carbohydrate, 5g total fat (1g saturated), 4mg cholesterol, 535mg sodium**

## FRENCH LENTILS WITH SHALLOTS AND BRANDY

*Prep: 10 minutes    Cook: 30 to 35 minutes*
*Makes 6 accompaniment servings*

| | |
|---|---|
| 1 cup small green French | ⅓ cup finely chopped shallots |
| lentils | 2 tablespoons brandy |
| Salt | ¼ teaspoon ground black |
| 2 tablespoons margarine or | pepper |
| butter | ¼ cup chopped fresh parsley |

◆ Rinse lentils with cold running water and discard any stones or shriveled lentils.

◆ In 2-quart saucepan, heat lentils and *2 cups water* to boiling over high heat. Reduce heat to low; cover and simmer 20 to 25 minutes, until lentils are just tender, adding ½ teaspoon salt halfway through cooking. Drain lentils. Wipe saucepan clean.

◆ In same saucepan, melt margarine over medium heat. Add shallots; cook 3 minutes, or until tender. Stir in brandy; cook 1 minute longer, until almost evaporated. Stir in lentils, pepper, and ¼ teaspoon salt and heat through. Stir in parsley.

**Each serving: About 100 calories, 6g protein, 14g carbohydrate, 4g total fat (1g saturated), 0mg cholesterol, 315mg sodium**

### LENTILS FOR LUCK

◆◆◆◆◆◆◆◆◆◆◆◆◆◆◆◆◆◆◆◆◆

In Italy, lentils are an indispensable part of the festivities for New Year's Eve. Associated with money because they resemble tiny coins, they symbolize prosperity in the coming year. In Tuscany, stewed lentils are served with *cotechino*, a lightly spiced pork sausage that is boiled and served in slices. Further north, in Bologna and Modena, lentils accompany *zampone*, a boned pig's foot stuffed with the same cotechino-sausage mixture.

# GLOSSARY

**Al dente** Italian for "to the tooth," describes perfectly cooked pasta and vegetables. If pasta is al dente, it is just tender but offers a slight resistance when it is bitten.

**Blanch** To cook foods briefly in boiling water. Blanching locks in textures for tender-crisp vegetables, loosens tomato skins for peeling, and mellows salty foods. Begin timing as soon as the food hits the water – the water needn't return to a boil – then cool in cold water to stop the cooking.

**Blind bake** To bake a piecrust before it's filled to create a crisper crust. To prevent puffing and slipping during baking, the pastry is lined with foil and filled with pie weights, dry beans, or uncooked rice; these are removed shortly before the end of baking time to allow the crust to brown.

**Boil** To heat a liquid until bubbles break vigorously on the surface. You can boil vegetables, cook pasta in boiling water, or reduce sauces by boiling them.

**Braise** To cook food in a small amount of liquid in a tightly covered pan, either in the oven or on the stove-top. Braising is an ideal way to prepare firm-fleshed vegetables.

**Broil** To cook food with intense, direct dry heat under a broiler. Always preheat the broiler, but don't preheat the pan and rack, or the food could stick.

**Caramelize** To heat sugar in a skillet until it becomes syrupy and deep amber brown. Onions can be caramelized by them sautéing slowly until deep golden and very tender.

**Chop** To cut food roughly into small pea-size pieces.

**Core** To remove the core or center of various fruits and vegetables. Coring eliminates small seeds or tough and woody centers (as in pineapple).

**Dice** To cut food into small cubes of about ¼ inch.

**Dot** To scatter bits of margarine or butter over a pie, casserole, or other dish before baking. This adds extra richness and flavor and helps promote browning.

**Drizzle** To slowly pour a liquid, such as melted butter or a glaze, in a fine stream, back and forth, over food.

**Fork-tender** A degree of doneness for cooked vegetables and meats. You should feel just a slight resistance when the food is pierced with a fork.

**Julienne** To cut vegetables, into thin, uniform matchsticks about 2 inches long.

**Marinate** To flavor and/or tenderize a food by letting it soak in a liquid that may contain an acid ingredient (e.g., lemon juice, wine, or vinegar), oil, herbs, and spices.

**Panfry** To cook food in a small amount of hot margarine, butter, or oil in a skillet until browned and cooked through.

**Parboil** To cook a food partially in boiling water. Slow-cooking foods, such as carrots, are often parboiled before they're added to a mixture made of quicker-cooking foods.

**Pare** To cut away the skin or rind of a fruit or vegetable. You can use a vegetable peeler or a paring knife – a small knife with a 3- to 4-inch blade.

**Pinch** The amount of a powdery ingredient you can hold between your thumb and forefinger – about ⅟₁₆ teaspoon.

**Poach** To cook food in gently simmering liquid; the surface should barely shimmer. If you plan to use the cooking liquid for a stock or sauce afterward, poach in a pan just large enough to hold the food. That way, you can add less liquid and avoid diluting flavors.

**Prick** To pierce a food in many or a few places. You can prick a food to prevent buckling – an empty piecrust before it's cooking in the oven, for example – or bursting – a potato before baking.

**Puree** To form a smooth mixture by whirling food, usually a fruit or vegetable, in a food processor or blender, or straining through a food mill.

**Reduce** To rapidly boil a liquid, especially a sauce, so a portion cooks off by evaporation. This creates a thicker sauce with a deeper, more concentrated flavor. If you use a wide pan, the liquid will evaporate faster.

**Roast** To cook food in the oven, in an uncovered pan, by the free circulation of dry heat, usually until the exterior is well browned. Many vegetables are suitable for roasting, such as potatoes, parsnips, peppers, and even tomatoes.

**Sauté** To cook or brown food quickly in a small amount of hot fat in a skillet; the term derives from the French *sauter* ("to jump"), and refers to the practice of shaking food in the pan so it browns evenly.

**Shred** To cut, tear, or grate food into narrow strips.

**Shave** To cut wide, paper-thin slices of food, especially Parmesan cheese, vegetables, or chocolate. Shave off slices with a vegetable peeler and use as a garnish.

**Simmer** To cook liquid gently, alone or with other ingredients, over low heat so it's just below the boiling point. A few small bubbles should be visible on the surface.

**Skim** To remove fat or froth from the surface of a liquid, such as stock or boiling jelly. A skimmer, with a flat mesh or perforated bowl at the end of a long handle, is the ideal tool for the job.

**Steam** To cook food, covered, in the vapor given off by boiling water. The food is set on a rack or in a basket so it's over, not in, boiling water – since it's not immersed, it retains more nutrients, bright colors, and fresh flavor.

**Stir-fry** To cook small pieces of food quickly in a small amount of oil over high heat, stirring and tossing almost constantly. Vegetables cooked in this way retain more nutrients because of the short cooking time. Stir-frying is much used in Asian cooking; a wok is the traditional pan, though a skillet or Dutch oven will do just as well.

**Tender-crisp** The ideal degree of doneness for many vegetables, especially green vegetables. Cook them until they're just tender but still retain some texture.

**Toss** To lift and drop pieces of food quickly and gently with two utensils, usually to coat them with a sauce (as for pasta) or dressing (as for salad).

**Whisk** To beat ingredients (e.g., salad dressings, sauces) with a fork or the looped wire utensil called a whisk to blend.

# INDEX